SETTING WORDS ON FIRE

Setting
WORDS
on Fire

PUTTING GOD
AT THE
CENTER OF THE SERMON

Paul Scott Wilson

Abingdon Press
Nashville

Library of Congress Cataloging-in-Publication Data

Wilson, Paul Scott, 1949–
    Setting words on fire : putting God at the center of the sermon / Paul Scott Wilson.
        p. cm.
    Includes bibliographical references.
    ISBN 978-0-687-64718-7 (pbk. : alk. paper)
    1. Preaching.   I. Title.
    BV4211.3.W555   2008
    251—dc22

2008035297

Copyright notices continued on page 293.

My speech and my proclamation were not
with plausible words of wisdom, but with a demon-
stration of the Spirit and of power,
so that your faith might rest not on human
wisdom but on the power of God.
1 Corinthians 2:4-5

Grant rather that the words of fire which you speak
to others through my mouth may equally bring
enlightenment and warmth to my inmost being,
that as a torch-bearer bringing light to others I may
likewise enlighten myself.
May true warmth be kindled in me.
Jean-Pierre Camus (1584–1652)[1]

Acknowledgments

I am deeply grateful to Princeton Theological Seminary for the opportunity to deliver the 2008 MacLeod Lectures; the invitation helped spur this project to completion, and I am grateful to many people there, including President Iain R. Torrance and colleagues in Homiletics and Speech Communication. In preparation, I also was blessed with an invitation from Andrews University to give the 2007 H. M. C. Richards Lectures in Preaching, and conversations there filtered into these pages. Many people contributed to this study in various ways, most notably graduate students over the years who have navigated with me the oceans of past sermons looking for useful places to land. Among them was Shin Suk Ko, who served as my graduate student assistant in the copyright stages of readying this manuscript for publication, and I am grateful for his careful work. I also thank Kerri Haggerman, Joni Sancken, Casey Barton, and numerous other doctoral students and colleagues at the Toronto School of Theology as well as students I have worked with at other schools on issues of proclamation, most recently those in the DMin in Biblical Preaching at Luther Seminary. Professor Terry Donaldson gave helpful counsel on exhortation in the New Testament. Professor John M. Rottman and the Reverend Dr. Andrew Sterling not only read the manuscript at a key stage and gave valuable input at various times; they also assisted in my obtaining grants to cover some of the research costs and costs of making the CD. Other colleagues from the Academy of Homiletics, including Professors Robert Reid, David Jacobsen, Luke Powery, Todd Townshend, and Art Van Seters, were generous in making time for conversation about matters here. Dr. Robert Ratcliff at Abingdon Press has been a kind mentor to this project from its inception several years ago. I am grateful to Victoria University in the University of Toronto and its president, Paul Gooch, and to its Board of Regents in granting me sabbatical leave, and to its Senate for granting me a research grant. The principal of Emmanuel College in Victoria University, Peter Wyatt, was always encouraging of preaching both in terms of its instruction at all levels and in terms of this project. The General Council of The United Church of Canada kindly awarded me the 2004 Davidson Award for Excellence in Teaching and Scholarship, and I have drawn on those funds in my work here. The Center for Excellence in Preaching at Calvin Seminary and its director, Scott Hoezee, provided an opportunity to test and record some of the ideas here and provided a generous grant to produce a master copy of the CD included in the back cover. Several individuals volunteered to read for it, and I thank them, Scott Hoezee, Margaret Jenista, John Rottman, and Luke Powery, the latter who traveled some distance to be of help. I thank also the staff in the audiovisual office at Calvin College for their recording and production work. My wife, Deanna, as usual has shown remarkable patience and kindness as I have worked through the material here, and she has served as a sounding board more times than she may have liked. Her wisdom and understanding plus her nurture are evident in these pages.

Contents

Introduction

For most of history preachers knew a difference between teaching and proclaiming and knew both how to teach and how to proclaim, but that may not be true today. The church in our time has many fine teachers yet often has put some aspects of teaching on the back burner that are necessary for proclamation. At the same time we have largely forgotten what proclamation is, much less how to do it. Both are needed. From the sermons of our forebears it is still possible to recover proclamation and the kinds of teaching needed to support it. In other words, the church has resources that it has not yet fully tapped for the renewal of preaching in our postmodern age. That, at least, is an exciting possibility raised in these pages. We will explore sermons through the ages for lessons we may learn to help us recover preaching as a dual art of teaching and proclamation.

Teaching at its best provides what people need to know about who God is; it helps them recognize God in their own lives and the world around them and involves many important subjects, including social justice. Generally teaching does not on its own introduce them directly to God; it introduces them to the ways that people have witnessed to and understood God through the ages. With that essential knowledge it becomes possible to know who God is and in faith to make claims about God's actions today. Teaching gives information *about* God for listeners to make sense of their experience of God, but teaching has limits. Teaching arguably stops short of providing people an encounter with God, though these matters are never fully in human control. Moreover, teaching leaves people with a sense of duty: they are to do something with the information they receive: they are to accept, believe, and integrate it; they are to act and live in certain ways. All of this is important, but it stops short of actual bestowal of God's grace.

Having information about someone is valuable, but it is no substitute for actually meeting the person and hearing that person speak. Proclamation introduces people to God. Like a sacrament, it offers God to the people. Acts of proclamation speak the heart of the gospel to listeners in loving, passionate, infectious ways such that in and through them they encounter God, who meets them not as ideas, but in the Spirit as a person who loves them and empowers them to be disciples. In proclamation at its best, people experience the greater truth that everything required is given to them in and through the cross and resurrection. People hear God saying words like "I love *you*," "I forgive *you*," "I died for *you*," "Death has no more power over you," and "Justice is mine." These are the words spoken from the other side of death that shape a ragtag group of individuals gathered in church into communities of faith. In and through proclamation people receive the Holy Spirit, and their lives are transformed in the shape of the cross.

My understanding of what might be helpful in the pulpit stems from my experience. Nowadays so much depends upon perspective, and some personal testimony might be in order. I grew up in the church. Most of my relatives were ministers. I left the church when I was eighteen and returned when I was twenty-four because through crisis, I had an experience of God in Jesus Christ. Some years later as I listened to sermons in my first years of teaching, I listened for what I had come to trust. Something was often missing. Students preached from the Bible. They did good exegesis of their texts, applied the texts to today, treated significant doctrines that linked with tradition, employed vivid images and metaphors, told fine stories, established important tensions within the sermon, addressed ethical, social justice, and pastoral issues, and revealed something of themselves as people, but something was often absent.

Perhaps I simply assumed that when the Bible was in the sermon, God was the subject. It slowly dawned on me that people were the main focus, and the reason many sermons had no power was that God was largely absent. One can preach for some time and offer historical insights on David killing Goliath, discuss David's lineage and family, and talk about how the Philistines were in the Iron Age and had advanced weapons, Israel was trapped in the Bronze Age, and David was in the Stone Age. Still, from a theological perspective, if God did not guide the pebble that David launched from his slingshot, if God did not cause the Philistine army to panic, there would be no obvious reason to preach that story apart from the fact that it is in the Bible. If the preacher is not willing or sufficiently daring to point to God in the Bible and the world, perhaps no one else will. Such pointing is a radical act because it takes faith to name where God acts and what God does. Sometimes the Bible does not mention God, and all too easily we turn biblical texts into human-centered, moralistic instructions that usually are not their intended purpose.

Many biblical scholars seem to be uncomfortable answering, How is the Bible the Word of God? How is it revelation? Many have good answers, but often unless they have a vocation as preachers, they may be reluctant to talk about faith issues in relation to their teaching. They have good reason: their discipline encourages history, fact, and documented evidence, and questions of faith seem to fall in the realm of the personal rather than the academic. Biblical scholars tend to read the Bible in historical-critical and literary ways, yet for it to be read as the church's book, as God's word, as Scripture, one needs to read it theologically as well, looking for God, for what God says, wants, does, and empowers.

In my first year of teaching I had in my class a student who challenged much that I said, if not by word then by the way he turned in his seat and stared out the window. He did not hand in his exegesis assignment showing scholarly study of his preaching text, explaining that *exegesis* meant "exit Jesus" (I thought my student at least showed wit). He did not show up on the day he was to preach. I have come to think that I failed him in two ways, in his final grade and in that I did not answer his deep fear that scholarship would destroy his faith. I did not lead him to appreciate the activity of the Holy Spirit even through scholarship. I now try to be deliberate in speaking in class about the strengths and the limitations of historical-critical study for the pulpit as well as what is needed beyond it by way of theological interpretation.

When I hear a student sermon, I silently ask, *Please give me a good reason in faith to believe what you say.* Very few people believe just because someone else does; otherwise more of our children and grandchildren (and even parents) would believe. Both seekers and members need to be given good reasons for believing, even though ultimately one must make a leap of faith, biblical texts read theologically often provide many reasons, and the fullest arguably relate to the resurrection of Jesus Christ. On whether he is alive or dead the faith stands or falls. One could argue then that the sermon needs to get to this issue each week, not just at Easter, and not just for seekers, though for them this can be crucial, but for ordinary believers as well, for presumably in that knowledge and affirmation, faith is renewed. This message needs to come not as "same old, same old," but afresh each week as the gospel is found both within texts and with texts.

This book is partly about providing good reasons for people to believe. Some people might assume that providing good reasons means providing tight arguments to persuade people to believe, and although such arguments from time to time may be helpful, that is not the norm advocated here. Many of the reasons arise out of good teaching about the Bible, God, faith, and contemporary life. Many of the reasons have to do with leading people in the sermon to the heart of the gospel where one encounters the risen Christ. Many of the reasons go beyond teaching to proclamation of the gospel in all its diverse forms that are present in the Bible and worship through the ages yet that have been largely lost from today's pulpit. Proclamation has to do with a sense of urgency, dynamic witness, encounter with God, restored faith, and inspired commitment. It has to do with allowing one's words as a preacher to catch fire in the Holy Spirit with excitement of the gospel, arising initially from one's biblical text.

Russell Maier, a British Columbia multimedia artist, photographs fire. For one picture he set the camera shutter speed at 1/650 of a second, and in that tiny flicker of time he captured a distinct image in the center of the frame (and flame) that looks like a dove (see this image on the cover of this book). Perceived one way, the dove is viewed from the side and seems to be stationary and fully attentive, its wings folded and almost resting on its back. Perceived another way, it is on the move, its wings powerfully unfurled to the edges of the picture, its underside exposed, and its tail outstretched and fanned, as though it is halting in one place, hovering for a moment in midflight, perhaps landing or taking off. Moreover, in the bottom left corner of the original is a hint of the cross.

The double illusion of the dove in fire can serve as a powerful image of the Holy Spirit. A friend who has suffered much in life looked at this photograph and said, "It's great that out of fire, the dove is seen to emerge." Had the artist been seeking a Christian title for his painting, he could have used any number of Bible verses, for example, "The light of Israel will become a fire, / and his Holy One a flame" (Isaiah 10:17). Along with numerous biblical references to the fiery throne of God and flames of righteousness that will cleanse the nations, the photograph calls to mind other images appropriate to proclamation: the flames of the burning bush that do not consume (Exodus 3:2); the Lord "in a pillar of fire" by night leading Israel to the Red Sea (Exodus 13:21); the live coal that touches Isaiah's lips and cleanses but does not burn (Isaiah 6:6-7); the fiery furnace where Shadrach, Meshach, and Abednego are found unbound, walking and unhurt, with a fourth man of divine appearance (Daniel 3:25); John the Baptist's prophecy that Jesus will baptize "with the Holy Spirit and fire" (Luke 3:16); the Holy Spirit who seems "like a dove" descending on Jesus at his baptism (Mark 1:10); the tongues of fire that rest upon the disciples at Pentecost (Acts 2:3); and the vision of Jesus Christ beheld by John of Patmos: "His eyes were like a flame of fire, his feet were like burnished bronze, refined as in a furnace" (Revelation 1:14-15).

When preachers proclaim the gospel, their words catch fire and, as Paul intimated, are filled with a "demonstration of the Spirit and of power." This power of the preached word is not oppressive or coercive, though it comes with "all authority in heaven and on earth" (Matthew 28:18). It is not the preacher's nor does it draw attention to the person of the preacher. This power is located in the Servant who wills to be known by the world not least through the weakness of our preaching. His light is to the nations, and he chooses weakness and humility even to death on the cross, "a bruised reed he will not break, / and a dimly burning wick he will not quench" (Isaiah 42:3; Matthew 12:20). As the Lord of hosts says in Zechariah 4:6, "Not by might, nor by power, but by my spirit."

The first section of this study draws lessons from the pulpit concerning how to teach. The second section reviews what it means to teach the gospel, both from a biblical perspective and from within homiletics. The third section gets to proclamation. Throughout, an attempt is made to explore the different roles of the Holy Spirit in teaching and in proclamation. Readers who are impatient and learn best by doing can jump to chapters 3 and 4 for lessons about teaching, and to chapters 9 through 17 for guidance with proclamation.

Readers can skim the many examples offered here, but they will then miss significant matters that have to do with sound, rhythm, emotion, form, content, and effect. A CD is provided to lift some of these historical examples into the air once again as an oral art. Most excerpts hark back to ages when preaching was not tied to the page the way so often it is today. In them we hear ways of thought that are rich in expression beyond most contemporary speech. Some excerpts address cultural matters that are now foreign. I have found that I often need to take time to read aloud these excerpts in order to appreciate them. I encourage readers to consider doing the same. One can thereby learn to do what these preachers did, and can learn in multiple ways that are often best, by seeing, hearing, speaking, and imitating. In so doing preachers can begin to reclaim some of the strength of their oral heritage. One might even consider using this book as a reference tool because of the models it presents.

As preachers, we do many things better than our ancestors, for example, dealing with the historical background of biblical texts, connecting with the needs of our listeners, and linking the faith to issues of social and environmental justice. After years of teaching the history of preaching and studying sermons from the past and present, I have gradually come to appreciate that past preachers often do some things better than we do today; in particular, they draw widely on the Bible, teach in significant ways about the faith, and use that teaching as a basis to proclaim. Several years into my teaching I took a half-year of sabbatical leave to read widely in sermons through the ages. I discovered anew what many preachers already know; most past sermons seem boring. I remember long hours of taking notes and trying to stay awake. At the end of that leave I did not know if I had wasted my time. I did not appreciate then that maybe I was in training. I was learning to see what was actually on the page, learning to read not merely as a historian who looks for biographical or historical connections, but as a pastoral theologian and teacher of preaching with a view to practice, for example, concerning social and hermeneutical issues and homiletical methods. Slowly I began to grasp what preachers in various ages were trying to do, and I started to recognize various patterned ways of speaking. Not least I started to realize that passion that is obvious in oral delivery in the pulpit actually leaves traces on the page of the written and often even translated sermon. I began to sense how some sermons might once have lived. Some passages were outstanding for their clear teaching while others seemed luminescent with deeper truth. The following chapters present some of that learning. I came to categorize and understand patterned ways of speaking on the page as particular genres within sermons, genres that serve the gospel.

I struggled with how many examples to include here. I needed enough to show the range and variety within each genre and enough to establish that these genres exist with frequency and are not just freaks of history. If I have erred, it may be in the direction of generosity. It is my hope that from the range of examples offered, the imagination of readers will be stirred, and they might be drawn to imitate and adapt at least a few examples in each genre in their preaching.

This project remains a challenge to me personally. Nearly every preacher today does proclaim from time to time, some more frequently than others, without necessarily knowing it or being intentional. In my sermons I have practiced some of what our forebears demonstrate, but often serendipitously without method. Rarely were my efforts sustained in the manner of many examples here. I still need these tutors to come into the study with me and instruct my preaching. In other words, it is one thing intellectually to understand what good teaching and proclamation are and can be, and it is a much longer task over many years to make them one's own.

No preacher ought to claim, "I have arrived," for we are always called to better witness. What sermons might evolve to look like in the future will be revealed in time with God's guidance, yet one hopes above all they will give ever more faithful witness. If preaching as a dual art of teaching and proclamation is worthy of recovery, the process is larger than any one of us and may take more than one generation of preachers. May we learn from each other, may we be willing to risk together, may our congregations be responsive and forgiving in the Spirit, and may it all be for the furtherance of the gospel of Jesus Christ.

Easter 2008
Emmanuel College
University of Toronto

CHAPTER ONE

A Challenge for Preaching

Preaching throughout history has had a dual focus, teaching and proclaiming, but lately this has not been the case. Teaching in most pulpits is alive and well, but not in the full range that may be needed for proclamation, and some dimensions of teaching that were important through the ages are now often missing. Published sermons today generally focus on human action and make important claims about what believers are to do by way of loving God and neighbor. However, more often than not they fail to focus on God in significant ways. Solid teaching is essential in every sermon, for as Jesus noted, a house is best built on rock. Teaching provides information that listeners can use to shape their thoughts and actions. Teaching gives people ways to think about the faith, God, and daily life. Teaching may even be said to generate consciousness by naming things we have not noticed, thereby opening them to experience. When a child learns that no two snowflakes are the same, or that through prayer a relationship with God is possible, a world of wonder may be opened.

Teaching, as we use it here, leads people toward faith and sets certain tasks before them that help them appropriate the teachings for their lives. Proclamation, on the other hand, is impassioned utterance that introduces people to God, makes faith a possibility, and allows them to be shaped by God's word. Proclamation may be said to have become largely a lost art. Proclamation makes God the center of the sermon and offers the fire of the Holy Spirit in transforming power. At its best it provides for Jesus Christ to speak in his true identity, as the one who died and rose again for the people whom God loves. In proclamation God in Christ takes the burden of responsibility from the hearer and accepts it as his own. God does what is needed, and hearers are invited and empowered to assent in faith and follow as disciples.

Proclamation appears in some new book titles, but one searches them largely in vain for the practice that our ancestors handed down to us. Many preachers today do proclaim. Others treat *preaching* and *proclaiming* as synonyms. Others may think of proclamation as a kind of old-fashioned harangue that insists on its own truth and way. In fact, it is akin to love in 1 Corinthians 13: it is not "boastful or arrogant or rude. It does not insist on its own way . . . but rejoices in the truth." Still, the word *proclaim* often evokes negative responses. *To proclaim* means "to declare or announce." It can connote a hierarchical notion of authority that is repugnant in circles today. Some of that understanding may carry over to Christian preaching, where the word *proclaim* may seem like a relic from the past. It is a little like the term *duplicating machine*, and while both terms are still in use, the cultural memory is mostly gone of what they actually were.

Proclamation Defined

Proclamation may be understood to consist of the most loving, life-affirming, Spirit-inspired words that anyone could ever hope to hear because they come from God. They announce God's redemptive activity in the moment, and in the announcement, also the fulfillment. Most preachers teach and do so best with the guidance of the Spirit. Proclamation is similarly Spirit-guided, yet it is also Spirit-filled. In it the self-giving of the Spirit is experienced, the same as is located in the cross. Proclamation in this sense has gone missing. Where it makes an appearance, it does so often without preachers being aware of it, of its history back to the early church, or of its many forms throughout the ages.

Teaching is absolutely critical for preaching and must be in place in order for proclamation to be heard. Teaching is like taking a bus tour to some royal estate that is wonderful in its own right, yet what a difference is made if by the journey's end, one actually meets the owner. Proclamation introduces people to God. They hear God speak. When preaching stops short of proclamation, arguably its main purpose is lost. Proclamation at its best is the loving announcement of the good news that has been accomplished in Jesus Christ, the articulation of words at the heart of the gospel that are spoken or received as being directly from God to the people of God. Proclamation is passionate, often almost musical speech that is intimate, urgent, and inspires confidence and faith. It actualizes the biblical text, brings the gospel to life, performs God's grace, and enacts God's liberation in the moment such that listeners experience that redemption is theirs in this present moment.

Proclamation refers not to a few words at the heart of the gospel, like key lines of classical creeds, but to a number of entire genres that center on the gospel and enable it to be heard, and that go beyond where most preaching stops today. If proclamation is conceived as only a quick reference to God's redemptive activity in each sermon, the people have a chance to experience almost nothing. What they get may be a kind of drive-by gospel; God seemingly wheels by the church and waves in the general direction of the open doors. Proclamation needs sustained treatment, and the words at the heart of the gospel have to be so framed or heard and received as divinely spoken, thereby setting faith and hope ablaze once more. The genres explored here offer a fresh vision of what is possible in the pulpit.

God at the Center

A homiletical storm arose in the 1950s that lingers to the present; its winds and surging tides have pummeled the preaching coastline. Sermons built on the seemingly "old" three points used different notions of authority from those popular today and did not weather well. Sermons designed according to what is called the New Homiletic have fared a little better. This school of thought argues, for example, that sermons should be structured according to the needs of those who will hear them, have fluid design, allow access to all, and provide ample windows to various perspectives. One of the New Homiletic's significant accomplishments was to ground sermons in the first instance in the bedrock of the Bible rather than in the shifting sand of topics and issues. In churches that follow the lectionary, for example, preachers tend to have become very good teachers of biblical texts, their settings and history, and their literary features. Congregations are now exposed to a wider range of Scripture than they were when preachers chose their favorite texts to preach. Still, all schools have their weaknesses, and it is clear now that having the Bible as a foundation is not necessarily the same thing as having God. Ostensibly, one can preach the Bible and not arrive at God's word, one can preach God's word and not arrive at the gospel, and one might even teach the gospel and still not proclaim it. In right balance, teaching leads to proclamation, and proclamation grows out of good teaching. It cannot exist without it. When teaching and proclamation are linked, preaching moves beyond giving information about the divine to giving the triune God. Teaching and proclamation as dual arts provide room for a meeting with God to take place.

No preacher presumably wants pancakelike sermons that are flat emotionally, lacking reason for excitement; flat rhetorically, lacking energy and music; and flat theologically and prophetically, lacking substantial focus on God. Most of us struggle to be good orators, compelling speakers who have an art to make common ideas new again, who can turn communication into participation and information into inspired music. We are part of a generation of conversational preachers who speak in natural ways that are authentic, who are gifted at working with the Bible and applying the text to today. Advances have been made in many areas, yet most of us could benefit by increasing our range: in content (to make the gospel our deliberate goal); in style (to be even better teachers); and in voice (to speak in impassioned ways). Though preaching is often a long way from its oral roots, it may not be too late to recover some of the dynamic speech that characterized the best pulpits in the past. In so doing our sermons might express more joy and excitement, and offer more demonstration of the Spirit and God's power.

Here we speak of the possibility of recovering this joy and excitement, yet this is not a call to use any one model of impassioned speech or to imitate a particular style from the past or present. Whatever proclamation might sound like when it is designed for today, the preacher's manner must be natural, not false in any way, even though the words are on fire with the Spirit. When one thinks of passionate people, one is aware of all the differences in their personalities and expression. Proclamation similarly has various ways of speaking that can be natural to each preacher, each person finding her or his manner of embodied passionate speech that integrates heart, mind, body, and soul.

Nevertheless, recovery of preaching as a dual art of teaching and proclamation may be not so much a matter of the church finding passionate preachers as it is a matter of preachers finding the good news and allowing their passion for it to be expressed in the sermon. Passion in the pulpit appropriately is a matter not of emotion in the first instance but of good theology, strong faith, and personal integrity. To be emotional for the sake of passion is foolish and empty, like Paul's "noisy gong or clanging cymbal" (1 Corinthians 13:1). Likewise, to be excited in the pulpit about some ideology, no matter how good the cause, seems wrongheaded. Ideally everything preachers do in the sermon connects in some way to the good news that Jesus Christ came to give, and those gospel connections potentially give particular voice to the Spirit. As Jesus said, "Apart from me you can do nothing" (John 15:5). The Spirit in good teaching enlivens texts and our lives, but the Spirit's additional purpose in preaching arguably is communicating God and presenting the risen and reigning Christ. Passion is important for preaching, but it is secondary. When preachers have something important to offer, that is, God's saving grace and power, excitement is natural. Preaching then can be a lifeline to the dying person, 20/20 vision for those who see but are blind, and justice for all who are oppressed. Preachers are then right to be excited, have fire in the belly, and use words on fire. Those of us who try to communicate the gospel without fire might seem odd, like someone saying, "I love you," in monotone, with eyes averted and deadpan facial expression.

Can a Lost Oral Art Be Recovered?

When proclamation was common, it was an oral art, and that was its strength and a reason it may be largely lost to us. Some people may think that it should remain lost because the preaching of our ancestors at minimum was stiff and formalized and might seem authoritarian. This assessment has merit with some preachers more than others, yet amazingly old sermons keep presenting passages that are not just spent coals but have live embers with tongues of fire that still lick the pages without consuming them. We can hope that our sermons similarly might have holy fire to give light for future descendants.

We can no longer hear the actual voices of preachers of old. How then can we recover proclamation? Four ways may be named. First, one can go to written sermons from times and places where proclamation was common. The page is obviously a poor instrument for recording actual sound, but at times it is better than we think. It is a little like digital recording today that converts life first into a binary code of zeros and ones and in turn converts these numbers back into words, pictures, movement, and sounds. In sermons from the past, sounds are recorded in the letters that mark the page, and while the technology may seem primitive, the reader voices those sounds and may be said to "hear" the preachers preach as though present. The page itself affords clues to how things were spoken if we learn how to read it. Still today portions of old sermons lift off the page with what Paul called a "demonstration of the Spirit and of power" (1 Corinthians 2:4). For example, even now groups can catch fire listening to excerpts from one of the earliest recorded preachers outside the Bible, Melito of Sardis in the second century.

A second way to recover a lost art is to contrast it with an existing art, in this case contrasting proclamation with teaching. Because proclamation moves beyond the plain style of most teaching to more elevated and impassioned styles and forms of expression, the page still allows these stylistic differences to come through: phrases are often shorter and more rhythmic; they often show frequent use of rhetorical devices like parallel structure.

Most of the innovative principles of teaching identified in the New Homiletic add strength to teaching in the pulpit. It is also important to see how teaching has fallen short in some regards and therefore does not always supply a basis for proclamation. Heightened awareness of teaching can allow preachers to be more intentional about employing what is needed for proclamation. Historical examples cited here will clarify the difference between teaching and proclamation and provide preachers with models of both to emulate.

Third, one can go where proclamation is at least remembered, and that is to a few theologians in the last century. They knew proclamation when they heard it, and more than that, they knew how to write about it. They understood God's role in it and developed important theologies of the word that may be found to highlight preaching at its best. The theologians I identify here are from the Reformed and Lutheran traditions, yet evidence suggests that most denominations practiced proclamation, and one therefore presumes that some theological understanding of it extended to all. People in these two traditions engaged in explicit conversation about it. At minimum they offer ideas for proclamation that stretch our commonplace contemporary assumptions.

Finally, one can go where proclamation is still practiced. Probably all preachers from time to time proclaim, most obviously around Christmas and Easter, and at funerals. Many preachers proclaim without awareness, and they may not know they can develop proclamation such that their words catch fire with sufficient flame to warm the listeners' hands, hearts, and minds. Proclamation is notably found in some African American pulpits that practice celebration, the rousing rhetorical climax of a sermon that embodies the gospel and encourages congregational involvement.

Still, preachers ought not to think of proclamation as only celebration. The present study identifies, along with celebration, a total of nine genres of proclamation that arise from sermons of the past. These genres have some features in common. We are not used to talking about proclamation, much less to conceiving nine genres of it. They are from many traditions of preaching in recent centuries and date all of the way back to the early church and Bible roots.

One conclusion here will be that just as much of oral African American traditions came from Africa, so too some seem to have come from a common preaching heritage. Some friends in these traditions have said that in their communities, they have wondered whether there was not something that they brought from the churches of the slave masters. Here we can only lift up that possibility. Racial division in the United States kept African American preaching isolated; thus when other preaching traditions lost proclamation, for reasons we will explore much later, it seems to have been less vulnerable. Could it be that it has helped to preserve, enhance, and advance dimensions of proclamation that predate it and that its founders in part received? We can say with confidence that proclamation is not unique to African American preaching traditions, though particular expressions there may be unique. Proclamation belongs to all preachers.

Sermon Subforms

Homiletical discussion about sermon form has focused on outward, external, or overall forms; thus we have sermons that are named thematic, doctrinal, expository, deductive, propositional, inductive, and narrative, to name a few. Not much attention has been given to forms within the sermon: some basic categories are inherited from ancient rhetoric, like introduction, body, conclusion, examples, points, and poems, yet these are so obvious from elementary school as to merit little interest or discussion.[1] Here we will examine a fresh range of forms or genres within sermons that arise out of the practice of proclaiming and that are particular to homiletics as a discipline in its own right. Attention to genres within sermons not only may open new avenues of academic study; it can help reestablish proclamation in the church's practice, should that be a goal. We will call these genres *subforms* of preaching to distinguish them from *genres of sermons* or *sermon forms*, terms that imply overall form.

It is easier to find excellent passages in old sermons than it is to find entire sermons that still seem excellent. In many extracted passages the Spirit seems still to find voice. In the current work, samples are harvested from sermons not to persuade preachers ultimately to spend precious time reading more deeply in history, beneficial though this may be, but to stimulate the imaginations of preachers today if we allow ourselves greater freedom to emulate, adapt, and borrow from the past.

Why New Directions May Be Needed

Why might new directions be needed? The simplest answer is the church is in decline. Numbers can never be our primary concern—the Holy Spirit grows the church—but as preachers in an age of decline, we nonetheless rightly ask if we are being as faithful as possible. Many churches are thriving. However, in the big picture fewer children are being reached by the church through its teaching, and fewer youth and young adults are developing a lifelong, daily relationship with God. Many people brought up in the church no longer attend. People outside the church typically see little reason to cross the threshold. The challenges are obvious. The role of ministers, priests, and pastors is changing, not least because society increasingly may view the rites and services provided by the church (such as baptism, marriage, and funerals) as commodities or, worse, as inconveniences. The sermon itself is under scrutiny. The centrality of the word, long a cornerstone of life and worship, in many traditions is questioned. For congregations at one extreme, the Bible and preaching may no longer have any particular authority. For congregations at another extreme, worship centers on music and instructions about proper living that often fall short of searching Scripture for God's word.

Arguably all that the church has to offer the world is the gospel. Some of our best efforts can be devoted to recovering preaching as both teaching and proclamation, to helping people establish a relationship with the living God, who empowers us to serve others.

Church Decline

Church decline is across the board, including many evangelical churches.[2] Mainline denominations demonstrate major decline since 1960: the Institute on Religion and Democracy in the United States shows the United Methodists down by 20 percent from roughly ten million members to eight; the Presbyterian Church (U.S.A.) and the Christian Church (Disciples of Christ) are down between 40 and 50 percent.[3] Various reasons can be given for the decline, including religious diversity and a changing demographic because of immigration patterns, birth rates, and numerous economic factors. Some reasons lie within the church, as Nancy T. Ammerman recently wrote:

> Everybody does some equivalent of Sunday school (even Muslims and Buddhists); mainline Protestants, however, are the only group that routinely does nothing else. Everyone else has weekday programs or day schools or bar mitzvah classes, for instance; but mainline churches are more likely to sponsor a scout troop than to have a regular organized religious activity for their children.[4]

Evidence shows that mainline churches are not able to retain even the children of their members. The average adult age of mainline congregations is fifty-two and of evangelical congregations is forty-eight; across the board, adults in their twenties are being lost.[5]

My own denomination is not unusual in having many healthy churches while also closing church buildings, amalgamating congregations, and blending names, sometimes to regrettable humorous effect.[6] In Toronto the union of Bond Street Church and St. James Church produced St. James-Bond Church, a union that predated the 007 James Bond movies, but newcomers to the city did not know that. Now even amalgamated churches are closed, including that one. Theologian Douglas John Hall put a positive spin on the decline, hoping that what survives is a more faithful remnant,[7] and the church still belongs to God and all things are possible. Crisis language is not used in denominational communication; even in the midst of large financial and program cutbacks, business as usual seems to be the message. This may happen because many surviving congregations are viable for the present time, or because ministry staff at local, regional, and national levels are overwhelmed struggling to keep their heads above water. Still if there is a fire in the kitchen, only for so long can we keep closing doors behind us and moving to rooms farther from the flames.

Religion Overload

At the same time the world seems a trifle weary of traditional religion. Some congregations are willing to try almost anything to keep the doors open. One church recently advertised itself as an "Express Church, Out in 45 Minutes Guaranteed." There are drive-in churches with prepackaged Communion elements distributed as one drives in; presumably, if one does not like people, one can leave without greeting anyone. There are churches for people who hate religion, as it says on the Web page of the Meeting House, a megachurch that actually does an excellent job of reaching young people. Some churches have turned to technology, PowerPoint, 3-D holograms, and pyrotechnics. In Newmarket, Ontario, in 2003, the Reverend Dorian Baxter, an Elvis Presley impersonator who calls himself Elvis Priestley, left the Anglican Church to set up the Christ the King, Graceland Independent Anglican Church. He has his own version of "Blue Suede Shoes": "Well it's one for the Father, two for the Son, three for the Holy Spirit and your life has just begun."[8] Megachurches like Willow Creek, Saddleback, and Prestonwood Baptist Church in the United States have had considerable success in terms of numbers and organizational innovation. Many have become megabusinesses that offer things like gymnasiums, health and other clubs, restaurants, bookstores, and a variety of publications, resources, continuing education courses, and outreach programs. In this regard they can begin to look like other empires.

A job description for preachers today can be formidable: the successful candidate must be steeped in the Bible and tradition; well read; spiritual; CEO material; sensitive to diversity of cultures; a caregiver; a counselor; able to speak to the range of experience that people bring to church; contextual; and knowledgeable in how to deal with the range of social ills and social services. Most preachers cannot live up to such high expectations, but they can follow Jesus' mandate: "Go into all the world and proclaim the good news to the whole creation" (Mark 16:15). This understanding of the centrality of the gospel undergirds all the New Testament. One could argue that ministry today is so much more than preaching, but at the same time preaching centered on the gospel may be said to lead to the gifts needed for other aspects of ministry.

Ten Cultural Barriers to Sharing Faith

Jesus' commission is to the entire church, not just to preachers. If a tree falls in a forest and no one hears it, does it make a sound? If we live good lives and people see our joy, but no one knows our faith, have we proclaimed the gospel? Some may say yes, and they would be in agreement with words attributed to Saint Francis of Assisi, "Preach the gospel always and if necessary use words." Still, something more seems to be called for by way of spoken word, noncoercive utterance, and shared faith. As Paul said, "Faith comes from what is heard, and what is heard comes through the word of Christ" (Romans 10:17).

If the whole congregation is to proclaim the gospel, this can mean that we help one another. George Lindbeck spoke of a cultural linguistic model of doctrine in which the ordinary language of a community of faith helps to shape the habits and lives of its members.[9] In practical terms the preacher offers the congregation words and language to share. However, cultural barriers exist to speaking of faith, and these vary from person to person, congregation to congregation, and culture to culture. The following are just a few:

1. The Absence of Silence

Many claims compete with those of the church, including Sunday sports leagues, the Internet, and all manner of media, easy transportation, busy schedules, and wealth. Society has largely banished silence. Everywhere people are talking on cell phones, listening to headsets, moving to music. People do not have the time to meditate for long or to experience a hunger for God. Richard Lischer offers a related perspective: "Culture . . . is suffering a certain exhaustion with words. Mass violence overrides the significance of language."[10]

2. The Desire to Respect Others

Postmodern society celebrates diversity; thus the line is blurred between sharing the gospel in a loving way and respecting the viewpoints of others. How is one best to proceed? A crusty professor at Austin Seminary back in the 1970s had no time for what were then called Jesus freaks. On his way out of a football game he was swept by the exiting crowd straight toward one of these young men who was handing out flyers and said to him, "Jesus loves you and so do I," to which the acerbic professor replied, "Well at least half of that is good news." Sharing faith can be done in ways that are more respectful of others and that encourage respectful response.

3. Evangelism Is a Bad Word for Many People

Christians in the past have conducted a form of evangelism that has been characterized as cultural imperialism. God-talk is so common on television in North America that many are weary of it. Even mentioning God in a conversation can mean being labeled. Moreover, much media offers a poor representation of faith. Many people lack models of how to share faith in respectful and loving ways. Unfortunately some Christians might feel more comfortable giving directions to the nearest mall than sharing what is most important in their lives. If preachers do not proclaim the gospel, it is harder for others to do so.

4. Critical Assessment Seems Diminished

Our postmodern world may question every assumption, and since the Vietnam War, most authority has been mistrusted. Scripture, tradition, reason, experience, the church, ordered ministry—all are challenged. All opinion is treated as though it is of equal value. A cartoon had a picture of the prophet Isaiah preaching to Israel, "They shall beat their swords into ploughshares gradually so as not to cause unemployment." Nowadays a sermon is as likely to be evaluated by whether it is politically correct as by any other standard. Even personal witness is suspect.

5. Resistance to the Past

We live in a high-technology world in which the growth of scientific knowledge is exponential. As a result the center of gravity in culture seems to have shifted from present-past to present-future, anticipating the next software, the new CD, the latest fashion, the next advance in medicine or technology. The future matters, and what happened in the past, notably in the Bible and traditions of the church, seems of lesser value. For many people, including much of the media, God seems to belong to a primitive way of thought or to a past time and culture.

6. Uncertainty about the Purposes of Preaching

With a worldwide decline in Christianity in proportion to other faiths, it seems less likely that Christians will ever "make disciples of all nations," as Jesus instructed in Matthew 28:19. Jesus said in John 14:6 that "no one comes to the Father except through me," and many Christians take this literally, others explain it away, and still others say that Christ may be found in all the major faiths. Preachers of previous ages seemed to agree that the purpose of preaching was to save souls, but many preachers today seem uncertain of a purpose. Many Christians may wonder whether confessing Christ is necessary for salvation; thus much motivation for sharing the faith is gone.

7. Biblical Illiteracy

Many people feel that they do not know the Bible and are ill-equipped to talk about their faith with others. Because they do not know their Bibles, they feel they do not have primary words, stories, and images of faith to share.

8. The Foolishness of the Gospel

Sometimes we may be reluctant to speak of God or indeed of Jesus Christ. Sophisticated people may find such talk embarrassing, even if they do believe it. Moreover, the gospel has no rational proof, and people come to it not by earthly wisdom, as Paul stated, but "through the foolishness of our proclamation" (1 Corinthians 1:21). He also said that "the wisdom of this world is foolishness with God" (3:19). Many of us preachers want to explain what cannot be explained instead of simply witnessing, living as Christ's disciples, and making room for the Holy Spirit to work.

9. People Confuse Sharing Faith with Telling Others What to Do

Telling others about faith might seem bossy or intrusive, more likely to cause offense than be welcomed, for people may think they are being judged. People in the past often have been treated as objects of conversion more than people with whom to enter a mutual relationship. Under the right conditions, talking to others about faith is an intimate and loving gesture. It is not giving information as much as it is offering to be in a relationship with that person, God, and a faith community.

10. Underestimating Sin and Evil

Society has a general underestimation of evil as a power, and in a good many pulpits the word *sin* seems not to be used. Some people are convinced that salvation is not even necessary, or if it is needed, they believe it is something one can provide for oneself as a kind of self-help. Still, sin and evil are powers that express themselves in individual lives, human institutions, and social systems. One of the marks of evil is that it looks good, it masks itself as right, and it presents itself as innocent.

Of course, many other reasons may be cited about why Christians might hesitate to share the gospel. These at least indicate that there is an urgent need for good teaching centered on God and human relationships with God, just as there is a need for sermons to catch fire with the good news, in other words, for sermons that move beyond teaching *about* the gospel to bestowing it.

In the immediate chapters to which we now turn we explore in some depth first the subject of improving our teaching. We preach particular biblical texts, and we teach from them concerning how they intersect with our lives. When our teaching also extends to the gospel, which may not be the direct subject of a particular text, we have the opportunity to proclaim the gospel. The key to it all is good teaching, and to that subject we now turn.

SECTION ONE

Becoming Better Teachers

CHAPTER TWO

Preaching as Good Teaching?

Good teaching is a necessary and profound asset for any pulpit. Paul calls teaching a gift of the Spirit (Romans 12:7; 1 Corinthians 14:6, 26). Alan of Lille in the twelfth century defined preaching as teaching: "Preaching is an open and public instruction in faith and behavior whose purpose is the forming of men; it derives from the path of reason and from the fountainhead of the 'authorities.' "[1] The purpose of such instruction was threefold, to edify, to increase knowledge, and "to maintain the well-being of the community."[2] Still today, preaching is or ought to be substantially teaching about God and who humans are before God. Teaching provides the theological, historical, and cultural information that listeners need to understand who God is, has been, and will be; it explores the thought of our forebears and leads to new understandings appropriate for the present; and it guides life and prayer. Teaching is dynamic and involves informed use of many resources and topics related to today's world, including the social sciences, world affairs, the environment, and social justice, to name a few. Teaching is attentive and geared to listener needs and abilities; thus it employs rhetorical and communication strategies. Teaching has received a great deal of attention in the last fifty years, and the quality of teaching may be said to have improved. The question we will pursue in these next chapters is whether teaching about God and the gospel has kept up with other pedagogical improvements in this same period.

A Review of Teaching in the Pulpit

What is the state of the art of teaching in the pulpit today? One way we may get a handle on the subject is to review homiletics over the last decades. Preaching as teaching goes back to Bible times; in fact, the Bible uses the terms *teaching* and *preaching* almost interchangeably. C. H. Dodd received much criticism for making too sharp a distinction between biblical notions of teaching (*didache*) and preaching (*kerygma*) in his *The Apostolic Preaching and Its Developments* (1936). He assumed an original core kerygma that was very close to the Apostles' Creed. Though he assumed too much by way of uniformity and unanimity, he drew important attention to the didache/kerygma distinction.

The *New Homiletic* is a recent term that refers to a school of thought in the last fifty years. People date the beginning of the New Homiletic in different ways. The term was coined by Richard L. Eslinger only as recently as 1987 when he contrasted the "old homiletic" with the advocates of a "new homiletic."[3] The revolution to which he referred was already in full bloom by then. While the term *New Homiletic* could be taken to mean everything in homiletics that is not old, it is more safely restricted to those elements of change that by then had found general agreement: listener need is central; greater focus is on the Bible; sermon agenda is set by solid exegesis involving historical-critical and literary analysis; sermon forms echo the content, form, and effect of the biblical texts; narrative, metaphor, and image are used to capture and evoke experience; and deductive and propositional argument is less favored than organic forms that arise and grow out of the content and that employ conversational style. Matters such as these found broad acceptance.

When did the New Homiletic start? One could go to its roots and say the English Romantics in the first half of the 1800s, for they laid the foundation for nearly all of the changes that were to come. However, the Victorian era (1837–1901) quickly lost sight of their key Romantic insights. Only when scholars like I. A. Richards in the 1930s reexamined them—especially people like Samuel Taylor Coleridge and William Wordsworth—was their impact in art, literary criticism, philosophy, and rhetoric felt more broadly (later still in theology and homiletics). Some scholars might claim the revolution began in 1951 with W. E. Sangster, who conceived that one possible form for sermons was inductive;[4] however, it was an idea that he did not develop, and no one seemed to notice he said it until after Fred Craddock developed the notion in the 1970s. Others claim H. Grady Davis as the start; his *Design for Preaching* (1958), for the first time since the mid-1800s, brought to preaching Romantic principles about literature, art, imagination, language, and metaphor. He advocated organic form, the inseparability of form and content, the sermon as an idea that grows and that moves in time with sequence and plot in the manner of music, story, and drama.[5] Still others may say the New Homiletic began with David Randolph, who proposed a new direction for homiletics based on the New Hermeneutic in 1969. He proposed:

1. The sermon . . . proceeds from the Bible as God's Word to us and connects with the situation of the hearers; it does not arise from religion in general and address the universe.
2. The sermon moves fundamentally to *confirmation* from affirmation, rather than to evidence from axiom.

3. The sermon seeks *concretion* by bringing the meaning of the text to expression in the situation of the hearers, rather than abstraction by merely exhibiting the text against its own background.
4. The sermon seeks forms of *construction* and *communication* which are consistent with the message it intends to convey, not necessarily those which are most traditional, most readily available, or most "successful."[6]

Randolph called for preaching to relate to the experience or situation of the hearers and for new sermon forms that reflect experience. However one dates the beginning of the New Homiletic, it has changed the face of preaching in much of the English-speaking world and beyond.

The Decline of Point Form

Most changes that have been wrought by the New Homiletic have actually been changes in what and how teaching is offered from the pulpit. One of the biggest changes concerns the use of points. Prior to the late 1960s, the traditional propositional three-point sermon was standard. If sermons did not actually mention three points, they were often structured with three sections. This form through history was so common that it is often referred to as the "bread and butter" sermon of the church. In practice, it was often treated with the kind of reverence usually reserved for something that has actual biblical basis, yet it seems to have medieval origin in the recovery of Aristotle. His works, which put emphasis on logic, reason, and science, had been lost to the Western world and preserved in Arab libraries. When they were rediscovered, he gave guidance and encouragement to ordered thought. Robert of Basevorn around 1300 indicated humorously that already the three-point sermon was standard: "Only three statements, or the equivalent of three, are used in the theme either from respect to the Trinity, or because a threefold cord is not easily broken, or because this method is mostly followed by Bernard [of Clairvaux], or, as I think more likely, because it is more convenient for the set time of the sermon."[7] Preachers and listeners alike throughout the ages have found that three points are an excellent teaching tool that allows material to be easily heard and remembered.

Anything good can be abused, and history is rife with examples of excessive use of point form. One of the most extreme periods of misuse occurred with the Puritans. They favored sermons that placed attention on reason, wit, and a host of points and subpoints that to our time seem scarcely to merit attention. In preaching today we tend to say that less is more, sensing some value in brevity; they seem to have said that more is not enough, and they expected something of length and substance.

Richard Baxter in England was a Puritan branded a nonconformist because he favored religious tolerance. His "Sermon of Repentance" might have taken up to two hours to preach and shows his Puritan background: near the beginning, seven points move into a new series of five points (all in the space of around two thousand words); after an interval of several thousand more words, he has four enumerated points immediately followed by a new series of ten. All of this is the first half of his sermon. In the second half he has seven points, of which the last is broken into five, followed by a new series of six, plus two other series of four and eight, for a grand total of fifty-six.[8] Such a sermon represents a different notion of teaching in the pulpit than generally prevails today, though one modern-day preacher recently announced that his sermon had eighteen points and then proceeded through each one, more to the surprise than to the delight of his listeners. People in Baxter's more oral culture were better listeners and perhaps could appreciate and remember such divisions in an argument. Or perhaps points in those days were not so much to aid the memory as to indicate the organization and unity of sections.

Of course, the enormous resilience of points as a learning tool can be seen today in the profusion of PowerPoint presentations, not least in worship. Points can still have considerable appeal. The reasons that three-point sermons fell out of favor in some pulpits are several (that are listed as points!):

1. They imply that the sermon is primarily information to be received.
2. They may sound like a lecture.
3. They tend to encourage a deductive approach to sermon composition.
4. They became predictable, as though every biblical text had three points.
5. They were overused and sometimes seemed corny, especially when week after week the points were arranged on the basis of alliteration or end rhyme.
6. They imply to some listeners a vertical and sometimes male notion of authority with the preacher seeming to be above contradiction.

At the same time that three-point sermons were in decline, a number of changes were taking place in church and society:

1. Faith was appreciated as having important experiential and affective dimensions.

2. Experience could no longer be considered uniform or universal.
3. Truth came to be understood largely as contextual.
4. Mass media and culture affected ways of communication and learning.
5. Society was understood as diverse and multicultural.
6. Biblical and other texts were understood to have many meanings.
7. Various theologies arose, reflecting the experience of various groups.
8. Increased wealth and recreation time challenged the place of the church in society.
9. Authority in all of its expressions was challenged.
10. Language was understood to be largely rooted in metaphor and experience.

These and other factors led to enormous changes not least in preaching under the New Homiletic.

The Rise of Narrative

The New Homiletic changed how narrative is perceived and employed in the pulpit. In propositional sermons stories typically were illustrations that did just that: they illustrated points that were already made. Stories gave examples and added pictures, not new lines of thought. There was little sense that stories had a voice of their own and made their own statements in their own ways. Biblical narratives typically were reduced to propositions, their form unappreciated as part of their meaning.

Narratives move by plot, not points, as Eugene Lowry made clear in his *The Homiletical Plot*. When the term *narrative preaching* is used, people initially tend to think of one long story. In fact, narrative may refer to a sermon that

- has for its form a single or several stories
- uses stories not as illustrations of points but as devices that make their own points in their own ways
- is driven largely by plot as opposed to a linear progression of propositional points addressed to the intellect
- demonstrates interest in character, imagery, and metaphor
- uses imagination and evokes emotion and experience
- is sensitive to ways in which the form of a biblical text contributes to its meaning
- represents a form of teaching that is conversational in style

Inductive or narrative form gained support in the 1970s through the 1990s largely from its use by mass media and scholarly attention to narrative and parable in biblical studies, theology, and homiletics. Various scholars named several narrative forms, for example, a single story retold from the Bible for today, two contemporary stories framing a biblical one, sermons that move through various episodes, and a wide range of formats that could use narrative largely or in part. Traditional propositional sermons were not limited to three points and often followed a classical formula—introduction, exposition, bridge to today, application, and conclusion; new approaches sometimes reworked this using narrative principles to develop ideas. Probably the most difficult narrative form to pull off effectively is a single story, for two reasons. First, it may not clearly engage the Bible (if it is about today) or today (if it is about the Bible). Second, it may depend almost entirely upon listeners identifying with a character or persona the preacher adopts—the role of the preacher as pastor may be submerged. This form often requires exceptional narrative skill or an exceptional story; congregational members in urgent need might long for plainer address.

Biblical warrant may be found for both propositional (though not specifically three-point) and narrative sermons. Just as propositional sermons run the danger of being too geared for the intellect, so too, narrative sermons run the danger of being too imagistic or lacking direction.

Teaching Issues

Both propositional and narrative sermons have been students at teachers' colleges and know how to teach. Narrative teaches through aspects of authorship, narration, characterization, plot, outcome, points of view, implicit and explicit values, and background detail. For example, Stephen Frears's 2006 movie, *The Queen*, focuses on one week in early September 1997, in which the Windsor royal family and their subjects sharply diverge over the death of Princess Diana. A narrator does not list the features of the royal court; nonetheless, much can be learned of it by observing the setting and the way that the action transpires. Teaching is ongoing.

By the same token, both propositional and narrative sermons teach the Bible. Expository sermons wrestle with the biblical text and meanings for today, and then apply biblical truths to the congregation at hand. Where propositional form generally puts its conclusions up front and sets out to prove them, narrative teaches largely through induction, offering a variety of different experiences that gradually narrow by the end to a single point, often by a process of elimination: not this, not this, not this, but this. Fred Craddock noted that preachers gradually through the week come to the meaning of the biblical text that they will preach. He ventured that if this inductive process of discovery works for the preacher, it might also for the listener.[9]

An excellent instance of inductive argument is found in a sermon of Barbara Brown Taylor based on Jesus' appearance to his disciples, where he invites them to see his hands and feet (Luke 24:40). Here is the rough order of her sermon:

- the text, focusing on Jesus' hands and feet
- various experiences of people's hands
- a beautiful story of a friend of hers whose mechanic father died suddenly of a heart attack. When the friend went to the funeral home, he had to see his father's hands:

He kept a clean shop, and before he went home at night he scrubbed his hands with a boar's bristle brush, washing away the grime of the day.

But as careful as he was, his hands stayed stained in places, and it was that my friend was looking for. Turning his father's big hand over in his own, he saw the motor oil in the fingerprints, the callouses dark from years of hauling engines, and he smiled. "It's him," he said. "They tried to clean him up, but look, they couldn't. It's my daddy. It's really him."[10]

- a lengthy discussion of Jesus' hands, how the wounds testify to who he really is
- closing focus on the listener as follows:

"You are the witnesses of these things," he told them before he left them, entrusting the world to their care. When that world looks around for the risen Christ, when they want to know what that means, it is us they look at. Not our pretty faces and not our sincere eyes but our hands and feet—what we have done with them and where we have gone with them. We are witnesses of these things. We still are: the body of Christ.[11]

With inductive sermon movement such as Taylor used here, the entire sermon comes into sharp focus at the end.

Narrative has its own form of logic and its own ways of persuasion that are not limited to the intellect. Just as in deductive argument, things have to move and make sense, so too in narrative, things have to move and make sense. The logic in deduction is often something like, given *a* and *b*, therefore *c*; or this, this, and this all demonstrate this. With induction, the movement is akin to a plot that unfolds. Inductive logic often has to do with natural narrative sequence and coherence, compelling analogies, believable characters, plausible action, communication of an experience, and movement to something meaningful. Inductive argument portrays experience in ways that allow listeners to participate and that address more than the mind.

The revolution of preaching in the last fifty years has considerably expanded the range of possible sermon forms and methods of sermon composition. Narrative preaching today may be understood broadly as sermons that tend to use narrative principles in their composition. Point-form preaching has also changed, and sometimes has gone high-tech. Hybrid forms are common. Both propositions and narrative are valuable in their own ways. Both teach. The homiletical revolution is not from one kind of preaching that is teaching to another kind that is not. Rather, they represent two key ways of teaching, and both have value, just as each can be abused in the pulpit.

A Call for Teaching

The New Homiletic in large part represents changes in how teaching takes place in sermons. In 1995, Ronald J. Allen wrote *The Teaching Sermon*, a book that brought renewed contemporary interest to the sermon as a teaching instrument.[12] He believed the need for the teaching sermon was urgent. His vision is a good indication of teaching in the pulpit today.

Allen argued that fewer opportunities exist for the teaching ministry of the church to reach its members. The number of people in America with no church affiliation had risen by 350 percent since 1952. He found that baby boomers avoid institutional religion but are drawn to churches that provide meaningful links between experience and the Christian vision, and that artic-ulate "a distinctive statement of transcendent reality, through which the church can make sense of itself and of the world."[13] Allen felt that a new vision of the teaching sermon could meet the need. He looked to churches experiencing growth and saw teaching as often a major component; people are taught what to do and how to live their lives.

Allen wanted teaching to be viewed as part of every sermon.[14] He reacted against old ways of reducing teaching to just the intellect and emphasis on fact, explanation, logical reasoning, and argument.[15] His idea of teaching is holistic: "A perceptive Christian teacher knows that thought, heart, and will are so conjoined that when one is moved, all are moved. The whole self is affected."[16] The goal of Christian teaching, he says, "is to help the church become aware of, and responsive to, the gra-cious presence and purposes of the living God as revealed through Jesus Christ."[17]

Today we tend to have a holistic understanding of teaching. People learn in various ways, by seeing, hearing, and doing. Woman and men have different ways of knowing. Teaching has emotional and spiritual components. While teaching is primarily focused on communicating information, it is also about molding character and helping people better to live the lives that Christ calls disciples to live. As we will see in the next two chapters, many of these and other insights of the New Homiletic afford rich possibilities for teaching in the pulpit.

CHAPTER THREE
Teaching Principles from the New Homiletic

This section is devoted to what good teaching might look like in the pulpit, and in particular to lessons about teaching from the New Homiletic. Any new paradigm such as the New Homiletic emerges out of what came before, it does not just suddenly appear out of nowhere. We need not be surprised, therefore, to discover that many of these new principles concerning teaching are anticipated by our preaching forebears who may still serve as models for their practice today. The narrative emphasis in the New Homiletic in recent decades was only possible because there was already a foundation for it in various academic disciplines (e.g., literary studies), in the broader culture (e.g., in the rise of the novel and mass media), and as we will see, in the pulpit. In any paradigm shift, what previously was unnoticed now becomes highlighted and visa versa, and this is true for pulpit teaching. Signs of effective use of narrative in sermons were occasionally evident centuries ago, and the New Homiletic provided not least a vocabulary with which to identify and appreciate what some of our forbears did. Here we will highlight teaching principles in four key areas: Bible, theology, social justice, and, in a subsequent chapter, the tensive nature of language.

Teaching the Bible

Create a Picture in Words of the Biblical Scene Before Discussing the Text

Here is a good rule from the New Homiletic that was anticipated long ago: before commenting on any aspect of a biblical text, picture it for the listeners. If they can picture it, they are more likely to understand it. Preachers today frequently make the mistake of launching into an evaluation of a text without reconstructing it. Hearing it read once in worship is not enough to place it into the minds of most hearers. One of the first preachers to demonstrate the importance of this principle was Laurence Sterne (1713–68), a country parson and early novelist (*The Life and*

Opinions of Tristram Shandy, Gentleman). In one sermon Sterne took time to picture the prodigal son, an act that was unusual in an age in which preachers put so much emphasis on reason:

> I see the picture of his departure—the camels and asses laden with his substance, detached on one side of the piece, and already on their way: the prodigal son standing on the foreground with a forced sedateness, struggling against the fluttering movement of joy, upon his deliverance from restraint: the elder brother holding his hand, as if unwilling to let it go:—the father,—sad moment! with a firm look, covering a prophetic sentiment, "that all would not go well with his child,"—approaching to embrace him, and bid him adieu. Poor inconsiderate youth! From whose arms art thou flying?[1]

Every time a preacher changes the geographical location in a sermon, the new setting needs to be described first, as Sterne does here, so that listeners can picture the events. He does not spend long on description, per se, and he offers it as part of the action, but various words he uses help the congregation clearly to see the events described. Today we might speak of a preacher teaching by "making a movie" in the sermon or "creating an event"; David Buttrick speaks of a photograph coming into focus in the lens of a camera. In Sterne's day the metaphor might have been "painting a picture." Sterne demonstrates several additional excellent teaching principles in this short passage: write in the present tense for more vivid narrative; concentrate on action instead of description; depict people doing things; create the event rather than report it; pick one scene in the story as a vantage point rather than summarizing the whole at once.

Sterne also gives us a lesson in perspective. He recognizes that his narrative retelling of the story is itself an interpretation, as indeed is any retelling. Effective narrative communicates the narrator's/preacher's perspective that highlights the sermon's larger purpose. In this case the detail about the elder brother loving the younger is not explicit in the biblical story, but it is a plausible and fresh interpretation to take. Without distorting the original text it adds depth and interest to the character of the elder brother.

Ascribe Theological Thoughts to a Biblical Character

An important way to enliven the teaching of a biblical text is to place on the lips of a character theological material that might have been presented more abstractly. In the mid 1900s, the great Scottish preacher James S. Stewart puts some of his argument in Hosea's mouth, and later in our own mouths. Hosea reflects on the parallel sorrow of what is happening both in his own house and in the nation of Israel:

> Was it not inevitable, as the prophets of doom were declaring, that the national fate was sealed, and judgment at the door? But stay! thought Hosea, "Here am I, crucified in the region of my affections: and yet knowing that, if Gomer came back to me tomorrow, I would sing for joy and take her to my arms and forgive everything—I love her still so utterly. *Shall God love less?* If I would do that for my dearest possession, will God do less for *His*?" This was the swift insight which made this man a prophet, this daring logic of faith rising from the human to the divine. "If human love can know such agony, how much more love divine! If I can suffer so much for Gomer, how much more God for Isreal!"
>
>   That was Hosea's argument. Is it valid? He argued, you see, from what was deepest in his own nature to what he believed must be in the heart of God. Is that kind of reasoning valid? Are we entitled to start from what is noblest in human nature, and say, "That must be what God is like"? Is this "how much more" legitimate? The answer is that it is Christ's own argument. "If ye, being evil, know how to give good gifts to your children, how much more will your heavenly Father give good things to them that ask Him?" And when Jesus thus argued from the human to the divine, He gave us a sacred warrant for doing the same. It is not fallacy. It is the soundest logic."[2]

Of course, Hosea did not literally say these words, but they reflect a legitimate interpretation. In a very short space of time, Stewart makes explicit an argument that is only implicit in his text. In presenting his material, he avoids abstraction; his argument is not about something remote but about the concrete life situation before him, Hosea's own empty home and the situation of Israel in rejecting their home in God. This excellent narrative technique is not to be confused with a very poor one of attributing things to biblical characters that are unwarranted by the text; or of taking the listeners into the mind, thoughts, feelings, or dreams of characters instead of staying with the action and the theology arising out of it. Note also that in using the word crucifixion ("Here am I, crucified in the region of my affections"), Stewart intentionally draws a parallel between God's love for Israel in the time of Hosea and God's love for us in Christ on the cross. In other words, no degree of apostasy is beyond God's redemptive power. This is a good example of how teaching can lay a foundation for proclaiming the gospel.

Teaching Theology

A large part of the purpose of preaching is to teach about the triune God and living lives of faith. When H. Grady Davis wrote his *Design for*

Preaching at the early stages of the New Homiletic, his notions of organic form were drawn from the English Romantic poets like Coleridge (also a preacher) and Wordsworth. They understood that form is fluid and unique to each act of composition, that form and content are related, and that images, metaphors, and symbols are not disposable, as Aristotle had claimed, and cannot be exchanged for plain speech. Rather, each part of a work relates to the whole and the removal of any part affects the whole. Meaning is produced not by individual words as building blocks but as parts of a web of interconnecting thoughts and codes. Texts do not have one meaning but many. These meanings are not limited to authorial intent and include what the words generate in the eyes and experience of the beholder. Such understandings were eventually appropriated by the New Homiletic and led to new ways of teaching theology in sermons, some of which we see were heralded in brilliant fashion.

Allow a Biblical Image to Bear Theological Freight

The New Homiletic helped preachers appreciate the value of images, metaphors, and stories. An apt image taken from a biblical text can be developed in such a way that the whole text and its theological meaning comes into focus. St. John Fisher (1469–1535) was the founder of St. John's College, Cambridge University, and was eventually put to death by Henry VIII for his loyalty to the Pope. Fisher may have provided the model for Jonathan Edwards to produce, two centuries later, the most famous image in American sermons—sinners as spiders in the hands of an angry God who holds them dangling over the pit of hell. Fisher's text was Ecclesiastes 12:5-6, "because all must go to their eternal home . . . ; before the silver cord is snapped, and . . . the pitcher is broken at the fountain. . . ." Of key interest to us is how he took an image from the text, the silver cord, and constructed an entire sermon around it, from the first line throughout. (Edwards, by contrast, developed his image only at the end.) The image gives unity and brings sharp focus to his theology, in this case a theology of judgment. Here is a portion from the middle of that sermon:

> Have mind on Thy Creator and Maker in the time of thy young age, or ever the pot be broken upon the fountain, that is to say, thy body and thou peradventure fall into the well, that is to say into the deepness of hell. This pot, man's body, hangeth by a very weak cord, which . . . Solomon . . . calleth a cord or line made of silver. . . . Take heed, he saith, or ever the silver cord be broken. Truly this silver cord whereby our soul hangeth and is holden up in this pot, in this frail vessel our body, is the life of man. For a little cord or line is made or woven of a few threads, so is the life of man knit together by four humors, that as long as they be knit together in a right order so long is

man's life whole and sound. This cord also hangeth by the hand and power of God. . . . The deepness of hell is under us, greatly to be abhorred, full of devils. Our sins and wickedness be afore us. Behind us be the times and spaces that were offered to do satisfaction and penance, which we have negligently lost. On our right hand be all the benefits of our most good and meek lord, Almighty God, given unto us. And on our left hand be innumerable misfortunes that might have happed if that Almighty God had not defended us by his goodness and meekness. Within us is the most stinking abomination of our sin, whereby the image of Almighty God in us is very foul deformed, and by that we made unto Him very enemies. By all these things before rehearsed we have provoked the dreadful majesty of Him unto so great wrath that we must needs fear, lest that He let fall this line our life from His hands, and the pot our body be broken, and we then fall into the deep dungeon of hell. Therefore what shall we wretched sinners do?[3]

Many preachers might not feel comfortable preaching about judgment in this manner, yet this serves nonetheless as an example of how a biblical image can teach theology. A textual image can be a vehicle, providing a visual framework that helps listeners to picture, experience, and remember what is said instead of just receiving abstract discourse.

In teaching theology in this way today, a preacher might be guided by several principles that Fisher demonstrates. Use a key image from the text, not an incidental one. Use the image to say something about God or human relationships to God. Keep the focus primarily on one image so as not to try to say too many things or confuse listeners. Some of the things one says will be expository about the image's meaning in the text, and some will be by way of application to life today.

Application is very important, for it offers the preacher freedom to say what is needed from the standpoint of the larger Christian story, led but not strictly bound by what the text says. Note how much of the above excerpt is of this sort. Fisher does not rush to a new idea, he simply allows the image to develop, grow, and control his thought as he explores the depth of its possible applications. The image both holds the sermon together and gives it movement and direction. Good teachers take their time.

Use an Image from the Biblical Text to Connect to the Christ Event

The New Homiletic teaches how one image can lead to another in the way that one story calls up another in conversation. Preachers have demonstrated the value of this from the early church, only their focus was on how one image or story can be used to lead to Christ.

The church offers the world the good news that Jesus Christ is risen from the dead and is alive, in glory, and gives us his power. All of the other teachings about faith and life stem from that. Contemporary notions of what is a text sometimes limit the ability of preachers to speak of Jesus Christ. Many preachers seem convinced that they must be faithful biblical exegetes and not stray from the boundaries of the text at hand. Throughout most of history preachers knew that they could not preach simply the text. The church conceived of "preaching texts" as single verses or portions of verses, sometimes only a couple of words. The approach of many of our forebears had obvious weaknesses: they used allegory in ways that distorted the texts and often did not treat texts in their contexts; of course, they did not have the historical tools we have to discover what the texts meant in their own time. They were nonetheless adept teachers of theology, not least concerning the significance of Jesus Christ for the world, and they were adept at connecting Bible verses to him.

One of their devices was to use textual images to link with some aspect of his story—the word for their practice was typology. Gregory the Great (540–640) used a biblical image to interpret the Christ event in the following passage. It is a brilliant early example of an imaginative reworking of the atonement, a doctrine that continues to need fresh imagery and interpretation today. The image Gregory (and others)[4] chose is that of leviathan who in the Old Testament is the chaos monster or serpent that God put to death in ordering creation (see Job 3:8, 26:5-13; Psalm 74:14; Psalm 89: 10-11; Isaiah 27:1). Here Gregory used leviathan as a symbol for Satan who is put to death by Jesus Christ in the resurrection. Specifically, Christ is the fishing bait who does leviathan in.

> The Lord revealed this [to] Job when he said: *Will you catch leviathan* with a fishhook? (Job 41:1.) Leviathan . . . designates that fish-like destroyer of the human race which, when he promised to bestow divinity upon human beings, took away their immortality. . . . On a fishhook, the food is evident, the barb is concealed. The all-powerful Father caught this fish-like creature by means of a fishhook, because he sent his only begotten Son, who had become a human being, to his death. The Son had both a visible body which could suffer, and an invisible nature which could not. When, through the actions of his persecutors the serpent bit the food of his body, the barb of his divine nature pierced him. . . . It is, then, as if the fishhook got caught in his throat as he was swallowing. The food of the Lord's body, which the destroyer craved, was visible on it; at the same time of his passion his divine nature, which the destroyer would do away with, lay hidden. He was caught by the fishhook of the Lord's incarnation because while he was craving the food of his body, he was pierced by the barb of his divine nature. There was in the Lord a human nature which would lead the destroyer to him, and there was a divine nature which would pierce him; there was in

him the obvious weakness which would entice him, and there was the hidden power which would pierce the throat of the one who seized him. Therefore was the destroyer caught by a fishhook, because the cause of his destruction was where he bit. And he lost the mortal human beings whom he rightfully held because he dared to crave the death of one who was immortal, over whom he had no claim.[5]

This excerpt is a set-piece, that is, it could have been used in any number of sermons by Gregory and is unrelated to the biblical text on which he bases his sermon. Like all set-pieces, it stands in a sense on its own, and can be incorporated into any sermon the way a piece of material is sewn into a patchwork quilt.

This passage needs to be read against the literary background of his time: postbiblical books like Enoch 60:7-9 identify leviathan as the primary dish at the messianic banquet.[6] While the metaphor of leviathan needs reworking for today, one can sense its appeal particularly for communities dependent upon fishing for their livelihoods, as many were in the Mediterranean. This extended fishing metaphor would stay with Gregory's congregation, they would talk about it, think of it when they fish or buy fish, and it might cause them to reflect on Christ. In fishing communities today it might not take a lot of reworking to be effective. The key here is the preacher's willingness to be imaginative and to teach with freshness on matters central to the faith.

The issue for preachers need not be *would I use leviathan?* Rather one might ask, what image in my own text might I use to enable me to include in my sermon some significant teaching about Jesus Christ? For example, in Genesis 32:22-32 Jacob wrestles with God, and Jacob comes away with a limp. One might choose to compare Jacob's burden to the cross we ourselves are to carry through being encountered by Christ. Alternatively, if preaching on God's plumb line in Amos 7:7-15, one might connect it with the cross of Christ that sets a new standard by which the world is to be measured. Such preaching is fine teaching, yet it stops short of proclamation if it does not yet cause listeners to meet Christ.

Keep the Focus on God Using Points to Guide Narrative

One of the most important lessons we can learn from our ancestors is to read biblical texts not only historically, but theologically as well. In part this means reading texts for what God is doing in or behind them. C. H. Spurgeon (1835–92) believed the point of preaching is to speak significantly of God. He preached in England in the century in which the novel became popular. The significance of narrative to communicate experience was felt even in the pulpit. Preachers today may tend to think of propositional sermons as one thing and narrative another, like two stark alternatives that can have no meeting or cross-fertilization. Spurgeon demonstrates how narrative can be structured around points to ensure a strong focus on God. Listen to how brilliantly in 1861 he found three points in one portion of his text and allowed them to aid in structuring a lengthy narrative paragraph of his sermon:

> And now we hear the voice of God as he cries, "Adam, where art thou?" Oh! there were two truths in that short sentence. It showed that *Adam was lost*, or God would not have needed to ask him where he was. Until we have lost a thing, we need not enquire about it; but when God said, "Adam, where art thou?" it was the voice of a shepherd enquiring for his lost sheep; or better still, the voice of a loving parent asking for his child that has ran away from him, "Where art thou?" There are but three words, but they contain the dread doctrine of our lost estate. When *God* asks, "Where art thou?" man must be lost. When God himself enquires where he is, he must be lost in a more awful sense that you and I have as yet fully known. But then, there was also mercy here, for it showed that God intended to have mercy upon man, or else he would have let him remain lost, and would not have said, "Where art thou?" Men do not enquire for what they do not value. There was a gospel sermon, I think, in those three divine words as they penetrated the dense parts of the thicket, and reached the tingling ears of the fugitives—"Where art thou?" Thy God is not willing to lose thee; he is come forth to seek thee, just as by-and-bye he means to come forth in the person of his Son, not only to seek but to save that which now is lost. . . .[7]

Spurgeon's points are: Adam was lost; Adam was lost even to God; and God was not willing to lose him. Because Spurgeon's focus is God, there is a surprising freshness to his interpretation. It is compelling even in our age when we are flooded with commentaries and preaching aids on Genesis and freshness is hard to find. Spurgeon's points do not protrude from the narrative, but are rather buried within it to give direction and purpose. He also avoids a common practice of his era, he does not reduce his narrative text to a proposition but allows the plot to carry the weight of what he says. He does not draw undue attention to the points, even with numbers, but simply allows the points to guide and shape his interpretation. His brilliance here (and in many other sermons) is marked in his meticulous reading of his text, trusting even the small textual details to produce fresh insight (e.g., Adam was more lost than we have been). Spurgeon not only demonstrates fine literary criticism ahead of his time, he uses a principle of what is called the jewel sermon. A preacher kept turning a biblical text like a diamond bringing different facets into view through which light might shine.

Teach the Gospel as Empowerment

A key idea about the performative nature of language came to the fore through the New Homiletic, in part through J. L. Austin in *How to Do Things with Words*.[8] Words do things, they perform actions, they cause things to happen. Preachers have always known this at some level, not least from Genesis 1:3 where God creates by speaking, and they demonstrate it in teaching the gospel as empowerment.

Too often preachers teach the gospel as information, instead of as a power and relationship. The Bible speaks of the Word as event, for instance in Isaiah 55:11. Paul says that the gospel "is the power of God for salvation" (Romans 1:16). Horace Bushnell argued that Christ is to be preached as "moral power . . . the power of God unto salvation," the possibilities of which are endless and have to do with "all that He was, did, and expressed in His life and death and resurrection."[9]

The gospel as empowerment is the focus in the following sermon of George Campbell Morgan, a noted Bible teacher and evangelist in the early 1900s. Listen for the sense of God's limitless power that Morgan communicates.

> The Gospel reveals the fact that God places righteousness at the disposal of men who in themselves are unrighteous; that he makes it possible for the unrighteous man to become a righteous man. That is the exposition of salvation. Salvation is righteousness made possible. If you tell me that salvation is deliverance from hell, I tell you that you have an utterly inadequate understanding of what salvation is. If you tell me that salvation is forgiveness of sins, I shall affirm that you have a very partial understanding of what salvation is. Unless there be more in salvation than deliverance from penalty and forgiveness of transgressions committed, then I solemnly say that salvation cannot satisfy my own heart and conscience. That is the meaning of the letter I received [from a parishoner]: mere forgiveness of sins and deliverance from some penalty cannot satisfy the profoundest [need] in human consciousness. Deep down in the common human consciousness there is a wonderful response to that which is of God. Man may not obey it, but there in the deeps of human consciousness there is a response to righteousness, an admission of its call, its beauty, its necessity. Salvation, then, is the making possible of that righteousness. Salvation is the power to do right. However enfeebled the will may be, however polluted the nature, the gospel comes bringing to men the message of power enabling them to do right. In the gospel there is revealed a righteousness of God; and as the apostle argues and makes quite plain as he goes on with his great letter, it is a righteousness which is placed at the disposal of the unrighteous man so that the unrighteous man may become righteous in heart, thought, will, and deed. Unless that is the gospel, there is no gospel. Paul affirms that was the gospel he was going to Rome to preach.[10]

In other words, the gospel makes a difference in people's lives, it is not just ideas. For Morgan faith is not just about a future life, it is about the difference salvation makes in this life. One of the most difficult things in preaching is generating theological movement, taking matters to a deeper level, challenging people to think yet not going above their heads. The tendency of inexperienced preachers is to make a theological point and then give repeated examples that do little to deepen thought or advance meaning. Morgan establishes movement by contrasting his own perspective with common understandings about salvation using Romans 1:16-17.

Morgan teaches about the gospel here in that what he says is *about* God, yet in other places he proclaims.

Teach Social Justice

Teaching social justice is not a recent thing in preaching, the prophets did it and Jesus committed himself to it in Luke 4:18. However, since Friedrich Schleiermacher's *On Religion: Speeches to Its Cultured Despisers* (1799) and Karl Marx's *Communist Manifesto* (1848), experience has become central in theology and has spawned many theologies based in social justice: liberation, black, womanist, feminist, Minjung (South Korean social justice), post-colonial, and so forth. Only gradually has social justice made its way into the pulpit in the last two centuries. Any student of history may wonder at the general absence of social commentary for instance in sermons of John Wesley. With a couple of exceptions (notably his sermon against slavery), they mention little of his social background, which is surprising given that (a) he was a social activist as well as an evangelist and (b) his Methodist movement was organized largely to meet the desperate social and spiritual needs of growing urban centers. It is as though in his age there was an unspoken understanding that the pulpit served to build up the faith that in turn fed the groups and programs of the church during the week that carried out its essential social and spiritual missions.[11]

The social gospel movement arose in the late 1800s, often associated with Christian socialism in Great Britain and Walter Rauschenbush in the Hell's Kitchen slum district in New York City. Even before its rise there were significant preachers who preached prototypes of it, like Henry C. Potter of Grace Episcopal Church, New York City.[12] With the social gospel, numerous preachers spoke on social issues in important ways. Preachers like Theodore Parker preached entire sermons on the subjects of "Poverty" and "Slavery." He preached, "The poor are miserable. Their food is the least that will sustain nature—not agreeable, not healthy; their clothing scanty and mean, their dwellings inconvenient and uncomfortable, with roof and walls that let in the cold and the rain—dwellings that are painful and unhealthy."[13] Such willingness to tackle difficult social problems in the pulpit was unusual in his day, and may have been made more acceptable by popular culture, for instance the novels of Charles Dickens that focused so significantly on the poor.

Many African American pulpits have managed to balance evangelism and justice, yet most other pulpits have tended to opt for one or the other. It could be argued that social justice was never a major part of the New Homiletic, although scholars like Art Van Seters, John McClure, Christine Smith, Charles Campbell, and others devoted themselves to important ethical and social justice issues. In general it remains an area needing much attention.

Teaching about social justice is an important way to provide a foundation for proclaiming the gospel. God cares about social suffering and economic injustice, as so many books of the Bible affirm, and those people who perpetrate oppression will receive their judgment before God. Before there can be effective proclamation of the gospel there must be teaching about the powers and principalities of this world. Once the forces that work against God are named Christ's greater power can be declared.

Some of the early expressions of social concern in sermons are still significant, for not only do they mark the historical growth of Christian social conscience, they put into perspective relatively recent historical understandings concerning the ability of people to effect social change.

Social Justice Concerns Can Be Raised Effectively in Single Paragraphs in Sermons

Issues of social justice are often controversial and controversial issues in the church need time and study. Even entire sermons typically are too short to deal effectively with a difficult subject needing action. The teaching ministry of the church cannot effectively be reduced to the sermon. Still, social ills are a concern of God, and they may frequently be raised even without analysis in short passages in any sermon, such that social concern becomes part of the regular vocabulary of preaching. The following brief excerpt is from a sermon by F. W. Robertson in England in 1852 on the character of Balaam. His distinctive feature, Robertson says, was his ability to hide his head like an ostrich:

> Such a character is not so uncommon as, perhaps, we think. There is many a lucrative business which involves misery and wrong to those who are employed in it. The man would be too benevolent to put the gold in his purse if he knew of his misery. But he takes care not to know. There is many a dishonourable thing done at an election, and the principal takes care not

to inquire. Many an oppression is exercised on a tenantry, and the landlord receives his rent, and asks no questions. Or there is some situation which depends upon the holding of certain religious opinions, and the candidate has a suspicion that if he were to examine, he could not conscientiously profess these opinions, and perchance he takes care not to examine.[14]

Robertson does not browbeat his congregation, he simply makes clear that concern for neighbors is a priority even in business. Courage and wisdom are needed to raise social issues effectively because as with most issues, there are differences of opinion; issues need to be raised in ways that do not simply drive people away but rather enable them to change. There will always be those who argue that the business of the church is saving souls. Ernest Campbell preached wise insight, "To follow Jesus is to have a plan. To follow Jesus is to face and embrace the future. To follow Jesus is to have a star by which to steer. Every time he comes across our way and bids us follow, he creates a crisis. And we can never be the same again. For when that command registers on our souls, we can choose to die to God and live to self, or to die to self and live to God."[15] Social justice puts the main responsibility on the people to act, as is the case even in this short passage. Special care is needed to move such sermons also to focus on God's actions that become a beginning place for proclamation.

Paint Pictures of Specific Social Ills

The New Homiletic reclaimed for preaching the value of concrete sensory language and word pictures. The old homiletic tended to value generalizations over specific instances and assumed that to speak in general terms reached the greatest number of people. Social ills are easily dismissed if they are presented in abstract fashion under various labels. However, if a preacher provides a specific person who is affected by a social ill, the issue gains importance. Moreover, those who likewise suffer are humanized.

Thomas Guthrie (1803–73) knew this. Anyone who has visited Edinburgh knows the Royal Mile or the Golden Mile of Princes Street. He describes it as running "from this neighboring castle to yonder palace" and calls it "the most picturesque street in Christendom" yet because of its human poverty and misery, "one of the most painful to travel":

With so many countenances that have misery stamped on them as plain as if it were burned in with a red-hot iron—hunger staring at us out of these hollow eyes, drink-palsied men, drink-blotched and bloated women; sad and sallow infants who pine away into slow death with their weary heads lying so pitifully on the shoulders of some half dehumanized woman—this poor little child who never smiles, without shoe or stocking on his ulcered feet, shivering, creeping, limping along with the bottle in his emaciated hand to buy a parent drink with the few pence that, poor hungry creature, he would wish to spend on a loaf of bread, but dare not—the whole scene is like the toll of the prophet, "written within and without, lamentations, mourning, and woe." [Ezekiel 2:10] How has it wrung out hearts to see a poor, ragged boy looking greedily in at a window on the food he has no one to give him and dare not touch, to watch him as he alternatively lifted his naked feet lest they should freeze to the icy pavement. He starves in the midst of abundance. Neglected among a people who would take more pity on an ill-used horse or dying dog, he is a castaway upon the land. Of the throngs that pass heedlessly by him to homes of comfort, intent on business or on pleasure, there is no one cares for him. Poor wretch! Oh if he knew a Bible which none has taught him, how might he plant himself before us and bar our way to church or prayer meeting, saying, as he fixed on us an imploring eye, "Pure religion and undefiled before God" is to feed me, is to clothe these naked limbs, is to fill up these hollow cheeks.[16]

Guthrie creates the event and provides an experience, he does not just report facts. He learned early from the youth in his church that they best remembered his illustrations, and thus he developed an illustrative style. His three homiletical and hence teaching criteria were what he called the "Three P's—Painting, Proving, and Persuading."[17] He seems to be one of the earliest preachers to bring this kind of vivid social painting into the pulpit. He provides descriptions of urban poverty as a moral issue for his congregation. He was likely influenced by Charles Dickens.

Poverty is an increasing issue today, yet how many of our pulpits keep it before their congregations as an issue of faith? Painting it so vividly and keeping the focus on the suffering of real people, prevents the issue from being lost in abstraction. Guthrie also knew that against this backdrop, proclamation of the gospel took on even greater significance.

Keep Justice and Piety United

As noted, many churches seem to have chosen social justice or congregational piety, as though they are exclusive of one another. Arguably the strongest social witness is made by preachers able to keep the two together. Because they call upon the resources of God, people are sent to their ministries with God's resources, not just their own. Charles Jefferson was a Congregational minister who ministered at Broadway Tabernacle in Manhattan from 1898 to near his death in 1937. His preaching was remarkable for uniting social justice and evangelical witness. In one sermon preached at the height of the coal strike of 1902 he spoke in favor of the miners, presumably answering specific negative comments against them in the press. He teaches about Christ's role in the strike:

> [They] spend their lives in the mines. They are our brethren. Christ died for them. They toil for us. If they foreigners and ignorant and depraved and dangerous, then their claim upon us is the greater. If the miner is at the rear of the procession, our Lord is by his side. It is His prayer that we may be with Him where He is and behold His glory. . . . The measure of a man's Christianity is not his attitude to the man above him, or to the man on his own level, but to the man who is below him. How do we feel toward the man at the rear of the procession? That is the test of our devotion to Christ.[18]

Jefferson shows considerable courage in speaking for the miners as brothers in a time when they were much vilified. He goes on to speak of the need for a "fresh vision of Jesus Christ and him crucified."[19] He then returns to teach "the truth that one is our Master and that we are all brethren":

> To talk about foreigners with the accent of scorn is wholly unchristian; to speak the word "American" in a tone which casts a shadow over the rest of the world is altogether pagan; to speak about the "ignorant masses," the "unwashed herd," with intonations of contempt is to fall into the ditch into which the Pharisees tumbled. There is too much ado about badges and ranks and distinction, and not enough genuine good-will and brotherly love.[20]

Christian practice, not doctrine is his focus, and the practice is both faith in Jesus Christ and acting for the neighbor in need.

In this chapter we spoke about key changes and excellent lessons that have been brought about by the New Homiletic in how to teach and how preachers anticipated those changes. We spoke of teaching the Bible, theology, and social justice. One additional key area of recent change remains to be discussed and it concerns the polar nature of language and the function of metaphor and imagination in teaching.

CHAPTER FOUR
Teaching and Polar Language

A mong the less heralded contributions of the New Homiletic is a change in how language is understood. The effect on teaching in the pulpit is dramatic. Words are not building blocks, as they were formerly conceived. Rather, they are part of a system of meanings that interact with and modify or magnify each other. Metaphor is no mere ornament, as Aristotle taught. It both participates in the reality it addresses and generates experience. Again, the Romantics were central. S. T. Coleridge saw metaphor not just as a figure of speech; it is how thought works. Metaphor (or what he called imagination) is the result of two identities brought together to form a new third identity. This new identity is the direct result of the tension between the initial ones. At a practical level, two people get married, each with his or her own identity, and the third identity is a product of their being together, in other words, who they are as a couple. He called this action in language the "reconciliation of opposites" and called it the signature action of the imagination. He did not mean literal reconciliation, of the sort that merges two identities so that one is lost in the other. Rather, he meant the dynamic and momentary harnessing of the two. He claimed that this principle of reconciliation of opposites is the basis of all consciousness and the highest means of individual poetic expression.[1] He was possibly the first in the English language to claim that language is tensive, that meaning arises because of polarity in language.

Two notable preachers helped to advance Coleridge's ideas in his century and claimed them for the pulpit. In England, the Anglican preacher F. W. Robertson (1816–53) said that "spiritual truth is discerned by the spirit, instead of intellectually in propositions: and therefore, Truth should be taught suggestively, not dogmatically."[2] Joseph R. Jeter Jr. describes Robertson's homiletic method: "He was ahead of his time in looking for truth in dialectical or polar structures of the text. He was more interested in encountering the tensions within a text than in trying to harmonize them. When most preachers of his day were laying dogmatic templates upon texts, his method anticipated the direction of biblical scholarship by more than a century."[3]

In the United States, Horace Bushnell (1802–76) was one of the first preachers to put into practice and expand Coleridge's ideas. "Human language," he says, "is a gift to the imagination so essentially metaphoric, warp and woof, that it has no exact blocks of meaning to build a science of."[4] He argued that there were many possible meanings of texts, that meanings "double and redouble" depending on the typologies, images, or analogies we develop.[5] Language is not univocal; it does not just mean what it says. It is multivocal and requires interpretation.

The New Homiletic adopted many of these ideas, though without necessarily acknowledging their origins. It placed new emphasis on the use of imagination, imagery, metaphor, and symbol. It understood language as having many meanings, addressing not simply the intellect but the whole person. It evokes experience and produces worlds in which people participate. Most important is the understanding that metaphor is not mere ornament, as Aristotle had claimed. It is the underlying structure of language, the way it works. Polarity is basic to language and thought; we know bad in contrast to good, right in contrast to wrong, one identity by its opposition to another.

In this chapter we examine several teaching devices that our preaching ancestors used that we might emulate, all of which make use of polarity in language to powerful effect. They move from the simplest practices, compare and contrast, to some of the most imaginative and powerful.

Teach Using Comparison and Contrast

One of the simplest and best ways to teach using polarity is by comparison or contrast. Classical rhetoric used this practice that Augustine called the use of contraries.[6] The Bible is filled with examples of comparison and contrast, not least Paul's opposition of the "spirit of the world" with the "Spirit of God" (1 Corinthians 2:6-16).

Teach Doctrine Using
Comparison and Contrast

Making comparisons obvious can be an effective means of instruction about church teachings. John Chrysostom in the early church sought in one sermon to teach the difference between Christ's followers and others on the topic of death. He did so in the following manner using a series of comparisons:

> We differ from unbelievers in our estimate of things. The unbeliever surveys the heavens and worships them, because he thinks them a divinity. . . . We

survey the heavens and admire Him that made them; for we do not believe them to be a god, but a work of God. I look on the whole creation, and am led by it to the Creator. He looks on wealth, and longs for it with earnest desire; I look on wealth, and contemn it. He sees poverty, and laments; I see poverty, and rejoice. I see things in one light; he in another. Just so in regard to death. He sees a corpse, and thinks of it as a corpse; I see a corpse, and behold sleep rather than death. And as in regard to books . . . to the unlearned the mere shapes of letters appear, while the learned discover the sense that lies within those letters—so with respect to affairs in general, we all see what takes place with the same eyes, but not with the same under-standing or judgment. Since, therefore, in all other things we differ from them, shall we agree with them in our sentiments respecting death?[7]

Might such a series be effective today? Yes, perhaps with very little alteration, though some clarification is needed concerning what he means by poverty. (Is it the condition of those the church serves or the situation of the blessed? He does not condone needless suffering, but he upholds the value of being unencumbered by wealth.) The main point is that preachers be intentional employing similar kinds of comparison.

Amplify Contrasts in a Text

The Beatitudes employ an implied contrast between what Jesus says and the conventional wisdom of his own and our day. In the next sermon Roman Catholic Bishop Fulton J. Sheen, the first notable preacher on American television, teaches the Beatitudes in the mid-1900s in brilliant fashion by amplifying the inherent contrast and making it explicit. His doctrinal point is clear by the end; the world and Christ are in opposition:

Contrast the Beatitudes with what we might call the beatitudes of the world; the one is the antithesis of the other. The world says: "Blessed are the rich"; Christ says: "Blessed are the poor in spirit." The world says: "Blessed are the mighty"; Our Lord says: "Blessed are the meek." The world says: "Laugh and the world laughs with you"; Christ says: "Blessed are they that mourn." The world says: "Be for yourself and your country right or wrong"; Christ says: "Blessed are they that hunger and thirst after justice." The world says: "Sow your wild oats, you are young only once; blessed is the sex appeal"; Christ says: "Blessed are the clean of heart." The world says: "In time of peace prepare for war"; Christ says: "Blessed are the peacemakers." The world says: "Blessed are those who never suffer persecution"; Christ says: "Blessed are they that suffer persecution." The world says: "Blessed is pop-ularity"; Christ says: "Blessed are ye when they shall revile you and perse-cute you and speak all that is evil against you for My sake."
In so many words the Sermon on the Mount placed an irreconcilable opposition between the world and Christ.[8]

Sheen combines two purposes: reminding the congregation what the text actually says, and making his own point about how different are Christ's values from ours. Sheen could have developed his argument in a linear and less interesting manner, teaching that Christ's values oppose the world, and explaining what that meant, but much interest and vibrancy would be lost. Any list could serve as a basis for similar comparisons, for example, the Ten Commandments or Paul's gifts of the Spirit.

Teach Using Paradox

If we heighten the tension of contrast a few degrees, we come to a second polarity for use in teaching, and that is paradox or apparent contradiction. Paul pointed to it in his experience and thought when he said, "For I do not do the good I want, but the evil I do not want is what I do" (Romans 7:19). Love of paradox goes back a long way and includes not least Pseudo-Dionysius and the tradition of apophatic theology, Luther and his juxtaposition of law and gospel, and the Romantics. Yet throughout history, paradox was generally perceived as an enemy to clear thinking, and still it can be. Arguments need to flow along logical routes, and contradictory arguments are naturally dismissed. Valuing paradox in the pulpit is not the same thing as valuing contradiction, for paradox can be an important way to communicate truth.

Many central teachings of the faith involve apparent paradox, for example, God is three in one; Jesus Christ is fully human and fully divine; the first shall be last and the last shall be first; we are sinners, yet saved; we must be born again; Christ died that we might have life through him; by dying to self, we gain life. Reason cannot resolve these seeming contradictions; they can be resolved only by the Holy Spirit acting in our lives through faith. Applying Coleridge's idea of imagination as "the reconciliation of opposites" to theological matters, we would say that faith reconciles the apparent contradictions and allows truth to emerge. F. W. Robertson said, "Truth is made up of two opposite propositions, and not found in a via media between the two."[9] Horace Bushnell stated, "Accordingly we never come so near to a truly well rounded view of any truth, as when it is offered paradoxically; that is under contradictions."[10] The advantage of contradiction of this sort is that the hearer must participate and determine the way in which the contradiction is true.

After Henry Ward Beecher and Phillips Brooks, in the 1870s, whatever impact the Romantics had upon the pulpit lessened, and the tensive nature of language was largely forgotten. Imagination regained its earlier reputation for being wild and unruly, not to be trusted. Only in the 1930s were Romantic ideas of imagination rediscovered, and then it took two decades for those learnings to reach the pulpit. By then German Romantic ideals had filtered into theological circles: Karl Barth and his colleagues embraced dialectical theology as the only method for theological discourse, which one theologian describes as "the method of statement and counterstatement, of 'yes' and 'no,' of paradox, in which polar pairs (whose unity cannot be thought) are held together only in the response of God-given faith—finite and infinite, time and eternity, wrath and grace."[11]

Teachers of creative writing know the importance of paradox. W. Foster-Harris taught its value in character portrayal: "Do not hesitate for an instant to give your hero or heroine . . . impulses to evil. . . . For these dark powers, fused with their opposites—the will to good, the moral impulses, the powers of the spirit—make your central character. The real purpose of the story is to test the fused contradictions which we cannot see but know to exist."[12] Anne Lamott advises writers to use contradiction. She uses it in her writing to create humor, for instance, when she says, "I became a socialist, for five weeks. Then the bus ride to my socialist meetings wore me out."[13] She says that the characters one writes about "shouldn't be too perfect; perfect means shallow and unreal and fatally uninteresting. . . . I like for them to have a nice sick sense of humor and to be concerned with important things. . . . I like them to be mentally ill in the same sorts of ways I am."[14] Dramatists have long known the importance of contradiction within character as a means to generate interest and plot.

Find Paradox within Biblical Characters to Make Them Real

When we speak of people being interesting or complex, it is often because of conflicting aspects of their personalities. When we speak of loving someone, we mean the entire package, warts and all. It is hard to find preachers prior to the mid-1800s exhibiting any interest in psychology. Phillips Brooks (1835–93) shows interest in the psychology of the rich man in 2 Samuel 12:4, and it is precisely the contradiction within his character that Brooks develops to make him real:

> In this old story from the book of Samuel we have a picture of a hospitable man, a man who really wanted to help the poor traveler who came to him, but who wanted to help him with another man's property, to feed him another man's sheep. There is real charity in the impulse. There is essential meanness in the act. "He spared to take of his own flock and his own herd to dress for the wayfaring man that was come unto him." Here is real kindliness and real selfishness in the same heart, not struggling with one another but in most peaceful compromise. "I am able to feed this guest of mine," the

rich man says. "How fortunate that I am able to do it without encroaching on myself, without taking of my own flock and my own herd." And by and by there sits the guest before the smoking feast, and the host's sheep are all heard safe and bleating through the open windows.[15]

Of course, one could argue that from an exegetical point of view, what Brooks has done here is not fully the point of the story, he deals with that elsewhere. Still, by highlighting the warring impulses of kindness and meanness in the rich man, he seems more real. Brooks criticizes the givers of charity in his own day, challenging them to go beyond easy giving and display self-sacrifice, calling them to an awareness of the contradiction in their behavior.

Find Paradox within Characters to Enhance Listener Identification

Rhetoric tells us that one of the most compelling features of any speech is identification, the ability of the listener to identify with what is said. Not a lot of pulpit time is available to develop character, yet even brief portraits are more convincing and real if some aspect of paradox or contradiction is evident. John Henry Newman (1801–90) demonstrates this in his psychological and theological analysis of the character of Baalam in Numbers 22:38:

> Balaam obeyed God from a sense of its being right to do so, but not from a *desire to please Him*, not from *fear and love*. He had other ends, aims, wishes of his own, distinct from God's will and purpose, and he would have effected these if he could. His endeavour was, not to please God, but to please self without displeasing God, to pursue his own ends *as far* as was consistent with his duty. In a word, he did not give his heart to God. . . .
>
> You will observe he *wished* to go with Balak's messengers, only he felt he *ought not* to go; and the problem which he attempted to solve was *how* to go and yet not offend God. He was quite resolved he *would* any how act religiously and conscientiously; he was too honourable a man to break any of his engagements; if he had given his word, it was sacred; if he had duties, they were imperative: he had a character to maintain, and an inward sense of propriety to satisfy; but he would have given the world to have got rid of his duties; and the question was, *how* to do so without violence; and he did not care about walking on the very brink of transgression, so that he could keep from falling over. Accordingly he was not content with *ascertaining* God's will, but he attempted to *change* it. He inquired of Him a *second* time, and this was to tempt Him. Hence, while God bade him go, His anger was kindled against him because he went.[16]

Almost anyone can identify with the inner conflict between individual will and God's will that Newman presents in Balaam. Moreover, it is exegetically sharp. Preachers today could learn much from Newman. No human being is without sin, and every individual has contradictory impulses that may manifest themselves as aspects of character and behavior. Only when a preacher portrays something of inner conflicts within a character is identification most possible because realism increases. Balaam's portrait is convincing and lifelike instead of wooden and stereotyped. Our tendency instead is to erase or ignore contradictions when we tell stories of biblical or contemporary people.

Newman demonstrates an early form of literary criticism at its best. His sensitive reading of Balaam, in fact, helps readers make sense of the seeming contradiction in the text: God permits Balaam to leave, and only later does the reader discover that God is still angry at Balaam. Even Newman's title for this sermon is brilliant, "Obedience Without Love," because it effectively names the heart of the issue that is never explicitly named in the text.

Preachers might ask themselves in any sermon, What contradiction is present that I might highlight in a biblical character in my text to increase listener identification?

Use Contradiction to Frame Mystery

The purpose of preaching is not to come up with all of the answers. Part of the purpose is to highlight the mystery that surrounds us in life, to raise questions, to alert hearers to the presence of the divine. Frederick Buechner once said that preaching puts a frame around the mystery. We see this framing of mystery in a passage from Dietrich Bonhoeffer, who finds his contradiction in the text:

> It is completely and utterly inexplicable, incomprehensible, it is an unfathomable riddle—and yet it was done. Judas, one of the twelve. That does not just mean that he was one who was with Jesus day and night, who had followed Jesus, who had sacrificed something, who had given up all to be with Jesus, a brother, a friend, a confidant of Peter, of John, of the Lord himself. It means something far more incomprehensible: Jesus himself called and chose Judas! That is the real mystery. For Jesus knew who would betray him from the beginning. In St. John's Gospel Jesus says, "Did I not choose you, the twelve, and one of you is a devil?" Judas, one of the twelve, and now the reader must look not only at Judas, but rather in great bewilderment at the Lord who chose him. And those whom he chose, he loved. He shared his whole life with them, he shared with them the mystery of his person, and in the same way he sent them out to preach the Gospel. He gave them authority to drive out demons and to heal—and Judas was in their midst. In fact,

by his office of keeping charge of the disciples' purse, Judas seemed to have been marked out above the others.

. . . John has one more completely mysterious sign of Jesus' closeness with Judas to tell. On the night of the Last Supper, Jesus offers Judas a sop dipped in the dish, and with this sign of the closest community Satan enters into Judas. Thereupon Jesus says to Judas, half as a request, half as a command, "What you are going to do, do quickly." No one else understood what was happening. Everything remained between Jesus and Judas.[17]

Bonhoeffer does not try to give answers about why Jesus behaves as he does toward Judas (which would in any case be unwarranted speculation on the text), nor does he launch into the larger question of why God permits evil. Rather, he simply gives guidance to a part of the mystery. The only resolution he offers is that our own identity lies with Judas ("Is it I?"), and we need to seek refuge with the one who hangs on the cross for all of us.

Contradiction works in the same way that metaphor works. One enters it in what Coleridge called "the willing suspension of disbelief."[18] Love both is and is not a red, red rose. On the one hand it is not true, and on the other hand it is. Some preachers try to avoid the contradiction in texts or explain away biblical miracles. The danger is that texts can be rendered into mere history, sanded smooth so that they have no edge, all mystery is gone, any conflict with reason is resolved, any summons to faith is silenced, and the text's ability to communicate God can be emptied. Christian novelist Ron Hansen says, "To fully understand a symbol is to kill it."[19]

Enhance the Contradictions of Christian Truths in Preaching

Contradiction is sometimes the best way to express profound truth, and sometimes contradiction needs to be heightened in preaching for truth to be more apparent. Reinhold Niebuhr was attuned to the importance of contradiction for the faith when he preached on joy through sorrow:

In the Bible there is a great deal about joy and about sorrow but very little about happiness. We read, "if ye will not die with him, neither will you live with him." We are crucified with Christ and nevertheless we live. Life comes through death, joy through sorrow, "Blessed are they that mourn for they shall be comforted." Peace comes out of strife, "Blessed are ye when men shall revile you and speak all manner of evil against you falsely." Fulfillment through hunger, "Blessed are ye that hunger and thirst after righteousness." There is no simple peace; Christianity is the religion of the cross. A cross is revelation of the heart of God and a cross is at the heart of human existence.

Is not this morbid? Could we not have something simpler? The fact is that all of us look for something simpler and the Christian faith has at many times been rejected until the moment of sorrow when there is no other way of finding joy except through sorrow. It is in sorrow that the truth of the Christian faith becomes known. But every one of us instinctively would like to have happiness, simple happiness, rather than this complex thing of joy through sorrow.[20]

Listeners who seek understanding of faith are honored when the seeming contradictions are acknowledged, not ignored or simplistically resolved. The cross and resurrection is the place that so many apparent contradictions find their resolution in the Spirit. In preaching to postmodern people, greater controlled use of contradiction ought to be one of the best teaching tools.

Use Theology to Heighten Contradiction in a Biblical Text

An excellent demonstration of using theology to heighten contradiction in a biblical text is found in Frederick Buechner, who understands that God's love demands our all. He preaches on Jacob wrestling with a stranger at the Jabbok (Genesis 32:22-31):

The darkness has faded just enough so that for the first time he can dimly see his opponent's face. What he sees is something more terrible than the face of death—the face of love. It is vast and strong, half ruined with suffering and fierce with joy, the face a man flees down all the darkness of his days until at last he cries out, "I will not let you go, unless you bless me!" Not a blessing that he can have now by the strength of his cunning or the force of his will, but a blessing that he can have only as a gift.

Power, success, happiness, as the world knows them, are his who will fight for them hard enough; but peace, love, joy are only from God. And God is the enemy whom Jacob fought there by the river, of course, and whom in one way or another we all of us fight—God, the beloved enemy. Our enemy because, before giving us everything, he demands of us everything; before giving us life, he demands our lives—our selves, our wills, our treasure.[21]

Peace, joy, and love are the gifts of a God who knows both suffering and joy. Obviously the profound contradiction here is that God is both adversary and advocate. To preach one or the other independently might be false, yet when the two are held together and reconciled by the larger gospel story of God's limitless love, they become an important means of teaching faith. Preachers might consider whether they have domesticated God too much and not tended to portray God as both adversary and advocate.

Teach Using Trouble and Grace as a Theological Lens

Law and gospel have been important theological categories since Paul's discussion of them in Romans. Many homileticians teach the importance of both trouble and grace (or law and gospel, or judgment and grace, or crucifixion and resurrection) as categories to shape the sermon, and even those who do not acknowledge them still commonly practice them. The entire sermon may move from one to the other, to help ensure that the gospel is preached and to mirror the hopeful nature of God's word. Regardless of whether they are used in a portion of a sermon or as its overall structure, they work by contradiction. They serve as two hermeneutical perspectives identified by Paul (Romans) and Augustine (*On the Spirit and the Letter*). Trouble puts the burden on humanity to do something, and grace puts the burden on God in Christ. They establish contrasting statements of truth, for example, we are sinners and we are saved, and one does not cancel the other, but both are true. Faith emerges from the tension between them (Philippians 2:12).

Barbara Brown Taylor offers a fine example of how facility with trouble and grace allows one to discover grace in texts of trouble (or alternatively, trouble in texts of grace). She preaches on the laborers in the vineyard who come at different times and are paid the same wage (Matthew 20:1-16):

> God is not fair. For reasons we may never know, God seems to love us indiscriminately, and seems also to enjoy reversing the systems we set up to explain why God should love some of us more than others of us. By starting at the end of our lines [i.e., with the laborers who came last], with the last and the least, God lets us know that his ways are not our ways, and that if we want to see things his way we might question our own notions of what is fair, and why we get so upset when our lines do not work.
>
> God is not fair, but depending on where you are in line that can sound like powerful good news, because if God is not fair then there is a chance that we will get paid more than we are worth, that we will get more than we deserve, that we will make it through the doors even though we are last in line—not because of who *we* are but because of who *God* is.
>
> God is not fair; God is *generous*, and when we begrudge that generosity it is only because we have forgotten where we stand. On any given day of our lives, when the sun goes down and a cool breeze stirs the dusk, when the work is done and the steward heads toward the end of the line to hand out the pay, there is a very good chance that the cheers and backslapping, the laughter and the gratitude with which he is greeted will turn out to be our own.[22]

Taylor compares the parable to waiting in line for a theater. We like to think we are at the head of the line, but God may have us halfway around the block behind more deserving folks. The sermon progresses from one truth, to a contradictory truth, and finally to their reconciliation in God's love: "God is not fair" is at first a judgment against us, then it is God's grace toward us, and finally it becomes a celebration of the gospel. Reading a text from both perspectives of trouble and grace, and of finding in the larger gospel story its truth, is a demonstration of Coleridge's reconciliation of opposites.

Teach Using Faith as a Key Perspective

In our postmodern era, preachers understand that biblical texts have as many meanings as there are perspectives we bring to them. Bushnell discovered rich meanings, "even as a stalk of corn pushes out leaf from within leaf by a growth that is its unsheathing."[23] Texts are now recognized as multivocal, and preachers now seek not one interpretation, but various interpretations, in order to speak to the mixed concerns of congregations living in a pluralist world. Texts can be read from a host of perspectives like age, gender, economy, race, culture, and religion. One of the most valuable and least discussed is this: the text may be read as a mirror of the community of faith. By finding the community's identity in the text, it teaches faith.

Treat the Text as a Metaphor of Faith

Preaching should inspire faith. Every time we consider a text we should ask, In what way might this serve as a metaphor of faith? What can it teach about faith? That is what Phillips Brooks does in the following sermon on Aaron making the golden calf in Exodus 32:24, "So they gave it me: then I cast it into the fire, and there came out this calf" (KJV):

> Aaron was frightened at what he had done. He was afraid of the act itself, and of what Moses would say. Like all timid men, he trembled before the storm which he had raised. As so he tried to persuade Moses, and perhaps in some degree even to persuade himself, that it was not he that had done this thing. He lays the blame upon the furnace. "The fire did it," he declares. He will blankly face his sin, and yet he will not tell a lie in words. He tells what is literally true. He had cast the earrings into the fire, and this calf had come out. But he leaves out the one important point, his own personal agency in it all; the fact that he had molded the earrings into the calf's shape, and that he had taken it out and set it on its pedestal for the people to adore. He tells it so that it shall all look automatic. It is a curious, ingenious, but transparent lie.

Let us look at Aaron's speech a little while this morning and see what it represents, for it does represents something. There never was a speech more true to our human nature. We are all ready to lay blame upon the furnaces. "The fire did it," we are all of us ready to say. Here is a man.[24]

Brooks retells the biblical story, takes an image central to it, the furnace, and brilliantly converts it into a metaphor of his listeners and his time, "We are all ready to lay blame upon the furnaces." By rendering the text as a metaphor of faith, he now has something that will preach. If we as preachers follow Brooks's example, we will similarly find in our biblical texts some image or echo of faith, some way of tying our text to great questions or struggles with faith.

Treat the People in the Text as Having Issues of Faith

One of the great errors of modern biblical criticism is to treat people in the Bible as though they are not people of doubt and faith or at least people who are called to live out their lives in awareness of God. In seminary preachers are taught to read Scripture as much as possible without the bias of theology using the best historical-critical and literary tools available. Less discussed is when theology actually is to be engaged with texts, even though this is most needed by preachers. To some extent the creeds of the church always guide the reading of Scripture for the pulpit—the church has never read Jesus' entry into Jerusalem as suicide, though from a strictly literary perspective that is a possible interpretation. As a general rule, once scholarly study of a biblical text is done, the preacher is called to treat the biblical characters as people with faith issues.

One function of doctrine is to read Scripture. Here is an instance from a sermon in which C. L. Franklin (the father of soul singer Aretha Franklin) uses the doctrine of faith to interpret the story of Doubting Thomas (John 20:24-29). Few biblical commentators speak about faith in the way Franklin does, yet preachers might be remiss in not doing so:

Thomas, called Didymus, which means the twin, has received a great deal of ridicule from the Christian world about his doubting position. But you know, you must give some respect to people who want to know, to people who are not satisfied with hearsay. You must give some respect to people who want to base their faith upon as much knowledge as they can acquire. You see, superstition, rumor and hearsay is not a sufficient foundation for faith. I know that faith transcends knowledge, but you get all the knowledge you can get before you stop. For you see, Thomas was moving on fact. And you see fact can carry you just so far. It was a fact that Jesus was put to death, that he was hanged to a tree. It was a fact that he dropped his head and died, and declared, "It is finished." This was a fact. It was a fact that they took him down and laid him in a tomb. All of this was fact. But that was as far as fact could go. This is the reason that Thomas couldn't go any further: because he was proceeding on the basis of fact. You understand what I'm talking about. His whole operation was based on empiricism, investigation and what one can find out. But you see, faith—you understand what I mean—goes on beyond the grave. (I don't believe you know what I'm talking about). . . .

Faith doesn't stop at the grave. Faith didn't stop when he said, "It is finished." Faith didn't stop when they rolled the stone to the tomb. And faith didn't stop when the governor's seal was placed thereon. For you see faith goes beyond what I can see and what I know.[25]

Such speech is not so much an application of the text to a situation as it is explication of the authentic subject of the text for the church. Treating the text as the church's book means using historical criticism from a faith perspective. Franklin reads his text using his knowledge of what the church teaches, and in the process he testifies about faith.

In this and the previous chapters we talked about teaching and what we can draw from our preaching ancestors in light of the New Homiletic. The next section takes a closer look at the subject of the gospel from both biblical and homiletical perspectives. If we are to proclaim the gospel, we need first to remind ourselves what it is and how it might be understood and practiced.

Teaching about
the Gospel

What is the gospel may be so obvious as to make discussion of it here seem unnecessary; it is God's redeeming and renewing love. It is seen most clearly in the coming of Jesus Christ, his life, death, resurrection, ascension, and second coming to fulfill all promises and to establish the new creation. Even to say this is not to define or circumscribe the gospel but is to claim minimally that this is where any discussion of the gospel must start. What we do with this understanding may vary, but when we look to the four Gospels in the Bible, this is what they address, not something else. No one part of these narrative chains of events is fully the gospel, yet the cross and resurrection are central; all of the testimonies lead to and from it.

Still, people will respond with a surprising range of answers as to what is the gospel. Some people connect the gospel with the general truth the church believes or teaches. Some assume that the gospel is what is heard when a sermon moves them emotionally or spiritually. Others might say that when the Bible is preached, the gospel is heard. Some equate gospel with the word of God. Some speak of the social gospel while many Pentecostals speak of the full gospel. Presumably the church preaches the gospel, yet if one examines published sermons, one does not necessarily find what one might expect. Using sermon practice as a standard, one recognizes that some, if not most, sermons communicate that the gospel is what we do, for many sermons are anthropocentric. Those who preach this way inadvertently say, "I preach in the name of God, but everything is up to us." For other preachers the gospel would seem to be what emerges from allowing history and literary matters to be the final arbiter on the meaning of a biblical text. They in effect say, "The gospel is what science and history can verify in the Bible." For others who have accommodated the gospel to culture, the gospel is cultural values. They say, "The gospel is what culture defines as good." One of the most important questions for any preacher concerns the relationship between the gospel and Jesus Christ.

Our goal is ultimately to reclaim preaching as a dual art of both teaching and proclaiming the gospel. In a postmodern age, all assumptions need to be tested, and here we test what gospel might mean. In this section we consider first what the Bible actually says about gospel, and next what people in homiletics say about its practice. As long as we explore the content of the gospel in sermons, we teach about it.

CHAPTER FIVE
What Does the Bible Say
about the Gospel?

L
ack of clarity about the gospel is not new. Gerald Kennedy, bishop
of Los Angeles in The Methodist Church in the early 1950s,
preached a sermon on the gospel titled "God's Good News" in
which he presented these points: the gospel is the good news of (1) personality—that God is a person (not a system); (2) joy; (3) freedom; and
(4) power (to be happy; of Jeremiah he said, "There is a fellow who
needed a counselor if ever there was one").[1] There was one passing reference to Jesus Christ and the joy of conquest for him even in the cross. How
one conceives of the gospel affects one's entire way of preaching. By contrast, a few decades earlier, Southern Baptist evangelist R. G. Lee
preached in his outspoken and sometimes amusing way, "You can preach
sociology, or psychology, or any other form of *ology*, but if you leave Jesus
Christ out of it you hit the toboggan slide to hell."[2]

At one level, what one takes to be the gospel is whatever lies at the
heart of one's preaching. If preachers were to review their sermons over a
year, they might get a good sense of what their gospel actually is as
opposed to what they think it is. Everyone preaches something as the core
of his or her sermons, and listeners hear it; it would be interesting to see
if what we preach matches biblical or congregational perspectives. Is it the
identity and saving grace of Jesus Christ as established in the cross?

At another more reliable level, the gospel is what the Bible says it is, yet
even here there is some variety of response. In this chapter we will consider a range of possible biblical and theological answers to our question,
and in the chapter that follows this, we will contemplate what homiletics
has said by way of preaching practice.

The Epistles and the Gospel

Can one even speak of "the gospel" in a postmodern age? Does it imply
a singular notion? Gospel (*euangelion*) is a biblical term, and of the
seventy-six times it is used in the New Testament, forty-eight are in Paul
and none in Luke or John, where only related terms appear.[3] (The Greek

55

titles of the Gospels omit the term and read simply "According to . . ." [*kata*].) Before any of the Gospels were written, Paul wrote about "the gospel." Most references to gospel in the Bible are to "the gospel," but Paul also speaks of "my gospel" (Romans 2:16; 16:25; 2 Timothy 2:8), "our gospel" (2 Corinthians 4:3), and "a different gospel" (2 Corinthians 11:4; Galatians 1:6)—adding, "not that there is another gospel" (Galatians 1:7), although he does mention "a gospel contrary to what we proclaimed to you" (1:8).

Paul offers a short summary of what he means by gospel when he says, "My gospel and the proclamation of Jesus Christ, according to the revelation of the mystery that was kept secret for long ages but is now disclosed, and through the prophetic writings is made known to all the Gentiles, according to the command of the eternal God" (Romans 16:25-26). Elsewhere he draws on pre-Pauline compositions or confessions that speak of the gospel: in 1 Corinthians 15:1-5, he says of the good news he preached, "As of first importance . . . that Christ died for our sins in accordance with the scriptures, and that he was buried, and that he was raised on the third day in accordance with the scriptures" (vv. 3-4); in 1 Thessalonians 1:9b-10, a passage that was likely part of a baptismal tradition, Paul states, "You turned to God from idols, to serve a living and true God, and to wait for his Son from heaven, whom he raised from the dead—Jesus, who rescues us from the wrath that is coming"; and in Romans 1:3-4, Paul speaks of "the gospel concerning his Son, who was descended from David according to the flesh and was declared to be Son of God with power according to the spirit of holiness by resurrection from the dead, Jesus Christ our Lord."[4] Pauline letters contain seven references to "the gospel of God" (e.g., Romans 15:16; 1 Thessalonians 2:9) and ten to "the gospel of Christ" (e.g., 1 Corinthians 9:12; Galatians 1:7); "preaching the gospel" and "preaching Christ" seem interchangeable.[5]

The same Christic center is found in Paul's "for Christ did not send me to baptize but to proclaim the gospel . . . so that the cross of Christ might not be emptied of its power" (1 Corinthians 1:17) and in his "but we proclaim Christ crucified" (1 Corinthians 1:23). He also refers to what he preaches as "the mystery of God" (1 Corinthians 2:1). Though God in Christ is revealed, mystery remains, or "now we see in a mirror, dimly, but then we will see face to face" (1 Corinthians 13:12).

When Paul says, "According to my gospel" (Romans 2:16), he not only identifies to the church in Rome that what he preaches is centered on "God through Jesus Christ," but he also identifies that his perspective is that of a witness. His testimony is not just knowledge; it is "the power of God" leading to salvation for all who believed (Romans 1:16).

The writer of 2 Timothy 2:8 provides a concise summary of the gospel:

"Remember Jesus Christ, raised from the dead, a descendant of David—that is my gospel." The writer of Hebrews finds consistency in the gospel: "Jesus Christ is the same yesterday and today and forever" (13:8). Still, how one understands him changes; for many centuries the gospel did not extend to women's rights, to a ban on slavery, or to issues of social justice and environmental stewardship.

The Gospel and the Old Testament

Good news abounds in the Old Testament: in the covenants God makes with God's people; in God's rescue of Israel from Egypt in the exodus; in countless miracles and signs; in God's righteousness as saving action (*sedaqa*), for instance, in Isaiah 61:1-3 ("The Spirit of the Lord GOD is upon me . . . he has sent me to bring good news to the oppressed"); in the salvation and "good news" that is proclaimed both there and in Isaiah 52:7; and in the law upholding justice, mercy, and righteousness. There is only one God in both Testaments. While the church reads some passages such as Isaiah 53 as prophetic of Christ, the Old Testament is not an extensive secret code about Jesus Christ, as the early church believed. The gospel found there is not different in character from God's saving action most fully expressed in the life, death, resurrection, and ascension of Jesus Christ. Paul makes this clear when he says that "the gospel . . . is the power of God for salvation to everyone who has faith, to the Jew first and also to the Greek" (Romans 1:16). This "gospel," he says, was revealed to Abraham (Galatians 3:8), who first "believed God, and it was reckoned to him as righteousness" (3:6). Paul himself received this gospel "through a revelation of Jesus Christ" (Galatians 1:12). The gospel need only be accepted; thus when people believe, they are "justified by faith" (Romans 3:28; Galatians 3:24) and become "children of God through faith" (Galatians 3:26), receiving the promise given to Abraham (3:29).

In fact, the gospel in the Old Testament is echoed and clarified by what is found in the New Testament, and the gospel in the New Testament is echoed and clarified by what is found in the Old Testament. Brevard Childs states that our way of reading Scripture must be to read the Old Testament in light of the New and the New Testament in light of the Old.[6] Kevin J. Vanhoozer gets at the same perspective:

> The history of Jesus Christ, which culminates in death and resurrection, recapitulates—perfects and completes—the whole theo-drama. In particular, Jesus recapitulates—repeats differently—the history of Adam and the history of Israel. It is this recapitulation of central events in the drama of redemption—exodus, exile, entry to the promised land—that ultimately

provides a framework for understanding the saving significance of Jesus' death in terms of an even more "wondrous exchange" than has hitherto been thought.[7]

Likewise, Ellen Davis writes, "The Old Testament in all its parts speaks to us in ways that are Christianly coherent," by which she means they lead us into relationship with the triune God.[8]

The Gospels and the Gospel

The crucifixion and resurrection are the climax of each of the four canonical Gospels. Richard B. Hays briefly notes the distinctive features of each narrative:

> All four canonical Gospels reach their climax in the resurrection of Jesus, but each nuances the resurrection message differently. Mark maintains the solemn, mysterious character of his gospel by omitting any direct narrative of Jesus' resurrection appearances, but his proclamation of the resurrection remains explicit and emphatic (Mark 16:6-7). Matthew's account of the resurrection highlights Jesus as the triumphant Son of Man who has received "all authority in heaven and earth" and who sends his disciples out on a mission to declare his authority to the whole world (Matt 28:16-20; compare Dan 7:13-14). Luke's account emphasizes the mysterious presence of the risen Jesus with the disciples at table (Luke 24:30-31, 41-43), highlights his role in teaching his followers how to read Scripture (24:25-27, 44-47), and foreshadows the giving of the Spirit to the community (24:49). John links Jesus' resurrection with the disciples' mission, with the bestowal of the Spirit, and with forgiveness of sins (John 20:21-23). He also adds the distinctive stories of Jesus' appearances to Mary Magdalene (20:1-18) and Thomas (20:24-29); the latter narrative underscores both the bodily character of Jesus' resurrection and its pertinence to future generations "who have not seen and yet have come to believe."[9]

Faced with the variations in the gospel narratives, the task of the preacher is clear, says Hays: "Rather than explaining away these early accounts with demythologizing or rationalizing theories, the role of Christian preaching is to carry forward faithfully what was handed on by these traditions, and to reaffirm these stories as the true source of our hope."[10]

The Gospel and the Preaching of Jesus

One could say that the gospel is what Christ commissioned the church to preach. In Luke, Christ says, "Repentance and forgiveness of sins is to be proclaimed in his [the Messiah's] name to all nations" (24:47). The Great Commission in Matthew is to "make disciples of all nations, baptizing them in the name of the Father and of the Son and of the Holy Spirit, and teaching them to obey everything that I have commanded you" (28:19-20). Mark reads, "Go into all the world and preach the good news [*euangelion*] to all creation" (16:15, NIV), by which he means saving news, liberating news centered on God in Jesus Christ. It is an announcement that heralds what God has done, is doing, and will do.

Is the gospel what Jesus preached? There can be good reason for such thinking. One result of considerable biblical research on parables in recent decades was reclaiming the centrality of repentance and the coming of the kingdom of God in Jesus' teaching, especially in Matthew. God's realm breaks in any moment, and its marks are justice, peace, mercy, kindness, repentance, forgiveness, reconciliation, food for the hungry, water for the thirsty, clothing for the naked, visitors for the sick and imprisoned. In short these actions are fruits of the Spirit. Indeed, Jesus commands his followers to "go and proclaim the kingdom of God" (Luke 9:60).

However, the content of Jesus' words was not his full message. Though he preached of the resurrection, his words awaited the fulfillment of the event. The origin of preaching is not so much his preaching but the first Easter. Everything hinges there. In Luke, the resurrection enables the Bible to be understood; Christ opens the disciples' minds to the Scriptures: "Thus it is written, that the Messiah is to suffer and to rise from the dead on the third day, and that repentance and forgiveness of sins is to be proclaimed in his name to all nations, beginning from Jerusalem" (24:45-47). In Mark, the disciples repeatedly are commanded to keep Jesus' identity quiet because they cannot grasp his identity as Messiah until he is raised from the dead. In John, the Holy Spirit will be sent to teach the disciples what they cannot understand about Christ in his earthly life (14:26). It is not just the fullness of Jesus' identity that is revealed in the resurrection; it is the nature of God's entire realm and the goodness of the news of Christ.

G. D. Yarold sees the resurrection as inseparable from the larger story: "The Christian community owes its existence to the total act of God in Christ, which is expressed in the sequence: Incarnation, Passion, Resurrection, Ascension, and Pentecost. The initiative is entirely on the side of God."[11]

Thomas F. Torrance similarly insists on the need to conceive of the Christ event as a whole. Incarnation and atonement, he said, need to be thought into each other, such that the incarnation is from the beginning the act of atonement, and atonement is grounded in the act of God becoming one with us as we really are: "It is of the very essence of the gospel that salvation and justification are by the grace of Christ alone, in which he takes your place, that you may have his place."[12] This radical understanding of substitution implies that Christ, in love, takes our place before God in all aspects of life, not just in the depths of our human misery and perdition, but also in our believing, praying, and worshiping of God. We are upheld by him in all aspects of our human relations before God. Thus when we speak with Paul of being justified by faith, we speak not of our own faith or abilities, but of the faithfulness of God in Christ, who can take even our sins and use them as the means to bind us to himself: "It is in Christ's grasp of us rather than in our grasp of him that our salvation and certainty lie."[13] Torrance wants preachers to be unashamed of the nature of the theological task. He wants them to be bold in preaching Jesus Christ, not through brilliant preaching, but by bluntly directing people to Christ, and to Christ alone, who has taken their place that they might have his.

In other words, one could preach what Jesus preached and seldom get to his identity as the Son of God, who died on the cross and rose again to save the world, who sent his spirit in love to strengthen, equip, and empower God's children for ministry.

The Gospel Paired with Law

Paul understood gospel in relationship to law, and he wrestled with their connection most notably throughout Romans, for instance, when he says, "For the law of the Spirit of life in Christ Jesus has set you free from the law of sin and of death" (8:2). In 2 Corinthians he speaks of these two dispensations as "the ministry of Spirit" (3:8) and "the ministry of death" (3:7). For Paul, "no one will be justified by the works of the law" (Galatians 2:16); rather, "a person is justified by faith apart from works prescribed by the law" (Romans 3:28).

Perhaps no one more than Luther picked up on the implications of Paul's distinction. Preaching on 2 Corinthians 3:4-11, he spoke against preachers who fail to make the law "a tributary to faith in Christ, [and] misuse it to teach work-righteousness."[14] The law is the word of God given by revelation, yet it serves only to condemn to death those who try to keep it. By contrast, the gospel is "of the Spirit" and "is the agency whereby the Holy Spirit works in the heart":[15]

> It tells rather of the works of Christ, who is unique in that he was born of a virgin, died for sin and rose from the dead, something no other man has been able to do. This doctrine is revealed through none but the Holy Spirit, and none other confers the Holy Spirit. The Holy Spirit works in the hearts of them who hear and accept the doctrine. Therefore, this ministration is termed a ministration "of the Spirit."[16]

The "letter" of the law, Luther says of Paul, "is all manner of law, doctrine and message, which goes no farther than the oral or written word, which consists only of the powerless letter."[17] The gospel, by contrast, as

> a "ministration of the spirit" would call attention to its power to produce in the hearts of men an effect wholly different from that of the Law: it is accompanied by the Holy Spirit and it creates a new heart. . . . It points not to man's works, but to the works of Christ, and bids him confidently believe that for the sake of his Son God will forgive his sins and accept him as his child. And this message, when received in faith, immediately cheers and comforts the heart.[18]

Elsewhere Luther argues that we need the law to know our failings, and to know what God supplies: "Without the law, no one recognizes himself and what he is lacking; and he . . . does not seek grace."[19]

The Gospel as Scandal

Something about the nature of the gospel, in all its scandal and offense, makes it difficult to hear. It is a stumbling block that God became human in a man, that humans need a Savior, that we have limitations set upon us as creatures. It is a scandal that Jesus died for us. It is a scandal that the Messiah was killed as a criminal on the cross, that he rose from the dead, that he is alive today, that we drink his blood and eat his body unto eternal salvation. Jesus said, "Blessed is anyone who takes no offense at me" (Luke 7:23).

William Willimon reminds preachers that they need not preach as though it is possible to hear without conversion. Instead of taking upon themselves the responsibility for the gospel being heard, the gospel is given that responsibility, for a miracle is needed if the gospel is to be heard. Some messages should receive no confidence, like the tired messages of liberal Protestantism that encouraged people to leave the churches in droves. He wants preachers to expect more from the gospel. He wants us to be so faithful that we might again be interesting. Easter is the basis of our preaching, and we should preach requiring a miracle, a resurrection, to be understood. For Willimon, evangelism looks for, hopes for, and promises transformation for hearers. In this it contrasts apologetics and encourages preachers to have confidence in the message they preach.[20]

Resistance to the Gospel

Resistance to the gospel can come from many quarters, including individuals who have difficulty with the cross as the standard for theological reflection and Christian living. Feminist-critical studies that take women's experience as the starting point for theological reflection find in the cross an instrument of torture and a symbol of violence that implies acceptance of suffering today.[21] The most vulnerable in society are encouraged to bear their crosses and discouraged from liberation. Many scholars argue that in history, theologies of the cross have been used in society to contribute to oppression, for example, when Luther renounced the peasant uprising in the mid-1520s. Nonetheless, theologians like Deanna A. Thompson are finding ways to claim the liberating features of the cross at the center of the faith.[22] They do this by placing oppressive historical practices within their social settings and retrieving from traditions norms that are refurbished to hold promise for today. As a result, the cross can be reclaimed as a symbol appropriated in weakness in opposition to a theology of glory. Part of the liberationist reappropriation of the cross is portrayal of the Crucified One who suffers alongside his suffering people, and whose resurrection is both vindication of their suffering and judgment upon those responsible for it.

A number of specific doctrines related to Christ and the cross also cause resistance to the gospel. For example, atonement theories through history are notoriously troublesome: the ransom theory implied that Satan set a price that God needed to pay; Anselm's satisfaction theory implied an honor code that needed to be satisfied; and penal atonement theories implied an angry God who demanded sacrifice. The topic is too big for us here, but a growing number of contextual and feminist scholars suggest new approaches that balance hermeneutical suspicion and recovery of what is valuable; they do not simply reject tradition. Sally Brown advises not settling on a single understanding or theory. She invites students to challenge inadequate theories of God's saving work and reclaim multiple images or metaphors concerning the cross.[23]

Of course, resistance to the gospel can be even more basic, having to do with whether the historical accounts of the resurrection are true. An apologetic response might argue that if there was no resurrection, Jesus' words would not be remembered; they gain their significance now because of who he is. William Willimon responds another way: "Our intellectual problem with the gospel is not one of *meaning* but really is about power. Not the limited intellectual problem of 'How can I believe this?' But rather in what power configurations am I presently enslaved?"[24] Everyone lives by some story, and it is a question of which one we choose. A student asked if it was not possible just to preach the various events in Jesus' life and his words and miracles, and only to mention the resurrection at Easter. Of course, it is possible and it is done in some circles, but such preaching falls short of the gospel and may even call into question why one would bother to preach since it departs from Christ's commission.

Summaries of the Gospel

It is tempting, though dangerous, to opt readily for a summary of the gospel, whether it is in the form of a prayer, hymn, creed, or particular verses of Scripture. The danger is shutting down other expressions and closing one's ears to the Bible. Every biblical text offers a different perspective from which to view the cross and resurrection, hence, new windows on the gospel for our day. No summaries are fully adequate. The novelist was right in saying, "If I could have said it in a sentence, I would not have written a book." Among the best summaries are the classic church creeds (especially the Nicene and Apostles') that have been used through history not only as confessional statements but also as hermeneutical tools to guide preaching. They are sophisticated lenses for reading biblical texts.

How one determines gospel is part of how one reads the Bible, and Christians for centuries have read it with a view to how the entire paschal mystery (cross, resurrection, ascension, Pentecost) illuminates and is illuminated by individual biblical texts. As Carol Norén has beautifully said (adapting Christopher Seitz), "The relationship between Scripture and creed is mutually informing, mutually constraining, and mutually asserting."[25] The Bible guides creeds, and the creeds guide readings of the Bible. The prayers of great thanksgiving in the Communion liturgy of many denominations also provide effective summaries of the gospel, beginning with creation and moving through the prophets and the entire Christ event to the end times. Still, we need the entire Bible illuminated by the Holy Spirit to be able to articulate the gospel.

The gospel also cannot be reduced to a doctrine. Christ is central, not doctrine about Christ. Christ is the starting point of faith, the returning reference point, the ultimate end point. Harold Wells uses the unusual term *Christic center* to emphasize that "the very person of Christ and not Christology as such"[26] is central to theology. Douglas John Hall makes the same point: *"It is necessary to distinguish carefully and perpetually between Jesus Christ and doctrine concerning Jesus Christ.* The foundational confession of Christian faith . . . is that Jesus is the center, the 'cornerstone,' *not* that this or that Christology or soteriology constitute that *fundamentum."*[27] In fact, Hall can see "no reason why anyone would deliberately claim Christian identity apart from his or her conviction that Jesus of Nazareth is the bearer of ultimate significance for his or her life."[28]

The gospel also cannot be reduced to its implications for today. Every age discovers new implications of the gospel. Thus the gospel is now understood to extend to circumstances and issues that were not in the purview of the biblical writers: for example, the abolition of slavery, equal rights for women, and preferential concern for those denied a full place in society. Each of these represents good news and is a mark of the activity of the Spirit, yet each finds its roots in the saving work of Jesus Christ on the cross. Applications change, and ways of viewing the gospel alter, but what constitutes the gospel has consistency from age to age, hence the words in Hebrews, "Jesus Christ is the same yesterday and today and forever" (13:8). The consistency is not in what the gospel is per se, but in who Christ is.

By the same token the gospel cannot be translated into images and metaphors that are more palatable today, whether this is by way of moralisms and dogmatic assertions that fall along political or ideological lines, or innocuous analogies of the resurrection to springtime, as though it is something that occurs naturally and automatically. Any attempts to make the gospel sound reasonable are attempts to accommodate it to the reigning culture. People do not have to understand the gospel so much as be confronted by it, allowing the Holy Spirit to work. Conversion and transformation are needed to hear it. For the gospel to be what it is, the Bible accounts must be allowed to speak for themselves as much as possible.

We have considered teaching the gospel from a biblical and theological perspective. Much more remains to be said, and we turn now specifically to teachers of preaching to help us say it. They help us understand what teaching the gospel sounds like in the practice of sermons.

Practical Helps in Teaching the Gospel

We continue our examination of teaching the gospel by considering specifically some practical helps in teaching the gospel. As a step toward that goal, we first consider what homileticians have taught. How they define the gospel or perceive its role in the composition of sermons both reflects the preaching of the church and has an impact on it. Since the New Homiletic has not been specifically focused on the gospel, it is important to understand what assumptions guided it and what might be needed.

In the 1870s, the gospel may have needed little clarification, but perspectives on it nonetheless mattered a great deal. Phillips Brooks understood that the gospel makes preachers into poets: "Every true preacher must be a poet, at least in so far as to see behind all the imperfections of men a certain ideal. . . . A belief in the Incarnation, in the divine Son of Man makes such poets of us all."[1] He argues that words quickly fail if we try to describe too precisely the incarnation and resurrection of Jesus Christ at the heart of the gospel, and yet we fail the gospel if our witness moves away from Christ.

One may be surprised at how many introductory and advanced preaching books across the theological spectrum do not speak specifically about the gospel. Books that one might expect to discuss the gospel, indeed even with the word *gospel* in their titles, commonly do not engage the subject, or they do so only in limited ways, for example, without mention of the resurrection. Perhaps only recently is there a need for clarity in this regard. The point here is that if instructors today do not make gospel central, it may not be present in the sermons they nurture. While at one time it may have been safe to assume that everyone knew what gospel means, we have seen that that is no longer the case. In our era what constitutes the gospel can have different interpretations, and biblical understandings of the gospel no longer can be assumed to be the stated, conscious, or even desired goal of preaching.

On the other hand, numerous individuals have made important claims about the gospel.[2] In *Preaching Resurrection*, O. Wesley Allen Jr. analyzes the resurrection stories in each of the Gospels in turn, "the good news of Jesus Christ as being the claim that Christ is risen, not the claim that Jesus was risen."[3] David L. Bartlett similarly devoted a chapter to each gospel in *What's Good about This News? Preaching from the Gospels and Galatians.* He defends the unity of the gospel message: "There are important continuities in the way good news is understood throughout the New Testament. It is still always the herald's announcement of God's victory. That victory is always won through Jesus Christ."[4]

Some people have identified a problem with preaching in relation to the gospel,[5] including Charles L. Campbell, who called preachers to return to it. He encouraged preachers to heed that the "ascriptive logic" of the canonical Gospels is not about narrative per se but about the character of Jesus:

> The gospels are not stories about elemental human experiences, but rather stories that render the identity of a particular person whose life, death, and resurrection accomplish God's purposes for the world.
>
> Thus, what is important for Christian preaching is not "stories" in general or even "homiletical plots," but rather a specific story that renders the identity of a particular person. The ascriptive logic of the gospels provides both constraints and guidance for Christian preaching.[6]

In other words, a purpose of preaching is to communicate the identity of Jesus Christ, who he is and what he has done, and narrative is important insofar as it enables that. A challenge to us all is to be more intentional about the gospel.

A Polar Gospel

Among those who have been most deliberate in focusing on the gospel are those who have engaged the classic themes of law and gospel first highlighted by Paul in Romans. *Gospel* is a frequent term in André Resner's *Preacher and Cross: Person and Message in Theology and Rhetoric.*[7] Recently he added to his Christ-centered meaning:

> It is increasingly clear to me that how one defines "gospel" is key in the hermeneutical appropriation of scripture for preaching. I am defining it this way: the gospel is something that God does, that no human can do for him/herself, that concretely changes a situation. There is a from/to character to the gospel. The change may be from hate or indifference to love, or from injustice to justice, sin to salvation, loneliness to community, judgment to redemption, violence to peace and harmony, or it could be the change of void to creation, or blessing on a good situation. Even this last instance, where no "problem has been solved," no "law has been trumped by

gospel," the situation is not as it was before. God cannot be active in a situation and things remain the same. Joy can be deepened, or even understood and seen more completely.[8]

At the heart of the gospel are two dramas held together as one, the crucifixion and the resurrection of Jesus Christ. They function as poles in Christian thought, the one pointing to the depth of human disobedience, sin, injustice, and alienation from God and neighbor, and the other pointing to God's willingness to save us at all costs. The church remembers these events by reenacting them not only annually in the major celebrations of the church year but also on a weekly basis: Sunday is the day of the resurrection. Richard Lischer puts it this way:

> Death and resurrection—this fugal theme is at the center of Christian worship. The drama of the church year unfolds it; the Sunday service, which originated as a little Easter, reenacts it, and the Holy Communion represents it. Baptism as burial and rising in Christ, sacramentally recapitulates it, and the Holy Communion represents it. The first and only feast of the church was the Pasch, the two-day vigil that commemorated the death and resurrection of Jesus in a single, fused experience, beginning with baptisms on Holy Saturday and culminating in the Eucharist at Easter dawn. . . . The church . . . orchestrate[s] its preaching, spiritual discipline, and liturgical and sacramental life according to the rhythm of death and resurrection.[9]

Even in using the word *Pasch*, the church claims the unity of this drama with what preceded it in the Old Testament; Christ is the Passover Lamb, whose blood is the blood of a new covenant (1 Corinthians 11:25).

The gospel is popularly confused with what seems nice, polite, or good by cultural standards, but the gospel in fact both convicts and comforts. The word of conviction for one person can be the word of liberation for another. Repentance precedes forgiveness. The gospel message is offensive to many. Paul identifies the problem when he says, "We proclaim Christ crucified, a stumbling block [*skandalon*] to Jews and foolishness to Gentiles" (1 Corinthians 1:23). The gospel continues to scandalize.

The Gospel as a New Age

David Buttrick has been consistent in taking time to speak of the gospel in terms of a new age. It is the new order that Christ inaugurated in his own preaching: "The good news is of God's coming new order disrupting our social stability but promising redemption."[10] For Buttrick, "the resurrection certifies Jesus' message of the kingdom."[11] Preaching the gospel means preaching God's future, picturing the new age with vivid images of a world reconciled in God's love. Eschatology ought to assist preachers in preaching boldly about social injustice in the present.

James F. Kay testifies that something new occurred in Jesus Christ that marks a radical shift: "If the turn of the ages has taken place in the cross and continues to take place in the work of the cross, then what is required of preachers are not simply illustrations from history and nature, but illustrations that place history and nature, indeed all of life, into the crisis of the cross."[12] Business is not as usual. Christ's rising pronounces a death sentence on all the powers and principalities that seemed to have the final say and announces that their time is at an end. The way things once were done is challenged by the new order that has already broken into the present moment. Old assumptions need to be reexamined in light of a new two-world perspective. In other words, the resurrection makes a difference.

In a related manner, Stephen Webb calls for preachers to embrace the "hyperbolic imagination" one finds in Revelation that holds a vision of what is possible before the congregation, even when there is no evidence for it in the moment. He calls this the poetics of the impossible rather than what too often rules, the poetics of the probable.[13] Hyperbolic imagination is concerned with what was meant to be and will be in the final fulfillment of God's promises.

Five Radical Claims

We come then to five claims about the gospel and preaching that some people might find radical:

1. Bible Texts Are Not Necessarily the Gospel

In two significant companion essays, "Preaching the Bible and Gospel" and "Toward a New Paradigm for Preaching,"[14] Edward Farley encourages preachers not to think narrowly about preaching a text or unit of Scripture, but to concentrate on the theological task of preaching the gospel and to allow it to set the themes of the sermon.[15] Both Buttrick and Farley claim that sermons based on biblical texts do not necessarily preach the gospel.[16]

Michael Rogness and David Lose challenge those who assume that in preaching the Bible they have preached the gospel:

Certainly our sense of the gospel (in brief, what God has done through Jesus Christ for us and all the world) emerges from the biblical witness. At the same time, though, there is some value in realizing that we cannot simply equate the two. Luther had a nice way of putting this. The Bible is the

---

manger in which the Christ child rests. So while we should flee to the Bible to find Christ, Luther counseled, we should avoid falling on our knees to worship wood and straw. To put it another way, we value the Bible so highly precisely and primarily because it contains the gospel.

The preacher's primary task in dealing with any biblical passage, therefore, is to say a word about what God has done and is still doing through Jesus Christ for us and for all the world. . . . Whatever you're preaching on, somehow it relates to the ongoing work of the God we have come to know most fully through Jesus Christ.[17]

This instruction to seek the gospel in the Bible is a helpful correction and encouragement to those tempted to treat the Bible and gospel as synonyms. Lose encourages preachers to move toward "ultimate speech"[18] centered on the gospel, using phrases that are reminiscent of early creeds and confessions, such as "Jesus died for us," "Christ was raised," "God loves us," and "Jesus is Lord." Lose claims, "When you approach the heart or climax of your sermon, you are most likely to be speaking in ultimate language."[19]

2. The Gospel Is Larger than the Cross and Resurrection on Their Own

The cross and resurrection are central to the gospel, yet the gospel is larger than the events of Good Friday and Easter in that it includes the implications of these events. It includes the incarnation, ascension, and Pentecost; it includes the fulfillment of all God's promises in the second coming; and it includes trinitarian notions of a God who is one nature and three persons. The gospel avoids christomonism, the practice of centering exclusively on Christ; it is properly trinitarian and witnesses to all the persons of the Trinity. Christ cannot readily be understood apart from the intimacy of love that is shared in the communal love of the Trinity and that is extended to humanity in Christ through the Spirit. Gordon W. Lathrop says,

Preaching is a trinitarian event: enlivened by the Spirit, the words of the preacher draw the hearer into the truth of our need, into the encounter with the Crucified-Risen One and so into faith and hope in God, into the communal life that flows from the presence of the life-giving Trinity. . . . Faith in the triune God, after all, is faith in God coming now, into the midst of our death, and making, *giving* life.[20]

These truths likewise afford perspectives on both creation and the promises of the end times. Where Christ is diminished or eclipsed, so too is the triune God.

Every promise that God has made is confirmed by the resurrection. Every biblical text is like a lookout point on a mountain. Look one way and each text affords a view of God. Look another way and each offers direction for a particular human historical situation. Look to the far horizon and each text offers a view of the cross. Look once more and the text points to the Spirit's empowerment for mission.

When we say that the gospel is larger than the cross and resurrection, we mean simply that every text—Old Testament, gospel, epistle, or Revelation—tells us something about the gospel, about God and what it means to be human. No biblical text or event stands in isolation from the entire canon. The cross and resurrection have unique centrality for the gospel.

3. What We Identify as the Word of God Is Not Necessarily the Gospel

In Reformed understanding, the word of God is found in the reading and interpretation of Scripture. In some traditions, after the reading of Scripture, one says, "This is the word of God," yet even that phrase traditionally has a more refined understanding connected with discerning what God is saying to the church. For Calvin, "The Word becomes efficacious for our faith through the Holy Spirit. . . . Without the illumination of the Holy Spirit the Word can do nothing. . . . Only the Holy Spirit leads us to Christ."[21] Karl Barth famously spoke of the "threefold form" of the word of God as Jesus Christ, Scripture, and preaching.[22] Daniel Migliore notes, "Scripture is thus authoritative not in itself but, as the Reformers insisted, as it 'sets forth Christ,' as it functions in the community of faith by the power of the Spirit to create a liberating and renewing relationship with God through Christ."[23] Brevard Childs claims, "The hearing of God's Word is repeatedly confirmed by the Holy Spirit through its resonance with the church's christological rule-of-faith."[24] What is word of God in Scripture is what the Spirit testifies to or what points to Christ and in so doing points to the triune God.

The way we typically understand the word of God is often not gospel. We may conceive of the word

- as event, creating that of which it speaks, akin to creation being spoken into being by God's word (e.g., Genesis 1; Psalm 33:6; Isaiah 55:11);
- as that which is divine or prophetic, modeled after "the word of the LORD" coming to prophets (e.g., 1 Kings 17:2; Isaiah 38:4, Ezekiel 1:3; Luke 3:2);
- as command (Jeremiah 16:1), judgment (1:14), or promise (46:27).

The word is eventful, but what makes it so arguably is not the use of eventful language, persuasive argument, or narrative plot; it is eventful because in hearing the word, listeners hear and meet the one who loves them without condition. To the degree that preachers may claim a prophetic word,[25] it is not because of the office of preacher, but may be because the Word found in Scripture is Christ, who puts to death the old creation and establishes a new one in the midst of the old. By the same token, God may speak a word of simple condemnation, but it is not the gospel until the hope that is rooted in God overcoming the dominion of death is also offered.

4. What We Identify as Grace Is Not Necessarily a Complete Expression of the Gospel

Grace is God's action. I am among those who believe that preachers should look for God's empowering action in or behind a text as one of the first steps in preparing a sermon. Once this has been located, one has something that will preach, and one has a focus for the sermon that will be centered on God.[26] Grace may be found in or behind any text. On the one hand, we may affirm that wherever God's grace is found, whenever one discerns God's action of saving, sanctifying, or bringing forth justice and mercy, one has located gospel. Still if one preaches on Israel saved at the Red Sea, or on Jesus healing people with leprosy, is the gospel proclaimed in its fullness? One might say that gospel gains its sharpest focus in the cross and its loudest volume in the empty tomb. Where Christ is present in his death and in his resurrection, in judgment and in grace, the gospel is fully present.

5. Biblical Texts Become the Gospel

To find the gospel message, one needs to read the biblical texts not only in light of good historical exegesis; theological reading of Scripture is essential with discernment illumined by the Spirit, God needs to be in view, and the God sense of Scripture needs to be found.[27] It is too easy for us as preachers to think that we preach texts because, in fact, we do, but that is not the purpose. Jesus called us to preach the gospel, not a section of a psalm or a lesson from an epistle. Any particular text is an essential opening or access to the gospel. Too often preachers mine a text for a golden nugget, irrespective of whether it says anything about God, or as though individual units of scripture stand independent of the Bible as a whole. Texts sometimes do contain an apt encapsulation of the gospel, but most texts, at least as we cut them, make no direct mention of God or

Christ. The percentage of biblical texts that speak of the gospel in Christ-specific ways may be very low, yet if we followed that percentage as a guideline for preaching, we might speak of the gospel only a few Sundays each year. The historical-critical approach embraced so thoroughly by the New Homiletic encourages texts to be read as semiautonomous units, and we need also to treat them as Luther suggested, as tributaries to the gospel.

Preaching the Gospel

How then do we preach the gospel? Do we preach only texts that mention the cross and the resurrection? Do we wait for a funeral when resurrection texts abound, or until Good Friday and Easter? Do we preach gospel by chance, when our biblical text happens to speak directly of it? Do we preach it by whim, when we feel like it? Do we preach it by deferral, pointing away from the sermon to the hymns and prayers of the worship service? Do we tack the cross and the resurrection to the end of every sermon, "But the good news is . . ."? Biblical texts become gospel, if they do not already contain it, and they do so with the help of the Spirit and intentional acts on our part. Here are some suggestions to help in this regard:[28]

1. *Determine what God is doing in or behind the text.* The gospel becomes the focus in preaching by being the goal from the beginning of the homiletical process to the end. Thus the first matters to which one might attend in the sermon process can be to get God in view. Gardner Taylor said that preachers should start by asking of a text, "To what part of the life in Christ is it that we want to point and lead the worshippers?"[29]

Texts sometimes do contain an apt statement of the gospel, but most make no direct mention of God or Christ. The gospel is what God does, not what humans do. Thus we ask, What is God doing in or behind this text? The answer is ideally stated in a positive way identifying an action of grace on God's part, something that God does to save or strengthen or establish justice. By naming what God does by way of grace in a text, one can ultimately build on it and find a coherent gospel link.

2. *Use God's action of grace to determine the trouble it addresses.* The gospel is both trouble and grace, crucifixion and resurrection; thus sermons desiring to communicate the gospel may move from the one to the other. One may conceive of the sermon as four parts or pages: trouble in the biblical text, trouble in our world, grace in the biblical text, and grace in our world.

3. *Re-create the text in the sermon.* The text is a vehicle for the gospel; it either contains it or points effectively toward it when understood

---

theologically. As we have seen in our discussion of teaching, listeners need the text to be reproduced in the sermon before they can absorb abstractions from it, so we do well to try to set it in its life setting as much as possible. Even representing a text in this manner is an act of interpretation; we highlight some things and diminish others. Since the core of the gospel is both crucifixion and resurrection, the retelling can be from each perspective, using the grammar of four pages.

This process of creative representation of a text in a sermon follows scholarly deconstruction exegesis. Reconstruction involves representing the text faithfully in its details and background. It also involves using common sense, imagination, and theology to fill in details that may be missing, enough to make the text and its original meaning come alive for today. This involves presenting lifelike scenes in movielike ways, for example, in preaching from Paul, using textual and historical details to picture something of the scene or circumstance to which, from which, or about which he writes.

4. *Use God's action of grace to determine some link to the life, death, resurrection, and coming again of Jesus Christ.* Some biblical texts contain some aspect of the fullness of the gospel. However, with most texts we may need to use the particular text as a vantage point from which to view the cross. In doing this we allow the significance of what God has accomplished in Jesus Christ to modify, complete, or otherwise affect the final meaning of the text at hand. One reads one's text intertextually, allowing it to interpret or be interpreted by other biblical texts. Our preaching ancestors in practice understood the preaching "text" not simply as the text that prompted one's reflections, but more fully as the entire Bible. Thus one might draw on any passages that help illumine as gospel the word one finds in one's particular text.

5. *Interpret characters, events, or actions in the Bible text in terms of central symbols of faith.* One seeks echoes of one's text in key symbols and images of Christian life, worship practice, and theological themes, for instance, baptism, the cross, Eucharist, atonement, redemption, the church, mission, sanctification, and so forth. This practice is akin to finding types of Christ or the gospel. Any of these links allow one to speak more fully of the gospel.

Examples of Using One's Text to Teach the Fullness of the Gospel

The call of Isaiah can serve as one example. (1) Read the text for trouble and grace: Isaiah is a sinner. In his call the coal on his mouth is an instrument of his guilt removed, and he hears the angel say, "Now that this has touched your lips, your guilt has departed and your sin is blotted out" (Isaiah 6:7). (2) Discern if the grace is adequate as a statement of the gospel: in this case, the answer may be no. The coal is specific to Isaiah's vision and means little to us; it has no bearing on our lives apart from the fact that the angel carrying it to Isaiah is an agent of the one God who still acts in our lives in similar ways. (3) Bring the cross and resurrection to the text: Isaiah's cleansing is reminiscent of what Christ accomplished for us on the cross. From the cross and resurrection we hear spoken to us the same words that were spoken to Isaiah by the angel, "Your guilt has departed and your sin is blotted out." (4) Seek echoes of the text in Christian life and worship: the coal is an echo of Christ's body given in Communion. In this manner, while the gospel may indeed be found within a text, it is also found with a text.

A second example may be seen in Ellen F. Davis with the burning bush for Moses in Exodus 3:7-8. (1) Read the text for God's trouble and grace: Davis finds in this event the self-revelation of God delivered to an oppressed nation. (2) Discern if the grace is adequate as a statement of the gospel: God's coming to save is the gospel. (3) Bring the cross and resurrection to the text: Davis finds in God's words to Moses a direct parallel to the annunciation to Mary and the self-revelation of God in Christ. (4) Seek echoes of the text in Christian life and worship: Davis describes her own process:

> I have seen, I have heard, I have come down to deliver them from the power of Egypt and to bring them up to abundant life in a land of promise—is this not the gospel in a nutshell? In other words these two self-revelations of God are really one, separated only in time. Holding them together, we see that this is how God always "comes down" into our lives, moved beyond all reason by love and pain.[30]

We might tend to think that texts in the Gospels automatically testify to Christ, yet the same process is needed for them. A third example may be found in Jesus' parable of the Lost Coin in Luke 15:8-10, though I have developed further examples elsewhere.[31] (1) Read the text for God's trouble and grace: a coin is lost and with diligence it is found. (2) Discern if the grace is adequate as a statement of the gospel: the heavens rejoice at a single sinner being saved. (3) Bring the cross and resurrection to the text: Christ goes to the cross to find/save all. (4) Seek echoes of the text in Christian life and worship: all of us have been the lost coin that Christ came to save. The latter is not making an allegory of the text, saying the text really means this, for steps one and two already guaranteed the text. Rather, it allows the text also to stand as a symbol or metaphor for the gospel and falls under the rubric of applying the text.

Gospel Phrases

Are there particular phrases that signal the gospel? C. H. Dodd attempted to identify exactly this. His *The Apostolic Preaching and Its Developments* (1936) was controversial largely because of the overly clear distinction he made between teaching (*didache*) and preaching (*kerygma*) in the New Testament. Using various passages in Paul, sermons in Acts, and the Gospels, he provided a seven-point formula summary of what functioned as kerygma for the early church:

1. The prophecies are fulfilled, and the new age is inaugurated by the coming of Christ.
2. He was born of the seed of David.
3. He died according to the Scriptures, to deliver us out of the present evil age.
4. He was buried.
5. He rose on the third day according to the Scriptures.
6. He is exalted at the right hand of God, as Son of God and Lord of the quick and the dead.
7. He will come again as Judge and Savior of men.[32]

Dodd's point was that the earliest Christian tradition of preaching, prior to the Gospels, had an original kerygma. The biblical writers gave this "an immense range of variety in . . . interpretation,"[33] yet their writing "acted as a preservative of the tradition which conveyed the facts."[34] He encouraged preachers in his own day to be kerygmatic in the same way as the apostles.

Perhaps it is no coincidence that Dodd's summary of the kerygma coincides with the midsection of the Apostles' Creed. His recommendation may seem simplistic. It suggests that (a) the kerygma had both uniformity and consistency at a very early date, (b) this kerygma functioned to unify the church and its writers, and (c) the Bible has an extractable core that can be separated from its various narratives, sayings, and laws. David Buttrick may have been right about Dodd: "Is preaching to be nothing more than the recital of an early Christian credo? After all are there not more than thirty words in Christian scriptures used to describe what we call 'preaching' . . . ?"[35]

Lucy Rose claimed that the kerygma is neither fixed nor self-evident.[36] It may not be as fixed as Dodd implies, but it does have some fixedness. Rose may be trying to avoid reductionism: one does not want to reduce the gospel to a handful of predetermined phrases. Or she may have been pointing to the contextual nature of the gospel. Nonetheless, there is often a recognizable Christ-centered quality to the gospel, and solid teaching about it allows for preaching to become proclamation. Teaching as we frame it here is about the gospel. Proclamation, as we will see, is the offering of the gospel to the people. Ultimately it is intimate language spoken by God to God's children. Proclamation has a range of expressions, for God can say, "I love you," in a seemingly infinite number of ways.

Becoming Better Proclaimers

Our purpose in this project is to recover teaching and proclamation as dual preaching arts that are strengthened by being in the presence of the other. Why does teaching need to be recovered, given the remarkable strengths we have seen in teaching in the New Homiletic? Teaching would seem to be generally healthy, but ailments are not always obvious. If one surveys contemporary published sermons, one typically finds an impressive array of subjects that are regularly the subject of teaching emphasis: biblical interpretation; theological reflection; historical, cultural, and social analysis; ethical inquiry and discernment; as well as matters of social outreach and pastoral care. With such rich fare spread before congregations, suggesting that something is missing may seem a little like someone at a smorgasbord complaining about having to make one's own sandwich.

The New Homiletic, as it is understood here, refers to those aspects of the homiletical revolution of the past fifty years that have received general consensus having to do with narrative, tensive language, and so forth, matters that we have already discussed. That New Homiletic consensus does not generally extend to theological matters, for example, the need for the sermon to focus on God and the gospel. Because God and the gospel for the most part were not a deliberate focus, many sermons that the New Homiletic produced seemed to fall somewhere short of good news.[1] Thus when we speak of a need to recover teaching so that it may assist proclamation, we speak mainly of a need to recover for teaching an explicit theological focus and content.

To put this claim in context, let us consider several possible end products of sermons today. If one surveys published sermons, one can find examples of sermons that settle for various levels of theological engagement. Moving from what might be called low theological engagement to high, we commonly have sermons today that preach primarily the following:

1. *Social or moral analysis without explicit grounding in the Bible.* Such topical sermons gain their authority primarily in the person of the preacher and/or the perceived rightness of the issue or cause. They seek to persuade listeners to accept certain truths.

2. *Historical-critical or literary insights.* These exegetical sermons may do a good job of presenting the fruits of exegetical research; indeed they may teach the historical background or literary details of a biblical text quite well. The focus of teaching in such sermons is what the Bible says, on teaching the Bible content and morality. Theological engagement of the text, faith, or tradition may be missing: God may be mentioned if the text happens to mention God, but God is not a deliberate focus.

3. *Word of God, where the word is understood primarily as wisdom or command.* Though the word is of divine origin, the emphasis continues to rest

on human action: wisdom is to be appropriated, or the command is to be followed. Sermons in this category tend to be expository; they focus on human beings and may do an effective job of naming moral or theological lessons in the text and explaining the connection with today.

4. *Word of God as bifocal, as both trouble (law) and grace.* This approach draws on understandings of the polar nature of language and on the dual nature of God's word. Where law puts the burden upon humanity to act, grace identifies God's empowering actions to help humans meet the demands. Both are true: we are both sinners and saved. In our categories, this is the first one in which God's action is the explicit focus.

5. *A biblical text(s) combined with teaching the gospel.* Not all biblical texts contain the gospel. In fact, most do not. A text can be developed as both trouble and grace, and then grace can be used to point explicitly to the larger gospel story, thereby magnifying the grace in the text.

6. *Proclamation of the gospel.* Sermons that aim for this arguably highest of theological goals may include the previous five categories and move beyond teaching the gospel to bestowing it.

This list not only represents a spectrum of preaching possibilities; it is also one way to conceive of what it means to preach the gospel. In the view presented here, preaching the gospel is assumed to arise out of preaching specific biblical texts. One might say that sermons at any of the above levels might be rooted in the gospel and might even develop consequences of it, yet they might still fall short of offering it. At issue may be whether the good news can be good news if it is separated from God.

Another way of addressing this, as we have already seen, is to claim that sermons based in the Bible may not get to the word of God, and sermons that are the word of God may not get to the gospel. The word in its fullest expression presents the gospel. For this the sermon needs to center on God and God's actions; on people in relationship to God, not on their own; on how God graciously helps, not just admonishes and corrects; on what God accomplishes by way of saving action, not least in Jesus Christ, and not just what any one Bible text tells us about God; and on the true identity of Jesus as seen in the entire Christ event, incarnation to ascension and second coming, and not just in Bible passages that leave his identity in doubt. Even all of this can still be teaching if its thrust is communication of information.

When we speak of teaching, we think not of doctrine and propositional discourse, but of biblical texts in their full range of historical and literary features and how, guided by the Spirit, they may address contemporary experience using any theological tools that assist instruction and spiritual formation. Preaching as teaching lays a foundation without which proclamation would be ineffective or impossible. Yet if preaching stops at teaching, it can also be problematic, for it may not then offer an encounter with God that fosters faith. It is even possible that the inadvertent emphasis in churches today on preaching as teaching has contributed to the decline of preaching as proclamation, to ill effect for preaching and the church. The most powerful sermons may be those that combine teaching and proclamation, thereby nurturing a relationship with God, and do more than communicate about God.

Thus whatever else preaching may be, it needs a substantial, primary teaching component. It needs to be teaching before it can also become proclamation. As in ice hockey, the game is much more than the ability to skate, but without skating there is no game. If for some inconceivable reason one had to choose between skating and other elements of the game, skating would have to be the choice. All of the stick handling, checking, and passing of the puck are just empty gestures if they are not accompanied by the gliding movement of the body and the puck down the ice. Preaching is like that. If choice is needed, teaching can at least function on its own, as we have had plenty of evidence to see in our time, for teaching at least can lead people toward God. If proclamation had to stand on its own, it would fall down. Without a foundation in teaching it sounds like utter foolishness: one can give God's words of "I love you" only if one has already given a sense of who God is.

CHAPTER SEVEN

What Is Proclamation?

Good teaching is to be treasured and nourished, yet the purpose of preaching is not fully conceived if it is only in terms of communicating information or moral instruction, or speaking *about* the Bible, the gospel, theology, or even God. Preaching is also proclamation, *doing* the gospel in the Spirit and in power. Hence we may make a rough distinction between *about* sermons and *doing* sermons. Preaching that ignites with holy fire presumes solid teaching. Proclamation relies upon it, emerges from it, and cannot do without it. Teaching is the kindling that allows the fire to catch hold. This activity of the Spirit is the ultimate purpose of preaching, for as Paul said, "The gospel . . . is the power of God for salvation to everyone who has faith" (Romans 1:16); and Gerhard Ebeling echoed, "The process of preaching is what it claims to be, that is, the process of salvation."[1]

The gospel message when it is proclaimed may sound something like any one of the following statements—probably not said in this kind of list where they may sound foolish and trite—but said arising out of the language and imagery of specific texts. The words of the gospel need to be inspired by the Holy Spirit, shaped for the individual time and place, prepared for by solid teaching in the sermon as one might prepare caringly for dinner guests, such that these precious words are heard to be spoken by God: "I love you. I died for you. I will not let you go. I forgive you. Come to me, all of you that are weary and heavy-laden, and I will give you rest. Take heart! Do not be afraid! Your faith has made you well. I am your Shepherd. Let not your hearts be troubled; neither let them be afraid. Well done, my good and faithful servant. I am with you to the end of the age. This is my body, broken for you. This is my blood, poured out for you." Such intimate, liberating, supportive words are at the heart of the gospel we seek to proclaim. When such words emerge in dialogue with a biblical text, when they arise from the heart of the faith, the gospel is proclaimed. The gospel is thus performed, and it transforms communities in the cruciform image of Christ. Such is the nature of the gospel that from it all else follows: lives of faith, ethical living, social justice, and acts of love and mercy.

When the preacher dares to step beyond teaching, to offer God in substantial ways in the sermon, to speak on God's behalf wonderful words of reconciling love, to facilitate a meeting between God and hearers in light of the cross, to make space for Christ in the Holy Spirit to encounter hearers from beyond the grave, then the sermon catches fire and becomes proclamation. Christ is present anew in his self-giving love on the cross and in his rising from death. Where teaching leaves the load of responsibility on the hearer to do something, proclamation removes it, or rather Christ does, in and through proclamation. Christ says, "All that is required I have accomplished for you. All that you need I give you anew with Spirit-power."

The Heart of the Gospel

Proclamation at its very best is the announcement of the good news accomplished in Jesus Christ together with its consequences. When words at the heart of the gospel are heard in faith, it is as though they are spoken directly from God to the people of God, and this may well be the case. Proclamation enacts the gospel in the preaching moment and enrolls the congregation in God's saving, transforming, and liberating purposes. Proclamation has to do with the *kerygma,* a word that derives from the Greek *kerux* (herald), someone authorized to deliver the proclamations of the king. In this case the herald's proclamation is precise, at least as Karl Barth conceived it in his homiletics lectures of 1932 and 1933: "No matter what may be said in detail, this is the point from which every single line [of preaching] must be drawn. Not the mere word 'Christ,' not a mere description of Christ, but solely what God has done with us in Christ, Immanuel, God with us—this is the central point of all preaching."[2] Only when this is the message for delivery does the preacher speak with the full authority of the one "who sends the herald."[3] The herald and the one who is heralded are not equal partners; the one acts in obedience to the lordship of the other. Preachers are constantly tempted "to proclaim human sins instead of this event, instead of God's goodness."[4]

In 1936, when C. H. Dodd attempted to make a clear distinction between teaching (*didache*) and preaching (*kerygma*), he was criticized for drawing sharper distinctions than the New Testament warrants. He identifies the primitive *kerygma* this way:

> It begins by proclaiming that "this is that which was spoken by the prophets"; the age of fulfillment has dawned, and Christ is its Lord; it then proceeds to recall the historical facts, leading up to the resurrection and exaltation of Christ and the promise of his coming in glory; and it ends with the call to repentance and the offer of forgiveness.[5]

From a practical perspective Dodd's error may have been distilling apostolic preaching to too few words, too sharply drawn. James S. Stewart published his Yale Lyman Beecher Lectures in preaching in 1953, titled *A Faith to Proclaim*, and spoke on five topics of importance that cover what Dodd identified as *kerygma*, proclaiming the incarnation, forgiveness, the cross, the resurrection, and Christ. Stewart defined *kerygma* as "God's life manifested and offered";[6] it is not a means to an end but an end it itself, the doing of the saving act it proclaims.

Rudolf Bultmann invoked an eschatological perspective on proclamation. He argued that Christ comes in the preaching of the cross. In faith he encounters us as the one who is crucified and risen. In and through this existential encounter individuals must decide for themselves whom they will follow. Only through preaching do people come to believe in the cross of Christ as the "eschatological event *par excellence*" and in its saving efficacy.[7]

A Porous Boundary

The boundary between teaching and proclamation is necessarily porous. At a very basic level, the difference between teaching and preaching may be seen in comparing the two versions of the Beatitudes. In Matthew's Sermon on the Mount the words function as teaching, "Blessed are the poor in spirit . . ." (5:3-11), whereas in Luke's Sermon on the Plain they function more as proclamation, not just because of who speaks them, but also because Jesus addresses them directly to his hearers, "Blessed are you who are poor . . ." (6:20-22). Proclamation may judge, correct, empower, liberate—in other words, it enacts and actualizes the gospel. It is a word that shapes human lives in the form of the cross that is preached, and it is God's performance of the power of the cross in the lives of the hearers.

In the same way that treble and bass intermingle in recordings, proclamation can sometimes be heard in teaching, and proclamation inevitably also teaches. Karl Barth said theology is not proclamation, even though it is "language about God." Rather, "theology reflects proclamation."[8] Perhaps that intermingling keeps many homileticians from trying to distinguish between the two. For all of our human effort at effective and responsible theological communication, God alone decides what to speak, when, and to whom. One person might hear the Holy Spirit through what might seem to someone else to be a very dull and uninspired sermon. Still, God has promised that human efforts are a means of salvation for those who have faith.

Three Views on Proclamation

Three theologians in particular, Emil Brunner (1889–1966), Gerhard Ebeling (1912–2001), and Gerhard O. Forde (1927–2005), are helpful in distinguishing proclamation from theology, or preaching from theological teaching. Each writer has a particular viewpoint. Together they help to establish that proclamation is rooted in teaching yet has the character of a one-to-one relationship with God.

1. Emil Brunner: Faith-wooing Address

Emil Brunner was born in Switzerland, was ordained in the Swiss Reformed Church (as was his contemporary Karl Barth), and taught preaching and other subjects primarily at the University of Zurich. He was concerned with how young people are brought into the faith, a concern enlivened by the poor experience of his four sons. He challenged the Swiss model of catechism in his day that provided instruction and mediation of doctrine. He lamented that intellectual misunderstanding and knowledge were stressed over revelation and communion with God. The "actual function of doctrine" he identified is strengthening faith and deepening knowledge in the context of a believing and confessing congregation.[9]

The experience of his sons led him in 1937 to offer lectures that appeared in English in 1943 as *The Divine Human Encounter*, and again in expanded form in 1963 as *Truth as Encounter*.[10] Brunner later commented on these lectures as "my most important contribution to the theological concept of knowledge."[11] His thesis was that Christian notions of truth were dominated by the subject-object antithesis of Greek thought, yet biblical understandings of truth were rooted in truth as revelation, an event of divine encounter. Brunner, like Barth, was a dialectical theologian for whom theological method consisted of assertion and counterassertion of seeming opposites whose unity could be discerned and reconciled only in faith: for them the word can only be received as gift from outside oneself. God alone transcends the limits of human reason, and truth cannot be found apart from that divine relationship; thus even dogmatic propositions cannot identify divine truth.

Brunner made an important distinction between theological teaching and proclamation. Doctrine, he said, is overvalued in the faith of an individual and in the teaching of the church. Doctrine is unavoidably part of preaching and congregations must know doctrine, but not at the expense of faith; churches ought not to "pile doctrine upon doctrine, without troubling about practical results."[12] Proclamation, he said in a rather splendid definition, "is itself something other than doctrine. It is faith-awakening, faith-furthering, faith-wooing address."[13] Though preachers are not prophets, proclamation "always has a prophetic character" while pure doctrine "has a didactic character"[14] that is designed to provide "conceptual clarification of the Holy Scriptures."[15] Proclamation "means an event entirely personal, in the nature of a personal meeting."[16]

In a wonderful phrase, Brunner says that God meets us in the law, but "he does not meet us as himself."[17] Such an encounter is not transforming and only makes one aware of one's sin. The word of God in its truest expression reveals God's unconditional love on the cross and transforms us into the new creation in Christ's image.

2. Gerhard Ebeling: The Word that Brings Double Certainty

Gerhard Ebeling was a Lutheran pastor who became a member of the Confessing Church in Germany and was Brunner's successor at the University of Zurich. It was left to him to make more of Brunner's terms, and he did so primarily in his *Theology and Proclamation* (1966).[18] Ebeling was concerned that proclamation had largely lost its ability to bring forth certainty and joy;[19] as he saw it, "All the difficulties which face proclamation today have in some way to do with the transition to a radically historical way of thought."[20] He felt that historical-critical method was essential to safeguard the understanding of revelation upheld by the Reformers, yet "how can talk about God have any meaning if only the historical is real?"[21]

What keeps theology and proclamation from being separate entities is their common subject matter: "They are different ways of speaking responsibly about God."[22] As he says, "Theology without proclamation is empty, proclamation without theology is blind."[23] In contrast to many people in theology today, he felt that "theology ceases to be theology if it is no longer concerned to bring God to expression."[24] The task of dogmatic theology is not to give an historical presentation of the tradition: "It does not recite words that have already been spoken, but brings God's Word to expression. It is the language school of proclamation."[25]

For Ebeling the purpose of proclamation is to bring certainty to hearers. The failure of his contemporary church to do this was a key issue inseparable from Christology: "Jesus is known as the Word which brings certainty, this means that we come to know him as the Gospel and the basis of faith."[26] "Speaking boldly, with certainty, is the primary form of speech which we use when speaking of Christ, just because we confess Jesus Christ as God's Word; that is, as the Word which brings certainty, which gives us power to take up the language of faith."[27] The state of uncertainty is the state in which people live and is "the essence of sin."[28]

In order for the preacher to proclaim the word, mere interpretation of traditional Christology is insufficient: the traditional kerygma must be interpreted, and then guided by this interpretation, the preacher needs to have "felt the claims of the 'event' from which the christological kerygma derives its necessity."[29] It is not simply a matter of interpreting a particular formulation of the kerygma, for that can be little more than historical representation. In other words, the preacher must address the listeners "in such a way that they begin to see their situation is determined by the ground of the christological kerygma and to see in what way it is determined."[30] In other words, the listener must experience what is said as personal address.

Jesus Christ clarifies our relationship to reality and gives us certainty by illuminating the powers to which we have fallen. The problem of preaching for Ebeling is that people have so fallen subject to the law that they are no longer aware of it. Unless we are certain of the sin to which we are subject, how can we have certainty concerning our salvation? Thus he speaks of the "double certainty" that proclamation offers: "If we did not encounter in Jesus both the law and the Gospel alongside each other, [we could] not encounter him as the Word which brings a double certainty."[31] In proclamation we are convicted both of our need for God and of God's help.

3. Gerhard O. Forde: Akin to Sacrament: Doing the Text to the Hearer

Gerhard O. Forde served as Professor of Systematic Theology at Luther Seminary in St. Paul. His *Theology Is for Proclamation* argues that what is missing from many pulpits today is proclamation. He defines it ideally as "present-tense, first-to-second person unconditional promise authorized by what occurs in Jesus Christ according to the scriptures."[32] It is unconditional declaration of good news *from* God, a word of love set loose in the midst of the congregation to achieve its purpose. The most apt paradigm of it, he says, is absolution: "I declare unto you the gracious forgiveness of all your sins in the name of the Father, the Son, and the Holy Spirit."[33] It is "the saying and doing of the deed itself, for example, 'I baptize *you*.'"[34] It is the "I love you" that leads to the confession, "I love you too!"[35]

Too often what passes itself off as proclamation is systematic theology, secondary abstract past-tense discourse reflection *about* God, "albeit systematics of a second-rate or rather unsystematic sort."[36] What Forde calls theology is in part what we have been calling teaching. The ultimate persuasion is not the assent of reason but the assent of faith. He wants to see recovery of the proper correlation: systematic theology clarifies and gives order to abstract thought but must inevitably *lead to* proclamation. Proclaiming presents a radical discontinuity between law and gospel, between Jesus who puts to death the old ways and Jesus who calls us into new life. Proclamation is "more like a sacrament than other oral communication such as teaching or informing."[37] In administering the sacraments, he says, "We do not merely say something, we do not merely impart information, we do something, we wash in water, we give bread and wine, to those who come. . . . We give it flat out."[38] Forde calls for proclaiming to be "a *doing* of the text to the hearers, a doing of what the text authorizes the preacher to do in the living present."[39] He offers this wonderful example:

> Where the text on the healing of the paralytic ends, for instance, with words to the effect that the people were "afraid and glorified God who had given such authority to men" the text virtually insists on what the next move has to be. The proclaimer must exercise the authority so granted. The proclaimer must so announce the forgiveness to those gathered here and now as to amaze them with the audacity of it all. Perhaps they will even glorify God once again. The proclaimer must, on the authority of Jesus, have the guts to do again in the living present, what was done once upon a time. The proclaimer must dare to believe that the very moment of proclamation is the moment planned and counted on by the electing God himself. The proclaimer is there to do the deed authorized, not merely to explain the deeds of the past.[40]

Proclamation performs the text, brings it to its intended completion as a liberating, loving word of forgiveness and empowerment from God. It is an eschatological occurrence in the now that puts an end to the old and makes a new beginning of the present. For Forde, proclamation is "the necessary and indispensable final move in the argument."[41] The sacraments extend, seal, and deliver the proclamation; they work "by creating the faith which receives them."[42]

Forde's notion of "doing the text to the people" is intriguing, yet it might be more accurate to say that proclamation is Christ "doing the gospel to the people." Not all texts contain the gospel, but arguably they all point to it if one reads with the cross and resurrection in view. In the Spirit, Christ communicates his own identity to the hearers in transforming power.

Two Kinds of Proclamation

For Forde, there seems to be one kind of proclamation, that is, proclamation of the gospel. While proclamation of the gospel is a goal and purpose of preaching, proclamation of God's word of direction and correction, condemnation and destruction is also possible. This is a lower and incomplete form of proclamation that stops short of the gospel, but a form of address direct from God nonetheless. Brunner and Ebeling may allow for this. They agree that proclamation of the gospel is the goal, that it is different from teaching, that teaching precedes it, and that it is the word of personal address that liberates the hearer. Brunner talks of God meeting us in the law but "not as himself"; thus another kind of proclamation seems possible. The same is true of Ebeling's double certainty, meeting Jesus in both the knowledge of one's sin and the assurance of salvation. In any case, here we claim two kinds of proclamation, one that is less complete or fulsome that functions to invoke the law and one that functions to bestow the gospel. We might still claim that God's word is never just law or trouble. The cross and the resurrection are necessarily linked and in tension. Moreover, the word of law is not the origin of Christian preaching; Easter is.

Two kinds of proclamation, proclamation of law or trouble and proclamation of the gospel, need to be recognized. The term *trouble* avoids some of the negative and inappropriate associations of law and Old Testament and gospel as New Testament. The word *trouble* is broader than law: it includes human failure to obey God as well as the tragedy of innocent human suffering;[43] in fact, it includes everything that points to the fallen nature of creation. *Trouble in its simplest definition puts the burden on humanity to act.* Paul laments that "I do not do the good I want, but the evil I do not want is what I do" (Romans 7:19). That is our common lament, for we cannot do what the law requires. Even if we were literally able to do what is required, we would still resent the law and break it in our hearts. The law thus becomes our death sentence by our failure to keep it. By contrast, *gospel in its simplest definition puts the burden on God in Christ, who has already accomplished what is needed.* By his righteousness, he has fulfilled the law, and he gives us his innocence in exchange for our failure. He even takes care of our resentment of the law: "A new heart I will give you, and a new spirit I will put within you; and I will remove from your body the heart of stone and give you a heart of flesh" (Ezekiel 36:26).

Proclamation is a heightened or emotionally charged form of communication that leads to personal address from God in preaching. In proclamation of trouble, God says, "You have sinned," "The world is not as I intended, and you have some responsibility to change it" (for instance, in relationship to poor persons or victims of abuse), or "Your suffering is my own." In proclamation of the gospel, God says, "I forgive you," "In Christ I start anew," or "In Christ I have overcome even your pain." Both kinds of personal address are found in sermons past and present.

Examples of the Difference between Teaching and Proclamation

In a sermon preached as part of his prison ministry, Karl Barth spoke to the difference between teaching and proclamation without using the latter term, yet speaking of the joyous word that characterizes proclamation of the gospel:

Someone once said to me: "I need not go to church. I need not read the Bible. I know already what the Church teaches and what the Bible says: 'Do what is right and fear no one!'" Let me say at this point: If this were the message at stake, I would most certainly not have come here. My time is too precious and so is yours. To say that, neither the prophets nor apostles, neither Bible, Jesus Christ nor God are needed. Anybody is at liberty to say this to himself. By the same token, this saying is void of any new, of any very special and exciting message. It does not help anyone. I have never seen a smile in the face of a person reassuring himself with this kind of talk. As a rule, those who use it are a sad-looking lot, revealing all too easily that this word does not help them, does not comfort them, does not bring them joy.

Let us hear therefore what the Bible says and what we as Christians are called to hear together: *By grace you have been saved!* [Ephesians 2:5] No man can say this to himself. Neither can he say it to someone else. This can only be said by God to each one of us. It takes Jesus Christ to make this saying true. It takes the apostles to communicate it. And our gathering here as Christians is needed to spread it among us. This is why it is truly news, and very special news, the most exciting news of all, the most helpful thing also, indeed the only helpful thing.

"By grace *you* have been saved!" How strange to have this message addressed to us![44]

The personal nature of the address from God truly constitutes proclamation because it does the saving act.

Another example shows the effect of proclamation. Mike Graves cites Frederica Mathewes-Green's description of her conversion to Eastern Orthodoxy and the impact of an icon of Jesus in her new church:

From the first time I saw this Jesus' stern expression I felt awkward, as if facing someone who understood something about me that I didn't, someone who understood why I have a murky bag of disconnected guilt rambling about under the surface all the time. I know that I ping back and forth between this guilt, and oh-yeah? behaviors like overeating or showing off or gossiping or thinking luxuriously about how spiritual I am. . . . When I look into the eyes of this icon, I think he knows, and it makes him very serious. . . . I had looked at this icon, somewhat shrinkingly, for several years before I realized that his right hand is held up *in blessing*. That is his will for me; he wants to bless me.[45]

Graves adds, "That is where preaching begins, with the love and blessing of God." In our terms, the difference that woman experienced is the difference between the proclamation of law/trouble and the proclamation of gospel/grace.

Homileticians on Proclamation

Not much attention was paid to gospel in the New Homiletic; thus proclamation was ignored. Such attention as there has been has come mostly from Lutherans. Perhaps the reason is that Luther paid so much attention to the Word, and for a time in the mid-1900s most major homileticians in North America were Lutheran. Still, it is surprising that at least Barth's and Brunner's emphasis was not continued in Reformed circles since other aspects of their thought had lasting impact. William H. Willimon has written *Proclamation and Theology*, which hints at the best aspects of what we are calling proclamation, in part because he believes that God speaks through preaching, but he essentially treats proclamation and preaching synonymously.[46] Such discussions as there have been for the most part acknowledge only one kind of proclamation, that of the gospel.

H. Grady Davis identified four emphases of proclamation, depending upon the listener.

1. To the person who has never heard of Jesus Christ, it is an announcement that "waits to be heard and believed."
2. To the one who is alienated and separated from God, it is "the call of God to the wanderer to return and believe the gospel."
3. To those who are dead in their sin, it is "an offer of life—not merely the messenger's offer in God's name, but God's offer made directly and personally to the hearer, an offer of life from the Source of life."
4. And to those who are without God and in despair of the world or themselves, it is "the form of a promise, not a promise concerning God, but a promise made by God, a promise of forgiveness and help, of liberation and joy, of hope and of glory."

For Davis, proclamation effects something in the doing of it: it serves "as the channel of a personal transaction between God and the soul of the hearer, a transaction that creates a new life in Christ on the basis furnished by God's redemptive action in Christ."[47]

Richard A. Jensen agrees with Forde: preaching at some point needs to arrive at first- or second-person, present-tense language spoken on Christ's behalf. Jensen states, "This kind of proclamation is worlds removed from preaching that only explains what it was that Christ said and did at some point in the past. Understanding is not the goal. Proclamation is the goal. How that proclamation works itself out in the lives of people is the work of the Holy Spirit."[48] Proclamation makes preaching transformational. Jensen anticipated Forde in calling proclamation the "public office of absolution . . . a sacrament through which the grace of God happens to people."[49] Jensen connects proclamation to language issues; the stories that preachers use should be metaphors of participation, involving us in their world, not metaphors of illustration.[50]

Writers like Ebeling, Davis, Jensen, and Forde provide the Lutheran tradition with not just the memory but also the possibility of proclamation as a distinct act. David Lose lists four features of proclamation: (1) its content is biblical, (2) it is eventful, manifesting both the content and the effect of what it speaks, (3) it has an objective element, speaking to the truth of the gospel that is beyond the speaker and the hearer, and (4) it is relational, drawing listeners into a relationship with God mediated through Jesus Christ.[51]

Numerous people have not spoken of proclamation as we use it here but have identified a problem with preaching in relation to the gospel,[52] including Charles L. Campbell, who calls preachers to return to it. He wants preachers to heed that the "ascriptive logic" of the Gospels is about the character of Jesus, not about narrative per se:

> The gospels are not stories about elemental human experiences, but rather stories that render the identity of a particular person whose life, death, and resurrection accomplish God's purposes for the world.
>
> Thus, what is important for Christian preaching is not "stories" in general or even "homiletical plots," but rather a specific story that renders the identity of a particular person. The ascriptive logic of the gospels provides both constraints and guidance for Christian preaching.[53]

For him a key purpose of preaching is to communicate the identity of Jesus Christ, who he is and what he has done, and narrative is important only insofar as it enables that.

Contrasting Views

For Lucy Rose, the biased nature of language "precludes the preacher's discovering an intention, voice, or experience of God, or a paradigmatic gospel experience"; thus the possibility of proclamation may be foreclosed in her approach.[54] Eugene Lowry distinguishes preaching from proclamation and says we cannot do the latter, for we can only evoke God's word:

Preaching I can do. I choose it; I prepare for it. Prayerfully I engage it, and I perform it. I do it. I will do it Sunday next. Proclaiming the Word is what I *hope* will happen next Sunday. . . . Nobody has the grip of control for it. You cannot capture it; you cannot possess it; you cannot package it; you cannot deliver it; and you cannot control the receipt of it. Sorry. Preaching the sermon is a *task*; proclaiming the Word is the hoped-for *goal*.[55]

Ideally for Lowry, preaching evokes proclamation. God is ineffable and cannot be possessed by language; thus one seeks the kind of language that "best says what cannot be spoken and gives what cannot be possessed."[56] He advocates the nonpropositional language of narrative, metaphor, and analogy. Language evokes mystery and awe, yet one wonders if it is helpful to speak of proclamation as being evoked. What are properly evoked are confession of Jesus Christ and other acts of human response. Proclamation might be said to belong to God.

Teaching and Proclamation

Teaching provides the theological, historical, and cultural information that people need about who God is now and in history, but it does not on its own introduce them to God. Information about someone is no substitute for actually meeting the person. Teaching provides the informational basis, understanding, and guidance for such an encounter, but to meet God, people need not just information *about* God—they need communication *from* God. They need to hear God speaking. They need to experience the presence and love of God directing and shaping them as individuals and into communities of faith. Effective proclaimers say words like, "Change your ways. I love *you*. I forgive *you*. I died for *you*. Death has no more power over you." That is proclamation. Without foundation in teaching, it may sound frivolous, naïve, irrelevant, or offensive. Proclamation picks up where teaching leaves off and brings it to its necessary completion.

Proclamation is testimony or confessional in the sense that it involves speaking from one's most deeply held beliefs,[57] while teaching is typically nonconfessional, explaining commonly held understandings. Graduate student Joni Sancken says that in teaching, people are the agenda, that is, their learning is central, but in proclamation, God is the agenda—people meet God.[58] Without using our terms *teaching* and *proclamation*, Todd Townshend distinguishes between them in brilliant fashion:

There is a great difference between the response [to teaching], "Ah, now I know this or that! Thank you preacher," and the response [to proclamation], "Ah, now I am redeemed! Thank you God!" The responder to a proposition about God can only affirm or deny agreement with the speaker. The responder to a redeeming encounter with God is a new creation. Both responses are necessary and may be considered two levels of response to two "poles" found in preaching.[59]

What happens with proclamation is the same thing that happened when Jesus preached his first sermon at Nazareth and he said, "Today this scripture has been fulfilled in your hearing" (Luke 4:21). We may say this because we read any biblical text looking for the gospel, in it or in relation to it. No matter what any text highlights by way of commandment, sin, injustice, or any other kind of trouble, the need is met in the identity and person of Jesus of Nazareth as established on Easter.

The Role of the Spirit in Teaching and Proclamation

We have already noted a difference between our key terms in the role of the Spirit. Many of us have assumed the Spirit's general involvement in the act of preaching without more precise discernment of the Spirit's work. For example, a preacher typically prays for guidance in preparing a sermon and in worship often offers a prayer of illumination prior to preaching, asking God to speak through it. In fact, the Spirit guides teaching in the same way that the Spirit guides life (Paul says, "If we live by the Spirit, let us also be guided by the Spirit" [Galatians 5:25]). Teaching is a gift of the Spirit, yet not all teaching is so blessed, only that which guides people in the ways God would have them follow. Teaching in the sermon is appropriately in service to the higher goal of proclamation of the gospel.

Proclamation testifies to who Christ is from his being the Word with God from the beginning, to his incarnation, ministry, crucifixion, and resurrection, to his coming again in the end times, with Good Friday and Easter as the decisive focal point. Proclamation gives voice to Christ and brings him to expression. A different kind of activity of the Spirit from what is involved in teaching accompanies proclamation. It continues to be guided by the Spirit, yet in proclamation the Spirit takes over. The Spirit gives testimony to who Christ is and utters his words. Jesus said, "When the Advocate comes, whom I will send to you from the Father, the Spirit of truth who comes from the Father, he will testify on my behalf" (John 15:26). The preacher mouths the words, but they are breathed out by and infused with the Spirit, who carries them with power into the world.

In claiming that the Spirit takes over in proclamation, one recognizes that no one can give testimony to Christ on one's own: "No one can say 'Jesus is Lord,' except by the Holy Spirit" (1 Corinthians 12:3).

This is not to deny that some so-called preachers, acting by other principalities and powers, may turn the gift of such testimony into something that is manipulative, self-serving, oppressive, or harmful to God's children, even in the sermon. The test of the Spirit is by its fruit: "The fruit of the Spirit is love, joy, peace, patience, kindness, generosity, faithfulness, gentleness, and self-control" (Galatians 5:22-23). These qualities are authentic marks of proclamation in affirmation of what Jesus said: "That my joy may be in you, and that your joy may be complete" (John 15:11). Such preaching, afire in the Spirit, forges disciples who choose servanthood as their model for ministry and find their strength in the weakness and humility of the cross.

The Spirit guides preachers when talking *about* the gospel and takes over when the preacher offers Christ in *doing* the gospel. This can be a big relief for the preacher. God is in charge, and everything does not rest on the preacher's shoulders to perform. By the same token, from the perspective of the people, the burden of walking in God's path is removed and becomes a joy in Christ. He takes the burden on himself in the cross. The Spirit proclaims and, in so doing, performs gospel miracles in the lives of the hearers.

Proclamation of Trouble and Proclamation of Gospel

In this chapter we said that proclamation is a function of preaching that leads to God's personal address being received. We have identified two kinds of proclamation, trouble and gospel. Proclamation of trouble pronounces God's word of trouble or law and is necessarily incomplete as an expression of who God is. It is not instruction *about* the law, for that is teaching; it is allowing the consequences of departure from the law to be experienced, God's words of rebuke or lament to be heard and felt. It is hearing and experiencing God's words of destruction upon Israel for making the golden calf without experiencing God's repentance at Moses' plea (Exodus 32:14). It is encountering God in crucifixion without experiencing resurrection. Such proclamation is the *doing* of "God against us" to the congregation, or better still, it is enacting God as enemy of sin and injustice.

Proclamation of the good news is not mere recital of past news of God in Jesus Christ; it is administering the one who is the gospel to the congregation. God's true self meets us. In this, every person may know that the word spoken is "for me," empowering each to do what is right. In that no one is excluded, a vulnerable community is formed of liberation and forgiveness, justice and mercy, and the new creation is experienced as already begun in Christ. Proclamation of the law is our death; we cannot do what is required. Yet proclamation of the gospel puts an end to death and is the beginning of new life. In return one may feel compelled in faith simply to say in praise and confession, "My Lord and my God."

CHAPTER EIGHT

Proclamation and Sermon Subforms
THREE PRECEDENTS

W ith what language may we speak of the shape, content, style, function, and goal of proclamation in the sermon? Preachers discuss sermons in our own time by their various overall forms, and discussion of the sermon's parts is typically limited to introduction, body and conclusion, points and subpoints. While important, these do not merit much attention, and they do not take a preacher very far toward composing a sermon. Identification and discussion of genres within the sermon are needed.

Proclamation is not a formless something that happens in a sermon, nor is it putting a sentence or two into the sermon near the end that speak to the gospel. Proclamation is more than saying in a sermon on Zaccheus that Jesus is coming to dine at your home. That may begin to teach the gospel; it mentions, indicates, and promises but does not proclaim because it does not offer Jesus. Proclamation, as we use it, is more than a brief declaration here or there; it is a section or more of a sermon devoted to providing a setting and context for the Spirit to utter words aflame with love. These sermon sections we call subforms or genres. They are designed so that content, form, and style work together to a desired effect, the hearing of the gospel. Proclamation is as much a matter of form and style as it is content. It is more robust than single lines or sentences; it is more passionate than a simple declaration; it is more fulsome than teaching and has many genres that communicate God's redemptive purposes.

Three precedents enable us to speak of these matters more substantially. They are in effect three case studies on sermon form: Phillips Brooks on sermon subforms; Bible genres and the New Homiletic; and Augustine on styles of speech.

Phillips Brooks and the Idea of Sermon Subforms

Phillips Brooks (1835–93) of Trinity Episcopal Church in Boston gave the Lyman Beecher Lectureship in Preaching at Yale Divinity School in January and February of 1877. In his lectures he advocated a new approach to sermon form that was never picked up in homiletics yet that helps provide a foundation for thinking of proclamation within the sermon. When Brooks received his invitation to give the lectures "some months" before they were due,[1] he must have retrieved from his library shelf a copy of the inaugural lectures by Henry Ward Beecher (his first of three lecture series in three consecutive years, 1871–74), which was published in 1872. Brooks looked in them for some clue to a topic that he himself might address. A couple of pages into Beecher's first lecture, Brooks must have been arrested by this passage:

> The preacher is one who is aiming directly at the enobling of his hearer. He seeks to do this . . . by giving to such truth the glow and colour and intensity which are derived from his own soul. If one may so say, he digests the truth and makes it personal, and then brings his own being to bear on that of his hearers. . . . The truth is that which is represented in the historical Jesus Christ, but it is that truth "*in you*," or as it exists in each man's distinctive personality, which must make it a living force.[2]

The idea struck Brooks with such force that without mentioning Beecher, he developed it and made it the theme of his entire lectures. In fact, if Brooks is remembered for one thing, it is his stated theme: preaching is "the communication of truth by man to men. It has in it two essential elements, truth and personality. . . . Preaching is the bringing of truth through personality."[3] Moreover, shaping personality is a goal of preaching: "The salvation of men's souls from sin, the renewing of their characters, is the great end of all," and since "that is done by Christ,"[4] the goal is to lead people to him. One aspect of Brooks's thought, the effect of personality on sermon form, has all but been overlooked.

Brooks is suspicious of the sermon forms of his day that he names as *expository, topical, practical,* and *hortatory,* for they do not fit his theology or his personality. Preaching that is "wholly exposition" he compares to "heat lightning that quivers over many topics but strikes nowhere." Topical preaching is unsatisfactory "because it does not fasten itself to the authority of Scripture," and it sends people away "with a feeling that they have heard him [the preacher] more than they have heard God." Like Beecher, he cautions that the sermon that "only argues is almost sure to argue in vain." Likewise, the sermon that "only exhorts is like a man who blows the wood and coal to which he has not first put a light."[5]

For Brooks, as for the Romantics, form and unity ought to be conceived organically, not mechanically. He advised against making the sermon idea "too specific, wishing to conform it to some preëstablished [*sic*] type of what a sermon ought to be";[6] instead, "let the end for which you preach play freely in and modify the form of your preaching."[7] He found the model for organic form in the Bible itself and believed that an enormous change had taken place in his own day concerning how Scripture is to be employed in the sermon: "The unity of the Bible, the relation of its parts, its organic life, the essentialness of every part and yet the distinct difference in worth and dignity of the several parts, these are now familiar ideas as they were not a few years ago."[8] Prior to higher criticism, people mistakenly treated all verses, no matter what their context, as though they were equally the word of God, "all true, all edifying, all vital with the gospel."[9] Brooks presented a powerful image in favor of treating Bible verses in their context: "The single verse is no longer like a jewel set in a wall which one may pluck out and carry off as an independent thing. It is a window by which we may look through the wall and see the richness it incloses. . . . Go up and look through them and then tell the people what you see. Keep them in their places in the wall of truth."[10]

Brooks's solution to rigid sermon forms is not to try one form one week and another the next. His suggestion is to be slave to no form and allow the message to shape the form. Let the function and content determine shape:

> But what I plead for is, that in all your desire to create good sermons you should think no sermon good that does not do its work. Let the end for which you preach play freely in and modify the form of your preaching. . . . He who freely uses the types which he finds, and yet compels them to bend to the purposes for which he uses them, he is their true master, and not their slave.[11]

He understands that these forms originated in practice because they were useful and only later were a name and value attached to them.[12] Some sermon forms are suspect on their own, for "every sermon must have a solid rest on Scripture";[13] a biblically based sermon ought not to be just one type among many. Sermon style ought to be appropriate to the person and vary from person to person.[14] His solution is revolutionary: all forms are needed in any single sermon:

> I am inclined to think that the idea of a sermon is so properly a unit, that a sermon involves of necessity such elements in combination, the absence of any one of which weakens the sermon-nature, that the ordinary classifications of sermons are of little consequence. We hear of expository preaching and topical sermons, of practical sermons, or hortatory discourses, each separate species seeming to stand by itself. It seems as if the preacher were expected to determine each week what kind of sermon the next Sunday was to enjoy and set himself deliberately to produce it. . . . No sermon seems complete that does not include all these elements, and . . . the attempt to make a sermon of one sort alone mangles the idea and produces a one-sided thing. One element will preponderate in every sermon according to the nature of the subject that is treated, and the structure of the sermon will vary.[15]

Learning from Brooks

In our time preachers have a similar, though expanded, array of possible sermon forms from which to choose that include exegetical, expository, point form, topical, doctrinal, narrative (with its own various forms), inductive, conversational, testimonial, and hybrid. Brooks's argument is not that such forms and functions need to be sermons; they better represent subforms or genres within the sermon:

> And so that preaching which most harmoniously blends in the single sermon all these varieties of which men make their classifications, the preaching which is strong in its appeal to authority, wide in its grasp of truth, convincing in its appeal to reason, and earnest in its address to the conscience and the heart, all of these at once, that preaching comes nearest to the type of apostolical epistles, is the most complete and so the most powerful approach of truth to the whole man.[16]

In looking to the Epistles, he finds biblical precedent for each of his various sermon forms.

Brooks proposed three new forms that acknowledge the sermon is about God. He said new forms are needed that relate to how God is cast in the sermon, in three categories, whether it is to the beauty and balance of God's creation, the righteousness of God's ways, or the usefulness of God's laws for peace and well-being.[17] If we hear Brooks correctly, he is proposing three subforms that include teaching and relate to doxology and nurturing exhortation, the latter two being among the subforms of proclamation that we will propose.

The radical and innovative dimension of Brooks is fourfold. First, sermons are unique to each person, subject, and moment. Second, they are organic and have a life and unity of their own. Third, sermons should be holistic, addressing more than just the intellect. Fourth, common categories of sermon form are best conceived as dynamic sermon subforms. One then thinks of preaching not as a chunk of thought that one chisels to a predetermined pattern but as an undetermined pattern, a living form, employing all the best forms of preaching as needed by the content. One could think of preaching as the performance of subforms each in its own way and time within each sermon. For Brooks, one might variously teach the Bible, praise God in relation to creation, speak on a topic such as righteous living, address pastoral concerns, encourage believers, and argue a case. To think of form in this way is to think of diverse theological, biblical, and pastoral functions within the sermon, each taking its own shape.

Brooks adapted poetic principles from Coleridge and Wordsworth to the practice of preaching. He was ahead of his time, for his words were soon forgotten and such organic notions of form would not be voiced again in homiletics until H. Grady Davis in the 1950s.[18] The homiletical revolution of the last fifty years adopted many of the principles behind Brooks's notions, but it did not return to his idea of external form determined by interior subforms.[19]

Bible Genres and the New Homiletic

Another precedent for speaking of sermon subforms is the subject of genres of the Bible, to which the New Homiletic has been attentive. Homiletics does not generally speak of genres within the sermon,[20] but it does speak of Bible genres. Apart from kinds of sermons (point form, narrative, inductive, deductive, and so forth), significant discussion of genre has been limited to biblical texts. The New Homiletic has helped to establish that biblical texts are holistic; their thoughts, images, and words cannot be separated from their meaning as though meaning is only informational content. Meaning can be rational, cognitive, discursive, intuitive, kinesthetic, and emotive. The literary form, expression, and rhetorical purpose of a biblical text are part of its meaning, and sermons need to be sensitive to this.

Discussion of genres in the Bible has not transferred into genres within the sermon, perhaps with good reason: the discussion was focused on how the form of a text affected the form of the sermon as a whole. The approach was sometimes lampooned to imply that a sermon on an epistle be a letter, a sermon on a biblical hymn be sung, a sermon on a prayer be prayed, and a sermon on Wisdom literature be a series of sayings. A preacher once proposed replicating the effect of his text, Jesus' first sermon in Nazareth (Luke 4:16-30), by preaching to make the congregation angry at him. Literal replication of a text's form may be called a kind of "formal fundamentalism."[21] The original homiletical proposal was more subtle. The form of biblical texts affects their meaning and might help form the sermon.

The close connection between form and content is a Romantic idea that made its way into preaching circles largely through a landmark volume edited by Don Wardlaw, the title of which indicates its radical proposal for 1983, *Preaching Biblically: Creating Sermons in the Shape of the Text*. Various contributors made suggestions about what this might mean:

- Ron Allen suggested a sermon on the commandment "Thou shalt not kill" or on a wisdom saying might be treated not just in stenic fashion as information, but as "experience concentrated into the particular form of the text—as coal is concentrated into diamonds."[22]

- Don Wardlaw noted that the hymn in Philippians 2:6-11 follows the movement of a parabola from heaven to earth to heaven; the entire sermon might follow that movement.[23]
- Gardner Taylor said that no matter what structure is used, "a sermon must deal with two things: the 'revelant' . . . and the 'relevant.'" A sermon on 1 Corinthians 15:12-20 ("If Christ be not risen . . .") might proceed *via negativa* through a series of the text's implicit denials and then move to a reversal in "now is Christ risen" (15:20, KJV).[24]

The above suggestions about form focus on various aspects of biblical texts often overlooked in earlier eras: feeling aspects of biblical texts (intuitive, emotive, and behavioral elements) as well as thinking aspects (rational, cognitive, and discursive elements). The authors focus on movement and interplay of thought and feeling in texts and how these can be communicated in a sermon.

Tom Long, one of the original contributors, later wrote *Preaching and the Literary Forms of the Bible* and clarified that if one was preaching on a biblical hymn like a psalm, it might be important to find an image or metaphor central to the text that could serve a central role in the sermon; this would be to honor the poetic intent of the text and to avoid reducing it to a series of informational statements. The preacher is to ask of the text: its genre, its rhetorical function, its literary devices that allow it to achieve its effect, and "How may the sermon, in a new setting, say and do what the text says and does in its setting?"[25] Concerning the parables of Jesus, Long suggests that preachers discern whether the parable functions primarily as an allegory using a code, as a simile using a single point of comparison to establish a truth, or as a metaphor using principles of art and identification to draw the listener into an experience. The preacher then might shape a similar experience of the congregation.[26] In 1 Corinthians 12:4-30, Long finds a chiasmic structure that the preacher might imitate: the variety of spiritual gifts, the unity of the body of Christ, and the spiritual gifts reconsidered.[27]

It is one thing to allow a biblical text's form to influence in important ways how that text is understood. It is another thing to suggest that a preacher shape the sermon in the form of some aspect of the text. The one is required by responsible exegesis. The other is a rhetorical choice the preacher might make that is not required by the text. Arguably the purpose of preaching is not to imitate the shape of the text; it is to preach the gospel using the text in whatever ways are valid. If one chooses to allow a text to shape the sermon, presumably one does so to serve proclamation of the gospel.

Mike Graves criticized a writer who claims, "Preaching on miracle passages is no different from preaching on any other narrative material."[28] He compares biblical texts to musical scores[29] and to what Richard Ward identifies as performance, "form coming through."[30] Graves suggests that preachers be "form-sensitive," striving to echo primarily the text's mood and optionally the text's movement.[31] The text's movement is optional because otherwise a prophetic confrontation in the Bible would be turned into a sermon that is harsh and condemning. As Graves's professor once cautioned, "If the Gospel is the greatest love story ever told, why do so many preach it with a clenched fist?"[32] The shape of a biblical text expressed through sermon form ought not to preclude the gospel being heard. Still, the form of a text is part of its function and meaning.

Charles Rice said in the early 1980s, "What we look for in homiletics today are forms for the gospel that derive from what the gospel is, how it is communicated, and what God in Christ intends for our specific human communities."[33] Homileticians now appreciate that "Scripture offers us a variety of approaches to structure."[34]

Learning from the New Homiletic

Extending form from a biblical text to the sermon is a matter of rhetorical choice on the part of the preacher; the biblical text does not demand it. Preachers might think in a more limited way of form-sensitivity to conceive of sermon subforms, forms within the sermon that echo the biblical text. Mike Graves counts roughly thirty literary forms in the New Testament alone, depending upon how one classifies them.[35] Sermon subforms in theory could be as numerous as Bible forms: epistle, extended metaphor, psalm, proverb, parable, miracle story, aphorism, or whatever. A preacher might choose to allow the form and function of the Bible text to appear in the sermon, perhaps as a direct commentary on the text but an outgrowth of it. A sermon on a parable might have its own contemporary parable within it, a sermon on an epistle might contain a letter, a sermon on a psalm might contain a hymn, or a sermon on Jesus' sayings might also present, for example, the contemporary sayings of a parent to a teenager, or a teenager to a parent.

Such value as there may be in representing the actual form, function, and movement of a text in a sermon is easier to conceive in a portion of the sermon, not the whole. When Fred B. Craddock preaches on the list of names in Romans 16:3-16 in a sermon titled "When the Roll Is Called Down Here,"[36] he does not preach one long list; in fact, he basically talks about a series of lists beyond Paul's, a jury panel, his student church, a Vietnam memorial, and so on. In a different sermon, just one part might be devoted to a list. In other words, if one thinks of the sermon in parts or as modules, then the work of many homileticians on the literary forms of the Bible is enhanced.

The notion of sermon subforms based on Bible genres brings us closer to identifying possible forms of proclamation in the sermon. The Bible can provide important clues for identifying what subforms exist in sermons.

Augustine on Functions, Styles, and Goals of Preaching

Phillips Brooks identified the possibility of sermon subforms or genres within sermons. The New Homiletic has helped us conceive of how potential preaching subforms might find models in the Bible and connect to texts. We now need Augustine's help to find a precedent for distinguishing between proclamation subforms and teaching.

On what historical basis might preachers distinguish between teaching and genres of proclamation? Proclamation is impassioned utterance. It is a heightened form of teaching or everything beyond teaching that carries the gospel message home. Augustine, drawing on Cicero, said that the purpose of preaching is to teach, to delight, and to persuade or move.[37] Of the three, *to teach* is "a necessity" and is a prerequisite in order to move people to change, for by teaching we clarify that which is unclear.[38] He said that the primary emphasis in teaching is what we say as opposed to how we say it;[39] thus teaching is concerned not with "eloquence" but with clarity.[40] The appropriate style is "subdued," simple, or plain.[41] *To delight*, one uses the "moderate" or "temperate" style,[42] and this is primarily in the service of condemning or praising something. *To persuade* someone to change, one needs the grand style.[43] All three are necessary, and to some degree they are intermixed.[44] Speakers must modulate from one to the other, depending on whether the intention is to render a verdict (teach), blame or defend (delight), or call to action in part through communication of the speaker's commitment (persuade). Speakers nonetheless tend to excel in one style.

Plain Style

The plain style is just that, plain and simple. It teaches by laying out the facts as clearly as possible without verbal flare or appeal to the emotions. It primarily relies on logic and argument. It makes minimal use of metaphor and other figures of speech. Augustine calls it "subdued" and compares it to the manner of a lawyer,[45] the same kind of speech that is still dominant in courts today. He cites Paul in Galatians 3:15-22 to demonstrate teaching and the plain style:[46]

Brothers and sisters, I give an example from daily life: once a person's will has been ratified, no one adds to it or annuls it. Now the promises were made to Abraham and to his offspring; it does not say, "And to offsprings," as of many; but it says, "And to your offspring," that is, to one person, who is Christ. My point is this: the law, which came four hundred thirty years later, does not annul a covenant previously ratified by God, so as to nullify the promise. For if the inheritance comes from the law, it no longer comes from the promise; but God granted it to Abraham through the promise.

Why then the law? It was added because of transgressions, until the offspring would come to whom the promise had been made; and it was ordained through angels by a mediator. Now a mediator involves more than one party; but God is one. Is the law then opposed to the promises of God? Certainly not! For if a law had been given that could make alive, then righteousness would indeed come through the law. But the scripture has imprisoned all things under the power of sin, so that what was promised through faith in Jesus Christ might be given to those who believe.

The style here is clear and precise without emotional appeal, and Paul explains the facts at hand. Emphasis lies on the logic of the argument and the worthiness of the case being made. Augustine understood the plain sense to speak best to ordinary people; indeed the early and medieval church in general favored the moral sense of Scripture, the meaning of a text that gave instruction on how to live. Plain teaching improved lives. John Wesley spoke to his own plain style in a preface to his sermons when he said,

> I design plain truth for plain people. Therefore, of set purpose, I abstain from all nice and philosophical speculations; from all perplexed and intricate reasonings; and, as far as possible, from even the show of learning, unless in sometimes citing the original Scripture. I labor to avoid all words which are not easy to be understood, all which are not used in common life; and, in particular, those kinds of technical terms that so frequently occur in Bodies of Divinity.[47]

Moderate Style

Only when understanding is already present can the moderate style be used.[48] Augustine says that the moderate style is to please or delight, and to affect "willingness" to do something.[49] In our time it may be helpful to think of narrative as one example of moderate style. For Augustine, the moderate style has something to do with how listeners feel about a subject, with an address to the emotions yet that stops short of encouraging action (i.e., the grand style). Moderate style is used when a speaker condemns or praises things that are "to be desired or firmly adhered to."[50] It is descriptive. Of the three in Augustine's time it is most poetic, using metaphors, images, figures of speech, and various rhetorical schemes and tropes. It does not rely strictly on logical argument to accomplish its purposes. In our time hip-hop might be an example of the moderate style. An example Augustine uses is 1 Timothy 5:1-2: "Do not speak harshly to an older man, but speak to him as to a father, to younger men as brothers, to older women as mothers, to younger women as sisters—with absolute purity."[51] Augustine also cites Romans:

> We have gifts that differ according to the grace given to us: prophecy, in proportion to faith; ministry, in ministering; the teacher, in teaching; the exhorter, in exhortation; the giver, in generosity; the leader, in diligence; the compassionate, in cheerfulness. Let love be genuine; hate what is evil, hold fast to what is good; love one another with mutual affection; outdo one another in showing honor. Do not lag in zeal, be ardent in spirit, serve the Lord. Rejoice in hope, be patient in suffering, persevere in prayer. Contribute to the needs of the saints; extend hospitality to strangers. Bless those who persecute you; bless and do not curse them. Rejoice with those who rejoice, weep with those who weep. Live in harmony with one another; do not be haughty, but associate with the lowly; do not claim to be wiser than you are. (Romans 12:6-16)

The moderate style takes greatest care with rhetorical devices, not least the use of parallel phrases and sentences, balanced sentence structure, repetition of key words or phrases, and short phrases for emotional and rhythmic effect. Augustine said the moderate style delights the senses because of its beauty. He provides a sample from a sermon by Ambrose[52] that he explains is an example of the moderate style because Ambrose is not urging anyone toward action but is simply explaining how the virtuous should act.[53]

Grand Style

For Augustine the grand style is used "when something is to be done and [the speaker] is speaking to those who ought to do it" and may not be ready; hence its purpose is to persuade.[54] The grand style makes the most emotional appeal and is demonstrated for Augustine in 2 Corinthians 6:2-11:

> For he says,
>   "At an acceptable time I have listened to you,
>   and on a day of salvation I have helped you."
> See, now is the acceptable time; see, now is the day of salvation! We are putting no obstacle in anyone's way, so that no fault may be found with our

ministry, but as servants of God we have commended ourselves in every way: through great endurance, in afflictions, hardships, calamities, beatings, imprisonments, riots, labors, sleepless nights, hunger; by purity, knowledge, patience, kindness, holiness of spirit, genuine love, truthful speech, and the power of God; with the weapons of righteousness for the right hand and for the left; in honor and dishonor, in ill repute and good repute. We are treated as impostors, and yet are true; as unknown, and yet are well known; as dying, and see—we are alive; as punished, and yet not killed; as sorrowful, yet always rejoicing; as poor, yet making many rich; as having nothing, and yet possessing everything. We have spoken frankly to you Corinthians; our heart is wide open to you.

The import here is "change your ways." The grand style suggests a faster pace of speaking and more passionate expression and involves readers in the energy and musicality of the words. Rhetorical tropes and schema are used, as in the moderate style, yet with less attention to balance and beauty and more to building to emotional impact and moving toward a climax. The grand style "is carried along by its own impetus, and if the beauties of eloquence occur they are caught up by the force of things discussed and not deliberately assumed for decoration. It is enough for the matter being discussed that the appropriateness of the words be determined by the ardor of the heart rather than by careful choice."[55] Another of his examples is Romans 8:28-39:

We know that all things work together for good for those who love God, who are called according to his purpose. For those whom he foreknew he also predestined to be conformed to the image of his Son, in order that he might be the firstborn within a large family. And those whom he predestined he also called; and those whom he called he also justified; and those whom he justified he also glorified. What then are we to say about these things? If God is for us, who is against us? He who did not withhold his own Son, but gave him up for all of us, will he not with him also give us everything else? Who will bring any charge against God's elect? It is God who justifies. Who is to condemn? It is Christ Jesus, who died, yes, who was raised, who is at the right hand of God, who indeed intercedes for us. Who will separate us from the love of Christ? Will hardship, or distress, or persecution, or famine, or nakedness, or peril, or sword? As it is written,
   "For your sake we are being killed all day long;
      we are accounted as sheep to be slaughtered."
No, in all these things we are more than conquerors through him who loved us. For I am convinced that neither death, nor life, nor angels, nor rulers, nor things present, nor things to come, nor powers, nor height, nor depth, nor anything else in all creation, will be able to separate us from the love of God in Christ Jesus our Lord.

The grand style is the most emotional and emotive, yet from a rhetorical perspective, we can see that the moderate style may be more intricate, requiring greater care in composition.

Comparison of the Three

Augustine connects the plain style with "understanding" and being heard to speak with intelligence.[56] At least four factors seem to operate to separate the moderate from the grand: (1) the appeal of the moderate style is more poetic or beautiful while the grand is more emotional; (2) the moderate he associates with things arranged in progression, the use of opposites or "contrary words set against contraries," and the use of eloquence and care in phrasing, sentence structure, and complete thought units;[57] (3) the moderate encourages "willingness" or what we might call attitude or disposition, and it encourages the listener to identify with what is said while the grand persuades in the direction of action or "obedience";[58] and (4) the purpose of the moderate is to praise (for example, God or good actions of people) or blame, and the purpose of the grand is to motivate to action. Augustine said that the plain, moderate, and grand styles should be alternated in a sermon, that "when one style is maintained too long, it loses the listener."[59]

Augustine's Rhetorical Styles and Purposes

Style	Function	Goal
Plain	Teach	Render a verdict (establish the facts)
Moderate	Delight	Praise or blame (affect the will toward something)
Grand	Persuade	Action for or against something (motivate)[60]

Augustine and Homiletics Today

Of Augustine's three functions and styles of speech, the plain style is teaching and seems easiest for us to grasp and recognize in sermons; it is giving the facts, the straight goods. Distinguishing between the moderate and the grand styles is more difficult because so much separates us from his time, culture, and language. Most of our speech today is in the plain style, and this is one reason that recent homiletics has largely ignored Augustine's distinctions. Our preaching is flat, and we have largely forgotten the ways our ancestors spoke. Evaluations of style in the ancient world hinge on matters of harmony of words, rhythm, metrical qualities of spoken Latin that are lost to us, intimate knowledge of figures of speech, schemes, and tropes, matters of taste having to do with everything from his culture's notions of the ornate to the heroic. Further, no sharp line marks the division between styles even in Augustine's age, for they blend into one another.

If we adopt his comments on style, we need to do so in ways that make sense to our times and cultures. Most preaching is plain style. The most satisfying parts of narrative sermons in the New Homiletic are in the moderate style; they are designed to please, delight, and affect how listeners think and feel. They do so with poetic turns of phrase, powerful use of a dominant image or extended metaphor, the telling of a story in a particular way and connection, the highlighting of an unnoticed aspect of a biblical text, and the like. The moderate to grand styles we are most likely to associate with passionate and inspired utterance designed to get participation and action, for instance, as seen most frequently in some African American sermons that move to celebration at the end. Robert Stephen Reid says that "the grand or majestic style is brought to bear in those moments of black preaching when the speaker is unashamed of the intention to persuade listeners to act."[61]

Contemporary homiletics has not been sure what to make of Augustine's comments on function, style, and purposes of preaching. There is resistance in some circles to persuasion and argument. People want to identify with what is said and find their own reasons to follow. Contrasting positions on the merits of persuasion were taken by Lucy Hogan (for) and Richard Lischer (against).[62] David Lose is sympathetic to feminist critique of persuasion as "the conscious effort to change others" and opts instead for an "invitational rhetoric" that does not argue from the position of strength but "confesses" one's own stance from the position of the weakness of the cross.[63] He thus avoids "the 'strong' word of persuasion" in favor of "the 'weaker' words like 'confessing' and 'witnessing.' "[64] Preaching nonetheless should be persuasive, having trustworthy elements while having confession as its goal.[65] Mary E. Lyons has commented, "Some presumptions that underlie Augustine's homiletic theories on style clearly fall short of actual experience,"[66] most pointedly critiquing his understanding that the plain style appeals best to uneducated people.[67]

Learning from Augustine

The real gift of Augustine for this current project is that he provides a basis to distinguish between teaching and proclamation subforms in terms of function, style, and purpose. In adopting his criteria, the primary purpose of teaching is to communicate information clearly. It must be present before the other styles are used. The primary purpose of proclamation, by contrast, is both to delight and to persuade, a combination of moderate and grand styles, yet it is not to delight and to persuade about anything in general. Proclamation as we use it is concerned with the gospel. Our own language and culture probably cannot sustain Augustine's three categories. Apart from hip-hop we do not have the heavily ornate ways of speaking (or the appreciation of rhetorical devices) that often mark his moderate style; narrative may be considered moderate in terms of affecting how one feels about something. However, we can sustain at least two categories. Our notions of teaching range from plain to moderate, and our notions of proclamation (such as we propose them) range from moderate to grand. By condensing Augustine's three categories to two, the effective result is that teaching and proclamation become technical terms that allow us to read sermons critically. If we revise the earlier chart, we might group the plain to moderate styles to speak of teaching and the moderate to grand styles to speak of proclamation:

Styles and Purposes Adapted to Today

Style	Action	Function	Goal
Plain to moderate	Teaching	Informs/ affects the will	Establishes knowledge
Moderate to grand	Proclamation	Delights/ persuades	Praises or blames/ motivates

In this chapter we have explored precedents that enable us to speak of subforms of proclamation. We have heard Phillips Brooks, who implied that overall sermon forms might be better conceived as subforms. The New Homiletic allowed us (1) to review contemporary discussions of genre for the pulpit and (2) to suggest that when literary forms of the Bible help to shape just portions of a sermon, they provide a way to think of sermon subforms. Finally, Augustine provides a critical basis for differentiating teaching and proclamation that is rooted in style, function, and goals of speech. He gives us tools with which to speak of subforms beyond merely form and content. Now let us get to what all of this preparation has been for, naming and exploring the precise genres of proclamation that stand as subforms of the sermon. To this we now turn.

Trouble Genres
of Proclamation

*P*roclamation, as we define it here, is words on fire, everything beyond teaching that carries the gospel message home. It is a heightened or emotionally charged form of communication that leads to personal address from God in preaching. It is impassioned announcement of God's word in God's name such that God is heard speaking directly to the individual and the community, as much as this is humanly possible. Proclamation is designed either to delight listeners as a means of bringing their will in line with God's, or to persuade, to enlist them to action in Christ's mission. Because proclamation is in the moderate to grand style, it has a kind of eloquence. It may make sophisticated and powerful use of metaphor, image, story, figures of speech, and the like, and of short phrases, heightened pace, parallel sentence structure, repetition of key words or phrases, and other rhetorical devices that help communicate emotional intensity and urgency. Since God speaks both to condemn and to create, proclamation can function theologically either as a word of trouble, an incomplete form of proclamation, or as a word of grace, yet both are in service to the gospel.

What then are genres of proclamation? It would be convenient to say that they are the genres of the Bible, but it has many genres, major and minor, and some lend themselves to proclamation less than others, like genealogy. The Bible is not our sole guide here. We also name subforms by common sermon practice through the centuries. Here we restrict ourselves to nine genres chosen from practices that seem to be most common in history. Each one has its own emotional, intellectual, and theological thrusts, and we arrange them so that they move from deepest trouble (or law) to most exuberant grace. *Condemnation, lament,* and *stern exhortation* are trouble genres of proclamation. *Testimony, prayer, nurturing exhortation, proclamatory statements, doxology,* and *celebration* are genres of proclamation of the gospel. We present them here as one might present a rainbow of colors, a progression of musical chords, or a range of emotional expressions. Each one has preaching potential today.

Three facts about these genres of proclamation are of special interest:

1. They appear most often when sermons discuss their contemporary worlds, not in passages that comment directly on biblical texts—the latter in any case are typically teaching.
2. They are all relatives of parts of the worship service or aspects of prayer. In other words, they derive perhaps as much from the ongoing practice of worship as they do directly from the Bible.
3. Were these genres found only in history, one might tend to disregard them, but because they are part of living traditions, they may be said to be ever new.

Guidelines for Naming Genres

To steer our discussion, it is helpful to have before us formal character-istics of genres in general. Literary critic John Frow identifies six struc-tural features of genre. They help to clarify what a genre is, and we adapt them here to sermons to serve as a rough guide in our subsequent dis-cussions. Genres have the following:

1. "Formal features" that may include visual elements on a page (for instance, we will see that celebration has a shape on the page that is integral to its meaning)
2. A "thematic structure" that uses particular topics that reflect reality (for instance, lament commonly involves an unjust system, innocent children, sinful humanity)
3. A "situation of address" in which a speaker addresses listeners with a particular kind of authority (in this case a preacher addresses a congregation, generally in a church)
4. A "structure of implication" that presupposes certain background information (e.g., knowledge of the Bible or a Christian worldview)
5. A "rhetorical function" or purpose (in this case to cause hearers to believe or do something)
6. The above elements are found within a particular "regulative *frame*" that distinguishes this genre from others (in this case within preach-ing and proclamation within it).[1]

These guidelines help ensure that we speak about genres, not random features in a sermon. Other genres may exist in sermons that we will not name here, belonging both to proclamation and to teaching—they are simply beyond the current study. Moreover, not all genres are helpful to name, and if one names too many, they can become more of a hindrance than a help, more of an object of learning in themselves than tools to aid preaching.

The Larger Purpose of Retrieval

The purpose here is not just to identify proclamation as a practice that is largely lost; it is to encourage its recovery for renewal of the postmod-ern church. Whatever changes lie ahead for the church in a pluralistic world, whatever ventures will be tried with worship and congregational life, the gospel will need to be central for the Christian church to continue. Preachers who long to be creative often look toward the culture. They may try to preach sermons that seem more relevant by engaging movies, novels, art, and the like, or by engaging diverse groups and opinions in the congregation. Creative engagement with the world is part of what preaching is. One can imagine, for example, a series of biblical sermons on movies, popular books, or vocations in the community. How is being a Christian like being a mechanic, a teenager, a single mother, a CEO, a nurse, a homeless person, and so on? On the other hand, what would be the point of such an exercise if the gospel is not in view?

Proclaiming the gospel is an essential avenue for creativity that has not been explored. It involves finding beautiful and inspired ways to communicate what is core to the faith. It brings passion to the pulpit, God to voice, and holy fire to words that do what they say. The prophet knew this, and he said,

> How beautiful upon the mountains
>   are the feet of the messenger who announces peace,
> who brings good news,
>   who announces salvation,
>   who says to Zion, "Your God reigns." (Isaiah 52:7)

In the following pages, a chapter is devoted to each of our nine genres. This is not just to show what each looks and sounds like; it is to encourage preachers to adapt and imitate what is found here as an avenue to greater creativity and faithfulness. Adaptation is often necessary because these preachers proclaim from their own times, cultures, and theological perspectives. Imitation may seem like a strange avenue for creativity. On the other hand, throughout history, students of art learned painting by going to art galleries to imitate the masters. Even today a medical teaching doctor has her intern imitate the way she stitches a cut. A lawyer builds a case using previous similar cases. A theologian innovates by retrieving and refurbishing ideas from tradition. Preachers have always looked to one another for guidance and inspiration. Starting to proclaim through imitation of excellent forebears can be a good way to proceed.

In a later section we will consider proclamation of the gospel, but here we look at three trouble genres of proclamation, namely, *condemnation, lament,* and *stern exhortation.* These three genres set words on fire, but the fire is mostly different from what burns in proclaiming the gospel. Here the fire is sometimes the fire of rebuke and judgment: "The LORD will come in fire . . . and his rebuke in flames of fire" (Isaiah 66:15), and sometimes the fire is of wrath and destruction: "On the wicked he will rain coals of fire and sulfur [brimstone, KJV]" (Psalm 11:6).

Even a reader's possible initial reaction against terms like *condemnation* and *stern exhortation* may indicate they are trouble. They communicate the law, identify human sin and suffering, show humanity's fallen nature, stress human responsibility to act, or point to the help that only God can provide. They do not in themselves provide that help. In this they are like teaching, yet they offer more than that. They offer God in wrath, in grief, or in urgent appeal. They *do* judgment or law, yet in that they generally come short of *doing* gospel, they are lesser forms of proclamation. They proclaim because they are readily heard as spoken by God, they are heightened forms of expression, they try either to affect one's disposition toward something or to motivate action, and they are ultimate speech in that they do or perform what is spoken, for instance, condemnation renders God's wrath. Again, Christ is present in it, just not fully as himself.

CHAPTER NINE
Condemnation

Initial negative reaction even to the word *condemnation* may be loud and swift in many quarters. Such preaching may seem to typify the hellfire and brimstone kind of preaching that suggests an angry God and a faith that is stingy with God's love. Of course, preachers have been preaching such sermons since biblical times. They flourished again in the late Middle Ages when theological interest in hell was at a peak and countless great artists painted their visions of the awaiting torments. Dante wrote of it in his *Inferno*. Earlier as teaching, we saw that St. John Fisher preached a sermon in which he pictures humanity dangling at the end of a silver cord over the pit of hell: "This cord also hangeth by the hand and power of God."[1] Now we turn to what Jonathan Edwards did with Fisher's example in turning it into proclamation in arguably the most famous sermon in colonial America, "Sinners in the Hands of an Angry God," a sermon that was, however, atypical of Edwards's norm:

> The God that holds you over the pit of hell, much as one holds a spider, or some loathsome insect over the fire, abhors you and is dreadfully provoked. . . . O Sinner! Consider the fearful danger you are in: it is a great furnace of wrath, a wide and bottomless pit, full of the fire of wrath, that you are held over in the hand of that God, whose wrath is provoked and incensed as much against you, as against many of the damned in hell. You hang by a slender thread, with the flame of divine wrath flashing about it.[2]

The individual sinner hearing this sermon has no doubt that the condemnation described belongs to him or her because of the personal nature of the address.

C. H. Spurgeon knew that preachers must speak in more than one style and move beyond teaching. In the late 1800s he still seemed to condone preaching as condemnation when he lectured, "Sometimes, too, we must change our tone. Instead of instructing, reasoning, and persuading, we must come to *threatening*, and declare the wrath of God upon impenitent souls. We must lift the curtain and let them see the future. Show them their danger, and warn them to escape from the wrath to come."[3] Many people have fled from this kind of preaching because it feels manipulative; it makes them or others feel bad without hope. A joke tells of a preacher who moved to a new church and followed the hellfire tradition of the previous pastor, condemning to hell the people who would not change. When the congregation began to decline, the pastor asked why, since his message was the same as his predecessor. The elder replied, "He condemned, but he seemed sad about it."

Four clarifications are important:

1. We speak here of sermon subforms, not sermon forms; thus no encouragement is made here to return to sermons that in their entirety merely condemn, threaten, and fall short of the gospel.
2. We speak of God's condemnation, not a preacher's own of others. Personal and spiritual discernment is needed to know the difference.
3. Condemnation in the sermon best functions as judgment now for current actions, not as final judgment consigning some people eternally to hell and damnation, even though in our worst moments as preachers, we might so wish. Condemnation ideally is less an irrevocable sentence than a dire warning of the consequences to be paid for sin and disobedience. Repentance and forgiveness are still possible, as Jonah discovered with Nineveh, much to his initial distaste. In fact, repentance and forgiveness are key reasons for preaching, and only God determines when it is too late.
4. Though our own age seems to have trouble with God's sovereignty, many things in this world need condemnation and destruction, for they fall far short of God's intentions for creation. God is all-powerful and does condemn, judge, and even destroy. However, not all destruction is divine, and that which is, is not separate from God's righteousness.

The Bible speaks condemnation. God causes a flood to come on the world, destruction to come on the residents of Sodom, and annihilation to come to the armies opposing Israel in various locations (including at the Red Sea, and under the rules of Deborah and David). References to God's wrath in the Bible are common, not least in the Prophets, most frequently in relation to Israel's sin of idolatry, though God's anger may burn at other nations as well (e.g., Psalm 2:1-5; Jeremiah 50:13). Still, at Moses' plea, God repents the threat to destroy Israel (Exodus 32:14). Psalm 103:8-9 reads,

The LORD is merciful and gracious,
    slow to anger and abounding in steadfast love.
He will not always accuse,
    nor will he keep his anger forever.

Jesus preaches condemnation in the "Woe to you . . ." passages and in parables like the Great Feast and the Rich Man and Dives; he speaks of eternal punishment (*kolasis*) of the goats in Matthew 25:46. In Romans 8:3, God's condemnation (*katakrino*) of sin rests upon his own Son, who died under the judgment that was ours. Much of Revelation, with the exception of the last two chapters, functions as condemnation.

Even as a subform of sermons, condemnation needs careful use almost always to be balanced with proclamation of the gospel. The gospel is never just condemnation. Preachers too easily become frustrated in ministry or annoyed at some people in the congregation and then lash out in anger and disguise it as the word of God. Condemnation ought to be used with exceeding care. In any case, some condemnation belongs with each of us. Jesus said, "Do not judge, so that you may not be judged" (Matthew 7:1). We pray with him, "Forgive us our trespasses as we forgive." Thereby we make our forgiveness conditional upon our own forgiving, and we invite judgment by our failure. All of this is to say that we need to be clear, perhaps with the discerning aid of a counselor or of elders in the community, that the condemnation is in fact God's. Unresolved anger issues need to be worked out with a counselor, not the congregation. Moreover, as preachers, we are not mere dispensers of the truth, regardless of the outcome; we are careful communicators making wise decisions about how a message will best be received. At times we take the advice of Proverbs 15:1: "A soft answer turns away wrath, / but a harsh word stirs up anger." Nonetheless, sermons by being God's word do call people to repentance and obedience, and sometimes this word will be pronounced as condemnation. It is judgment for the wicked and punishment for those who harm.

Condemnation in Practice

Preach Condemnation and the End Times

Here is a remarkable example of condemnation from an anonymous homily written in Anglo-Saxon around A.D. 1000. It demonstrates surprising creativity using allusions to many biblical texts as well as rhetorical devices like parallelism and accumulation, piling description upon description. This extract is located roughly in the middle of a sermon that is otherwise prose:

On that day shall be manifested to us:
the open heaven   and might of angels
the destruction of all creatures   and ruin of the earth,
the hardships of the faithless   and fall of stars,

---

uproar of the thunder-road
the light of the sky
the creation of those groaning
the grim vision
the hot shower
and bursting of mountains
and the broad burning
and the great pestilence
and the painful sorrow
and the death-bearing dragon
and the narrow pit
and the burning abyss
and the great fear of fiends
and groaning of heathens
multitude of heaven-inhabitants
and that great council
and the harsh rod
and shame of sins
and the pale countenance
the fearful cry
and the shamed army
the groaning abyss
and the horror of serpents.

and the dark storm,
and the blast of flames,
and the strife of those spirits,
and the godly might
and mirth of hell-dwellers
and the song of trumpets,
and the bitter day
and the sins of men
and the separation of souls
and the destruction of devils
and the swarthy death
and the bloody stream
and the fiery rain
and the fall of armies
and the might of their lord
and the fearful army
and the right judgment
and the accusations of fiends
and trembling word,
and the weeping of the people
and the sinful throng
and the devouring hell

And then shall be manifested to each of us such fear.[4]

A quite different example of the condemnation of Armageddon is from the great Welsh preacher Christmas Evans (1766–1838), who blends the gospel into the condemnation. Evans dared to put the following words into the mouth of Jesus Christ:

The divine hero answers, "I have trodden the winepress alone; and of the people there was none with me. Even Peter has left me, with all his courage and affection; and as for John, to talk of love is all that he can do. I have triumphed over principalities and powers. I am wounded, but they are vanquished. Behold the blood which I have lost! Behold the spoils which I have won! Now will I mount my white horse, pursue after Satan, demolish his kingdom, and send him back to the land of darkness in everlasting chains, and all his allies shall be exiles with him forever. My own arm, which has gained the victory on Calvary and brought salvation to all my people from the sepulcher, is still strong enough to wield the golden scepter of love and break my foes on the field of Armageddon. I will destroy the works of the devil, and demolish all his hosts; I will dash them in pieces like a potter's vessel. For the day of vengeance is in my heart, and the year of my redeemed is come. My compassion is stirred for the captives of sin and death; my fury is kindled against the tyrants that oppress them. It is time for me to open the prisons and break off the fetters. I must gather my people to myself. I must seek that which was lost, and bring again that which was driven away. I must bind up that which was broken, and strengthen that which was weak. But I will destroy the fat and the strong, I will feed them with judgment; I will tread them in mine anger, trample them in my fury, bring down their strength to the earth, and stain all my raiment with their blood!"[5]

Suggestions for Creative Adaptation

The subject of both of these sermon extracts is the end of the world. Because this subject has often been misused in the pulpit as a means to frighten people into the faith, some preachers might decide not to imitate such a passage in a sermon, no matter how much the language or theology is updated. Apart from funerals and a few Sundays in the Christian Year, our own age or at least some of our traditions are not very good at preaching eschatology, the end times, yet it is hard to escape the biblical truth that history is moving toward a God-given purpose in which all of God's promises will be fulfilled, the old creation will end, and a new age has already begun in which Christ rules over all.

Preachers need to speak of the end times, and they must do so with integrity. That being the case, what does the end look like? What biblical images of the end times does the biblical text offer? Upon what other biblical images might one draw (both of the above preachers draw images and references from various places in the Bible)? What images from contemporary culture might help? Both of the above passages could easily be adapted to announce an end, for instance, to the destructive power of drugs, gambling, domestic violence, or any contemporary social sin, and in fact, Evans does this in speaking of those wrongly imprisoned.

In terms of style, we see in the Anglo-Saxon homily the same type of parallelism as is in numerous places in the Bible, notably Psalm 19:7-9 ("The law of the LORD is perfect, / reviving the soul; / the decrees of the LORD are sure, / making wise the simple . . ."). In imitating this parallel structure of column a and column b, the phrases in both columns need not be the same length, yet within each column they are roughly the same length for the sake of rhythm. The anonymous preacher allowed some variation in the starting words in column a (*the, and, uproar*), yet began every entry in column b with the same word (*and*). That said, this sermon was effective in its day because people were familiar with the various biblical and contemporary images of hell. People listening to this sermon today might not get caught up in its emotion and energy because they would not immediately understand the references, some of which in any case are too abstract (e.g., *the godly might, the bitter day, the swarthy death*). The preacher imitating this passage would need to find images immediate to the congregation that need little pondering because the smooth, rhythmic flow is crucial. Such images are readily at hand in the Bible and in places of suffering or poverty in the world.

Concerning the dominant rhetorical device of Evans, we experience the power of putting words directly into the mouth of Jesus Christ. Evans's excerpt calls to mind God's speech in the psalm: "The voice of the LORD flashes forth flames of fire" (29:7). Care obviously needs to be taken, for if the congregation were to hear Christ say hateful words contrary to the gospel, the preacher may sin against the Holy Spirit. Further, not everyone in the congregation needs to hear condemnation, so clarity is essential about the intended hearer. However, what better way is there for the sinner to be challenged than directly by God?

Allow Condemnation to Extend from a Biblical Narrative

The genres of proclamation do not need to arise from the biblical text at hand to have a place in the sermon, but if preachers think of using condemnation, it is usually because they find it in their biblical texts. T. DeWitt Talmage (1832–1902) preaches at a time when narrative in the pulpit is just starting to be used effectively, partly because of the rise of the novel and short story. Observe how vividly and passionately he paints his biblical scene at the end of this sermon from Judges 7:20-21:

> There is the army of the Midianites down in the valley of Jezreel. I suppose their mighty men are dreaming of victory. Mount Gilboa never stood sentinel for so large a host. The spears and the shields of the Midianites gleam in the moonlight, and glance on the eye of the Israelites, who hover like a battle of eagles, ready to swoop from the cliff. Sleep on, oh, army of the Midianites! With the night to hide them and the mountain to guard them and strong arms to defend them let no slumbering foeman dream of disaster! Peace to the captains and the spearmen!
>
> Crash go the pitchers! up flare the lamps! To the mountains! fly! fly! Troops running against troops, thousands trampling upon thousands. A wild stampede! Hark to the scream and groan of the routed foe, with the Lord God Almighty after them! How sudden the onset, how wild the consternation, how utter the defeat! I do not care so much what is against me, if God is not. . . .
>
> Alas for those who fight against God! Only two sides. Man immortal, which side are you on? Woman immortal, which side are you on? Do you belong to the three hundred that are going to win the day, or to the great host of Midianites asleep in the valley, only to be roused up in consternation and ruin? Suddenly the golden bowl of life will be broken, and the trumpet blown that will startle our souls into eternity. The day of the Lord cometh as a thief in the night, and as the God-armed Israelites upon the sleeping foe. Ha! canst thou pluck up courage for the day when the trumpet which hath never been blown shall speak the roll-call of the dead; and the earth, dashing against a lost meteor, have its mountains scattered to the stars and oceans emptied in the air? Oh, then, what will become of you? What will become of me?
>
> If the Midianites had only given up their swords the day before the disaster, all would have been well; and if you will now surrender the sins with

which you have been fighting against God, you will be safe. Oh, make peace with him now, through Jesus Christ the Lord. With the clutch of a drowning man seize the cross. Oh, surrender! Surrender! Christ, with his hand on his pierced side, asks you to.[6]

Suggestions for Creative Adaptation

Our cinematic age is apparently not the first to imagine earthly destruction from an asteroid. The question for many preachers today is what to do with images of violence as found not least in Judges. Does one preach them because they are in the Bible, or does one not preach them because they may contribute to a society of violence, especially against women and children? The compilers of the Revised Common Lectionary no doubt fought this battle among themselves when they included only one text from Judges in the three-year cycle: Judges 4:1-7 tells of Deborah, but stops short of her army killing every one of the soldiers of Sisera. Generally facts of violence have a place in the pulpit, but horrific details do not; they are too painful and hard to counter with the good news. One does not need to come to church to find them. Nonetheless, for those who tragically have suffered violence from others, the possibility of the perpetrators' destruction at the hands of God may be part of a healing process; it may be the beginning of their ability to hear the gospel, however incomplete destruction is as a statement of who God is. Talmage demonstrates true brilliance and inspiration in this passage from which we can learn. With any biblical text that expresses condemnation (say, for instance, Jesus condemning the Pharisees, or Lazarus and Dives), the following steps may be taken: (a) Set the action in motion with a lively narrative that turns the textual account into an event right now. Talmage creates the moonlit scene of the opposing armies with the glint of light off shields as though it is happening right now. (b) Develop the condemnation that falls on the guilty party. He describes the battle (he knows not to show the blood and guts). (c) Treat the scene theologically, as saying something about faith. It is not just Israel who routs the Midianites; it is the Lord God Almighty for their violation of the will of God. (d) Suddenly switch from talking about those condemned in the text to the congregation. Members of Talmage's congregation become the Midianites in the last two paragraphs above. They suddenly discover that the text into which they have been drawn so thoroughly is actually about them and their possible condemnation.

Preach Condemnation by Inversion

Poet Ralph Waldo Emerson (1803–82), in a Christmas sermon, uses condemnation as the climax and conclusion of what he says. He inverts the saving significance of Christmas to be a condemning event for others, and in so doing he preaches the gospel by inversion:

> Great is your reward in heaven. But if the exceeding great and precious promises which he [Christ] brought, have been slighted by you, if your days have been made dark by sin, if the immortal faculties that slumber in your breast have been neglected or abused, alas! My brother, alas! What is it to you that *squadrons of angels announced his birth*, what matters it though *the Almighty clothed him in power to bear witness to the truth of his mighty commission*, what is it to you that *death could not destroy him*, that *the tomb rendered back its trust, that he forsook it and arose*, or yet *that he ascended to his Father and ever liveth to make intercession for his faithful disciples*? What is it to you but another weight of sin which will be laid to your charge, inasmuch as you have sinned against this marvelous light?
>
> You have seen what prophets and kings desired but were not able, and have averted your eyes. The prevailing eloquence of his life, the wonders of his hand, have failed to move you. The *great tragedy of his death and the interposition of the Almighty for his resurrection* have failed to move you; then is this day an occasion of sorrow and danger, for the light of this day shall be remembered against you as an opportunity which you have slighted, as a warning which you defied. But no, I trust in God it shall not be so with us. Let us remember that life is short, and neglected opportunities will never return; that Christ will not again appear, till he comes to sit in judgment. Let him that in body was born in Bethlehem, in spirit be born in our hearts. Let us celebrate his nativity here.[7]

Suggestions for Creative Adaptation

For all of the excitement and passion of Emerson's delivery, the thrust of the passage is trouble or what the listener can or will do. God has sent Jesus Christ, and the rest is up to us. The short phrases suggesting rapid delivery and a mounting sense of lost opportunity are designed to help convince the listener to believe. At the same time the emphasis here is on condemnation of those who have failed to be moved by God's offering: "Another weight of sin which will be laid to your charge. . . . The light of this day shall be remembered against you as an opportunity which you have slighted, as a warning which you defied." In our own day, when people arrive at faith from different backgrounds and perspectives, one might need to avoid being heard to say, "Believe this or you are wrong." As an alternative to invoking condemnation on a vertical axis, with God up above and us down below, we could consider a more horizontal approach, speaking, for instance, of the neighbors we have failed to help, the suffering of others we have chosen to tolerate, and so forth.

Emerson makes a clever use of inversion in this passage. I italicized a number of his phrases (above) that are summaries of the gospel, phrases that typically might lead a preacher to praise. Instead, Emerson treats them in inverse fashion and uses each statement of God's glory to convict the unbeliever. Thus even as he praises God and communicates the gospel, he mounts the case against some of his hearers. We might use a similar manner of condemnation through praise with any passage that speaks of the mighty acts of God.

Proclaim the Gospel through Condemnation

Charles G. Adams of Hartford Baptist Church in Detroit preaches a powerful condemnation of contemporary attitudes to God, and yet manages to proclaim the gospel powerfully through it:

> We have lifted up Christ so high that we think him to be irrelevant to our everyday workday decisions and dilemmas. Isn't that the cutest way to get rid of God? That's exactly the way to do it.
>
> Straitjacket the living word into your own hard-line, atomistic, chopped-up, out-of-context interpretation of the written word. Transmute the story into a scheme. Fit and fix the Savior into a plan of salvation. Freeze the Christ into a creed. Harden gospel into a structure. Embalm amazing grace into stiff authority. Change love into law. Beat blessings into bureaucracies. Hammer faith into conformity. Ossify freedom into procedure, liquefy liberty into license, rationalize redemption into rhetoric, subvert Holy Spirit into religious habits, preempt resurrection into regimentation, pickle Jesus into ecclesiastical uniformity, wrap Christ up in the sacerdotal shroud of orthodoxy, lay Jesus out in a tomb of detached irrelevant ritual, keep Jesus out of the fight for freedom, out of the struggle for justice, out of the march for peace, and expect God to stay away from us.
>
> Expect Jesus to stay in the tomb fixed and fitted and frozen where we have put him. But it won't work. God will not stay away. Jesus will not remain dead. Faith cannot remain captive to politics. The Holy Spirit will not be obedient to our selfish economic interests. The voice of God will not be suppressed. The light of love cannot be extinguished. The challenge of Christ will not go away. Jesus will not lie still, will not keep quiet, will not stay put, will not be held down. . . . I see an angel standing at the open door of an empty tomb, saying, "He is not here. He is risen like he said." I hear a voice calling from beyond the sacred page and the sacred place saying, "Here I am."[8]

Suggestions for Creative Adaptation

In the first half of the passage Adams uses a process of inversion similar to Emerson; this time condemnation comes through satire rather than praise. Adams seems to praise people for what they have done to God, but his meaning is the opposite. Most significant is what happens in the second half. Adams shifts the focus from human actions to God's response to those actions. The condemnation continues, but the gospel is simultaneously proclaimed. Adams offers an even bolder proclamation of the gospel later in the same sermon (not cited here), but here he simply keeps the gospel central. Preachers can be bold in condemnation if they are similarly bold in the gospel. Thinking of condemnation as a genre that can have two parts (human and divine focus) is a particularly strong practice. The key to imitating Adams is to gain skill in the reversal. (We will see a similar two-part human and divine focus in the next chapter with lament.) The practice is made easier if we remember that the gospel typically provides the reversal.

Adams's use of wordplay and parallelism similarly can be instructive. Do not be afraid to imitate, loosely adapt, or even borrow. Just be sure to give credit, at least in published notes and in the church bulletin—but do not preach the footnotes.

CHAPTER TEN
Lament

We continue our exploration of trouble genres of proclamation by turning to lament. While the world defines it as a passionate expression of grief or sorrow, within Christian contexts it is commonly both addressed to God and inspired by God. Lament often arises out of a particular situation and tends to project the experience of grief and loss as universal—indeed that is often the effect of sorrow in life. One associates lament with the deepest kind of trouble, brokenness, or need. Usually one does not lament the loss of a pencil or the brief absence of a friend; one laments matters of substance in the big picture of things. The emotion matches the seriousness of the event. Lament is heartfelt; it is normally expressed on behalf of a community in such a way that the preacher enters the pain and is no mere detached observer. Lament is different from teaching about a tragic circumstance. Preachers are pastoral theologians who must speak out of their feelings, help listeners name theirs, and minister God to them. Lament manifests an elevated style and passion that differs from plain style.

The funeral sermon often is largely lament; in fact, among the most well-known contemporary words of lament in recent homiletics are these devastating words at the beginning of a sermon by William Sloane Coffin Jr. at Riverside Church in New York City on Tuesday, January 23, 1983:

> As almost all of you know, a week ago last Monday, a week ago last Monday night, driving in a terrible storm, my son Alexander—who to his friends was a real day-brightener, and to his family "fair as a star when only one is shining in the sky"—my twenty-four-year-old Alexander, who enjoyed beating his old man at every game and in every race, beat his father to the grave.[1]

At every funeral there can be lament. Even if the deceased was a miserable sort, that fact needs lament. Kathleen S. Smith encourages a wider role than is commonly practiced for lament in worship, and she defines it as "being sad and mad in worship."[2] She comments on the value of lament as pastoral care in any time of crisis: "Gathering up the feelings of anger, betrayal, and fear that accompany a crisis, lament provides a way to express them to God—not as doubt, but as an act of faith."[3]

Lament in the Old Testament is one of the oldest and most established genres and includes the funeral dirge (e.g., 2 Samuel 3:33-34), the lament for a city (e.g., Psalm 137:1, "By the rivers of Babylon . . ."; Isaiah 15–16), the individual lament (e.g., Psalms 3; 6; 13; 22; 28; 31; 51; 88; 102), and the communal lament originating in times of danger or days of fasting (e.g., Psalms 44; 58).[4] Paul laments his inner conflict in a lengthy passage in Romans 7:14-26 that contains his cry, "Wretched man that I am! Who will rescue me from this body of death?" Lament has received renewed scholarly attention in recent years, including an edited volume of essays, *Lament: Reclaiming Practices in the Pulpit, Pew, and Public Square.*[5] Two of these essays by C. Clifton Black and Robert C. Dykstra consider the crucified Christ as a statement of God's lament, God's anger and tears mixed with those of humanity.[6]

We want to think broadly when conceiving of lament as a subform of preaching. The practice of lament can include citing biblical laments or use any of their typical features, such as narrative that compares what was with what is now, assessment of responsibility in events leading to a loss, discussion of doubt, the seeming absence of God, address to God, complaint, statement of need, and plea for help. The psalms of lament can be a model for preaching because they normally contain a turn to praise God, an affirmation of trust or a confession of sin, and generally some form of muted hope. Psalms of lament have what Joachim Begrich called a sudden movement to praise or "an oracle of salvation" that typically begins with the word "But. . . ."[7] Clinton McCann Jr. and James C. Howell say that there is a movement "within virtually every Psalm of lament from plea to praise, from cry to trust."[8] Luke Powery speaks of a turn from lament to celebration, and he claims God's role in inspiring lament, "The voice of the Spirit resounds in sermonic lament but sermonic celebration also manifests the Spirit."[9]

James L. Mays names several features that the biblical laments have in common. An individual in urgent need speaks them. The main section is petitions for assistance. They are addressed to God. The trouble they describe is in relation to the self, to others, or to God. Reasons are given about why God should answer, and these have to do with the situation of the psalmist, the character and nature of God, and the psalmist's relationship to God. Laments include praise and/or a promise of sacrifice on the part of the psalmist.[10] Sally A. Brown recommends that sermon movement might follow the two-part literary movement of biblical lament, from plea (complaint, petition, and imprecation or curse) to praise (hope).[11]

What theological function does the lament subform serve? Sermons are like Sundays; ideally they celebrate the resurrection. Arguably every sermon nonetheless should lament something because there is so much wrong: sin, suffering, illness, injustice, violence, sexual abuse, oppression, environmental degradation, hardness of heart, other aspects of human behavior, and natural disaster. To preach without lament can deny that the congregation has pain, has members who have gone astray, has failed to live as the community of faith God wants it to be, or has membership in a global family that is hurting. To preach without lament can be to deny need for God; it can deny God.

Psalms of lament offer utterly unguarded frank and honest address to God, heartrending cries of suffering, anguish, anger, and despair. Although the actual social situations or locations of the psalmist cannot be determined,[12] they include sicknesses, betrayal, false accusation, and armed conflict.[13] The psalmist at times is exhausted or near death, languishing, moaning, or weeping. As in Psalm 6 the psalms sometimes identify God as the problem, and they often look to God to bring revenge. Psalms typically lay responsibility for the psalmist's plight on external forces. Jeremiah's laments blame God for his suffering because God set him apart as a prophet.[14]

Lament also provides an occasion to preach God. Carol M. Norén notes that in the Apostles' and Nicene Creeds, "belief in Jesus Christ and his Resurrection from the dead precede references to human destiny. This suggests that any statements about a Christian's life and death are made in reference to the nature and saving work of Christ."[15] The purpose of lament in the sermon is never to just complain or grieve, but is similarly to put life in appropriate perspective before God.

When is a complaint not just a complaint? When it is addressed to God and inspired by God. Although it arises out of despair, it is spoken to the only one who is the legitimate true source of hope. No book of the Bible is more frequently quoted than the Psalms with good reason; the 150 psalms are written for all manner of occasions and appeal to people in all circumstances in life. Nancy J. Duff notes that no type of psalm is more numerous than the individual psalm of lament, yet in her Presbyterian hymnbook, psalms of praise outnumber laments sixteen to six.[16] She implies that Christians today are not comfortable with lament.

Genres of proclamation unavoidably have a teaching component. What does lament teach? Like condemnation, it helps to teach what is wrong, but lament does so by protesting the pain, loss, or injustice in the world. Lament helps to teach what it means to be human: we are God's creatures, and we face the limitations of creaturehood, sin, and mortality. Lament includes arguing with God. People defy the laws of nature, government, or God and expect that there will be no cost to themselves or others. Because lament has a large emotional component, it teaches that what falls short of God's goodwill needs not just to be reported or argued as though we are distant from it; it needs to be entered and grieved. It is worthy of lament.

Nicholas Wolterstorff wrote his powerful *Lament for a Son* as a way of dealing with the tragic death of his twenty-five-year-old son, Eric, in a mountain-climbing accident. Published some twelve years after the death, he poignantly wrote, "The wound is no longer raw. But it has not disappeared. That is as it should be. If he was worth loving, he is worth grieving over. . . . I struggle indeed to go beyond merely owning my grief toward owning it *redemptively*. But I will not and cannot disown it. . . . Every lament is a love-song. Will love-songs one day no longer be laments?"[17]

Lament teaches not only that life involves suffering and loss, dying and death but also that these experiences are important. They are to be marked not just as times of protest, grief, and struggle, but as times of *redemptive suffering*, community support, prayer, and help. Communal lament extends beyond those most intimately affected to those who are involved or concerned. Reinhold Niebuhr was dean of the faculty at Union Seminary in New York when he preached on Matthew 11:16-19 on the importance of sorrow and joy, and linked them with the cross (we have no indication of his specific social context at the time):

> The point in the comment of Jesus is in the words, "We have piped unto you and you would not dance. We have mourned unto you and you would not lament." "Be careful," Jesus was saying. "You are the kind of people who can neither dance nor cry because dancing and song come out of the same sensitivity that tears come from." If there really is a sensitive heart which has been touched by God's grace, it will weep many a tear and will rejoice in many a song. The love, joy and peace of God all contain the pain and sorrow of the cross.[18]

Both lament and celebration are needed. Niebuhr's point is that we become hardened to them at our peril, for in so doing we become hardened to our neighbor, hardened to life as it is to be lived as Christ's disciples.

Lament functions as a warning, as a redemptive act recovering meaning, and as a turn to praise. Indeed, lament in the Bible is commonly a mode of prayer, and it is offered in the sermon in expectation of deliverance. For all of the apparent absence of God that many people like Job experience, and for all of the anger toward God that people like the psalmist feel, those feelings say something both about human pain and about God, who receives anger, has entered our suffering in Jesus Christ, whose Spirit acts as "a very present help in trouble" (Psalm 46:1), and to some extent gives us the appropriate words of lament to utter.

Lament in Practice

Lament a Public Action

One of the most famous historical examples of lament is by John Chrysostom in 387 when the people of Antioch rioted against new taxation by Emperor Theodosius I and desecrated statues of him. For a time the future of the marvelous city was in the balance, for no one knew how the emperor would respond. A trial date had been set, and destruction of the city was a possibility. Large numbers of the population had fled. The following is from the opening of the second in a series of twenty-one sermons during Lent on the crisis over the statues:

> 1. What shall I say, or what shall I speak of? The present season is one for tears, and not for words; for lamentation, not for discourse; for prayer, not for preaching. Such is the magnitude of the deeds daringly done; so incurable is the wound, so deep the blow, even beyond the power of all treatment, and craving assistance from above. Thus it was that Job, when he had lost all, sat himself down upon a dunghill; and his friends heard of it, and came, and seeing him, while yet afar off, they rent their garments and sprinkled themselves with ashes, and made great lamentation. The same thing now ought all the cities around to do, to come to our city and to lament with all sympathy what has befallen us. . . . Suffer me to mourn over our present state. We have been silent seven days, even as the friends of Job were. Suffer me to open my mouth today, and to bewail this common calamity.
>
> 2. Who, beloved, hath bewitched us? Who hath envied us? Whence hath all this change come over us? Nothing was more honourable than our city! Now, never was anything so deplorable! The populace so well ordered and quiet, yea, even like a tractable and good natured steed, always submissive to the hands of its rulers, hath now so suddenly started off with us, as to have wrought such evils, as one can hardly dare to mention. I mourn now and lament, not for the greatness of that wrath which is to be expected, but for the extremity of the madness that has been perpetrated! . . . How, I pray, are we to bear the shame of all that has been done? I find the word of instruction broken off by lamentation; scarcely am I able to open my mouth, to raise my lips, to move my tongue, or to utter a syllable! So, even like a curb, the weight of grief checks my tongue, and keeps back what I would say.
>
> 3. Aforetime there was nothing happier than our city; nothing more melancholy than it has now become. As bees buzzing round their hive, so before this the inhabitants flitted about the forum, and all pronounced us happy in being so numerous. But behold now, this hive hath become solitary! For even as smoke does those bees, so fear hath driven away our swarms.[19]

Chrysostom's sermon series had considerable effect on the people of Antioch, causing many to express remorse and many to become Christians. Partly as a result, the emperor's eventual punishment of the city was more restrained.

Suggestions for Creative Adaptation

Any lament must be geared to its situation and the desired outcome. Chrysostom shows remarkable skill, maturity, and restraint perhaps because he held his peace for seven days before this sermon and he did not preach out of anger. He is descriptive, not accusatory; compassionate, not vindictive; bewildered, not overcome. In the first sentence he turns to God in saying it is a time for prayer, not preaching, and later in invoking parallels with Job. He places himself firmly with the people, not over above them, even as he gently laments that their action is the reason for the troubles. Still, he empathizes with them and does not invoke vertical judgment of the condemning sort. He uses simple, clear, powerful imagery to depict their situation: first they are like riders on a good horse that has been spooked and bolted, and next like bees with smoke that have fled the hive. He is gentle in holding the people to account even as he is vulnerable to them, letting them experience his feelings of terrible loss. As he says, his need to give them instruction is overtaken by his need to lament. He says nothing to make his people defensive, and he speaks of his sense of shame, for if anything will aid the people's plight, it will be their communication of remorse to the emperor.

Frequently in the news we hear of some single event triggering fear, outrage, confrontation, riots, or war. Preachers need to anticipate preaching on public crises, including anything from the possibility of an unpopular court ruling, to a terrorist attack like 9/11, to a natural disaster. While lament can have a role in any sermon, it has a key role in sermons at such times. We might ask what kind of lament might we have made in preaching after, for example, September 11, 2001, though it was not a disaster of our making.

Is the above lament proclamation? It is not proclamation of the gospel, and it may not be possible to say with certainty if it was even proclamation in the more limited sense of a word from God. Arguably it was if its result was peace and reconciliation and if listeners heard the voice of God through the loving ways Chrysostom spoke when he could have been scathing. Moreover, what he says here could serve as proclamation if it is echoed or inverted by a gospel perspective later in the sermon or series.

Lament the Situation of Individuals

Lament an Individual's Sinful Life

John Wesley closes a sermon on the Sermon on the Mount with a paragraph of lament over human sin, particularly in relationship to the perils of hell. Though Christian "mourning is at an end, is lost in holy joy, by the return of the Comforter," disciples "still mourn for the sins and miseries" of humanity.[20] Listen as Wesley calls on listeners:

> Heaven and hell are in very deed open before you: and ye are on the edge of the great gulf. It has already swallowed up more than words can express, nations and kindreds and peoples and tongues and still yawns to devour, whether they see it or no, the giddy, miserable children of men. O cry aloud! Spare not! Lift up your voice to him who grasps both time and eternity, both for yourselves and your brethren, that ye may be counted worthy to escape the destruction that cometh as a whirlwind! That ye may be brought safe, through all the waves and storms, into the haven where you would be. Weep for yourselves, till he wipes away all the tears from your eyes. And even then weep for the miseries that come upon the earth, till the Lord of all shall put a period to misery and sin, shall wipe away the tears from all faces, and "the knowledge of the Lord shall cover the earth, as the waters cover the sea."[21]

Suggestions for Creative Adaptation

As a child, I heard a great-uncle preach; at times he sounded almost as though he was weeping. My father explained that for earlier generations, it was common for ministers in the pulpit to cry because of people's sins. Getting people to weep for their sins, also once a common practice, may still have virtue, though it easily can be seen as manipulative; the purpose should be repentance, not tears per se. The practice of calling people to weep might be most effective in suffering that affects the community as a whole, for in such circumstances they already are weeping. Following Wesley's model might be less effective, especially if people in the congregation find sin and hell foreign concepts, or if folks are suspicious of religious authority. In this type of lament God is above and humanity is below seeking forgiveness; the axis is vertical. The preacher communicates judgment, and the effect is to make the listeners both aware of their guilt in not accepting Jesus Christ and desirous of being reconciled to God. Should one seek an alternative, a preacher might name specific sins on a horizontal axis yet still before God, for instance, raising social and spiritual consequences of certain actions, like bullying, dealing drugs, distributing pornography, or inadequately funding Christian missions.

Lament a Pastoral Issue

A Scot, Hugh Martin, in the late 1800s uses lament as a way to empathize with a problem that might plague some of his congregants: Why do good people suffer? He becomes the lamenter:

The clouds of trial that intervene between [the believer] and his very life are not by any effort whatsoever to be rolled away; neither by impatience are they to be murmured at, as if some strange thing happened to him. It might be comfortable and delightful to see and enjoy here the unbroken felicity of eternal life. One may even ask, in agony, Why should it be so,—why, if I am a child of God,—why, if I am alive for evermore,—why, if I am not only a prospective heir, but a present possessor of eternal life? Why are so many things, if not all these things, against me? Why is it with me thus? Why cannot I do the things that I would? Why cannot I compel the acknowledgement of my high estate, my heavenly credit and renown? Why should I be in heaviness through manifold temptation? Why should I have to groan within myself, oppressed continually, with anomalous and seemingly unreconcilable conditions?

It is a state of feeling of which thousands of Christians have been conscious.[22]

Charles Booth in our own time uses lament in a similar fashion in preaching on the question of why good people do bad things, taking as his text the story of Hagar and Sarai (Genesis 16:1-6). He addresses the feelings of many of his congregants that they are unforgivable:

All of us have crooked ways that need to be made straight and rough plains that need to be smooth. We are "naughty by nature!" Education, economics, and pedigree are never enough. Hagar was a tease! Sarai mistreated Hagar! Abram lied! Jacob was deceptive! Moses was a murderer! Samson was sexually weak! David committed adultery! Solomon unfairly and unduly taxed his own people! James and John were egotists! Peter was impetuous! Paul persecuted the church! It is an undeniable fact of history that good people do bad things! But thanks be to God, this is not our eternal plight and destiny! There is one who is good totally and completely! There is one who is lovely altogether! There is one who is wonderful, counsellor, mighty God, and Prince of Peace! He is Jesus, the Christ! It is he who can do for us what we can never do for ourselves. He is the only one who can save us from our sins and from ourselves![23]

Suggestions for Creative Adaptation

Neither of these examples is designed to make members of the congregation feel guilty or judged per se, for the preachers assume that they already may feel judged. Rather, these laments are designed to help them feel seen, heard, and understood. This kind of lament requires the preacher to identify with the people and speak for them. Hugh Martin's very personal lament might need easier vocabulary and revised questions, but it is still remarkably effective in using heartfelt questions to God as a means to name the issues. Charles Booth's lament might be imitated for its turn midway to praise God, in the manner of the psalms, and for its proclamation of the gospel.

Lament Social Issues

John Watson was a fine preacher and a brilliant writer; under the pen name of Ian Maclaren, he published his popular short stories, *Beside the Bonnie Brier Bush* (1894). The beauty of his prose is plainly evident in his sermons, as is seen in this lament over city life that begins his sermon actually in praise of the city, based on the heavenly Jerusalem in Revelation 21:2:

> When one is in a healthy state of mind he must love the country with its wide distances, its varied colours, its wealth of animal life, its untainted air, its simple living; and he must resent the masterful aggression of the city as it covers the greenery with packed streets of monotonous houses, and replaces the quietness with the weary din of traffic. One almost hates the city for a wrong, and a sadder waste, because of the people it has devoured, who came up healthy, contented, simple-minded, and grew stunted, restless, bitter, each man pushing his own way, and knowing not his neighbours' names, wearing out his years in grinding toil, or flinging them away in riotous pleasure. The city seems to be like the fabled monster which lived upon a tribute of young life, because it is ever devouring our best and filling its shrunken veins with the red blood of the country. There are hours in every man's life when he longs to escape from the crowd and turmoil of the city, when he regards its problems with despair. . . .
> We mourn the sacrifice of bright lives which have been worn out by the exacting demands of the city, the men and women who have died before their time. It is the tragedy of the city. We might also mourn the men who have come to nothing in the country.[24]

Another Scot, Andrew Morton, was minister of James' Place United Presbyterian Church in the heart of Edinburgh in the 1870s, and in those days there were not yet laws against opium. Morton's sermon "The Unbearable Wound" is based on Proverbs 18:14 ("The spirit of a man will sustain his infirmity; but a wounded spirit who can bear?" [KJV]). He identifies several wounds the body can bear—bodily distress, mental trials, and spiritual depression—before lamenting the unbearable wound, the wounded spirit that works against the self:

> How amazing the all but universal acquiescence of men in sin, and all the "wounds" it can inflict! Sense reigns. They "eat and drink," and sooth their souls with every kind of opiate. Yet, amid all the transient glory of the present, are they not all carrying a burden? Are they not loaded with "infirmities," tottering under them, and sinking as they totter? If natural reason may hear, every moment, "the knell of departed hours," and may "start up alarmed," looking over "life's narrow verge," how may all the other questions arise? "What shall I do to be saved?" "How can a man be just with God?" Is there no one to take the load of guilt from the soul? Must this burden of

conscious sin, and its perpetual death-involving consequences, be my doom, hopelessly or for ever?

A "wounded spirit" is, therefore, a spirit that has no internal support. It is a consciously guilty spirit.[25]

Morton begins by condemning the sin, but moves by the fifth sentence to weep for the lost. Here is a good principle for lament: describe the wrong; empathize and weep for the afflicted; don't focus on judging. Stay with the feelings. In the final sentence above, Morton turns from lament back to teaching. The former is passionate and involved; the other is dispassionate and assessing. The one is filled with sorrow, and the other is descriptive and analytical.

Suggestions for Creative Adaptation

When lament is employed, it tends to function best in the first half of the sermon so that by the end, there is time to bring to the situations of lament a more fulsome expression of the gospel. By the end of Morton's sermon, he establishes that even the unbearable wound of self-destruction is curable and is "even as nothing" in Christ.[26] By the end of the first sermon extract above, Watson begins to praise the city for all that it enables, and by the end of the sermon, he challenges the church to a "social gospel" that cares for poor and needy persons with proper housing and fair wages for all in the spirit of Christ's love. Both sermons lament difficult social situations: one laments city life, and the other laments the self-destructive activities of people. Lament is not easy to find in much preaching through history, which is strange since every sermon arguably should lament something. Lament has been more common in African American preaching, where the history of slavery and continued racial injustice and deprived social opportunity provides no shortage of reason for lament. Lament is no stranger to situations of oppression and suffering. White preaching seems to teach *about* wrong, offering important instruction about such situations and exhortation or encouragement to change behavior. It stops short of actually *doing* lament in the name of God and in the power of the Spirit. Again, so much is lamentable in contemporary life, why is not lament frequent? As preachers contemplate using lament to proclaim, they might ask, What situation in my sermon is worthy of lament? Might the lament be rooted in the occasion of someone's broken heart? Might lament be centered on people's sin, the drug culture in so many schools today, domestic violence, or governmental waste of funds? Might the lament be centered on victims of things such as poverty, disease, racial injustice, or war? Might lament be for the environment?

In the Psalms, lament is often accompanied by curse—calling upon God to bring justice to the enemy. Imprecatory psalms (Psalm 109 and others) are so called because they are devoted to cursing enemies. While we moderns have trouble with this idea, it was essentially a way of recognizing that oppression requires justice, and that by voicing our curse to God, we are relinquishing the need to seek vengeance ourselves. Further, we are to love and pray for our enemies (Matthew 5:43). Might it still be possible for us to curse from the pulpit those things that oppress God's people, calling for divine judgment on them?

Proclaim the Gospel through Lament

Much African American preaching employs excellent models of lament in part because social concern is part of its fabric; evangelical fervor is matched with passion for justice. Leonard Lovett preached a sermon in 1980 comparing Moses and Martin Luther King Jr. in which, at the end, he has a stylized lament concerning the distance remaining to the promised land. Midway through the passage below, listen for how the lament changes to hope:

"How far is the Promised Land?" When we are reminded by educators and social scientists that there are more segregated schools in this nation than there were fifteen or twenty years ago, we must ask, how far is the Promised Land?

The Promised Land is as far away as our unwillingness to work seriously at genuine intergroup and interpersonal living. . . .

The Promised Land is as far away as our refusal to recognize that the choice is no longer that of violence or non-violence but it is, to use the words of King, "nonviolence or nonexistence."

The Promised Land is as far away as our unwillingness to expose and end the sophisticated forms of discrimination against minorities, the subtle forms of institutionalized racism that destroy the social fabric of our society.

The Promised Land is as far away as this nation's unwillingness to understand what real violence is. Violence occurs when farmers are paid not to farm while poor people go undernourished for lack of basics. Violence occurs. . . .

How far is the Promised Land?

It is as close as minorities getting together spiritually, educationally, and politically so that we can equally participate in the decision-making areas of this society.

It is as close as our ability to move against the wholesale misuse of dangerous drugs that destroy our best minds before they can fulfill their potential.

It is as close as our faith that truth will ultimately triumph over evil.

It is as close as minorities realizing that we must begin in our own communities to stop killing one another and ripping off one another. . . .

It is as close as our realization that as blacks in America we are still hold-ing a bad check in our hands marked insufficient funds because this nation has defaulted and refused to honor it at the Bank of Justice.

Since the kingdom of this world has not become the kingdom of our Lord and of his Christ, we must move forward.[27]

Suggestions for Creative Adaptation

Using Lovett as a model, one can imagine a lament in the season of Advent, How far is Bethlehem? or during Lent, How far to the empty tomb? or at Pentecost, How long until we feel the Spirit blowing? ("It's as soon . . ."), or if preaching on the parable of the Talents, How many times do we have to doubt our talents to . . . ? ("Jesus Christ is using his talents to . . ."), or on Matthew 17:20, How long until faith is the size of a mus-tard seed? ("It's big enough already to . . .").

Summary

Lament can be mentioned in a sentence, but to do it typically needs more substantial form that can be conceived as an entire paragraph or two. It needs to be long enough for its pain to be experienced. Its style is a heightened form of trouble, that is, it is not simply description: it is impassioned description with words set afire by God's righteousness and compassion. Its features can include measured or balanced phrases, par-allelism, concrete language, and sensory words that create pictures and evoke feeling. Its sound is distinctive in delivery; it is a kind of moaning, a speaking with sorrow, a form of the blues. Were lament to become a cursing of enemies or stern exhorting, it would move into other genres. Lament's rhetorical purpose is not to communicate information; it is to move people so that the lament becomes their own and they seek the assistance of God. Lament is best used as complaint addressed to God that finds some divine response by the end of the sermon. It gives voice to the sorrow that is in our hearts and God's and allows the word to illu-minate especially those places of deepest suffering and need.

CHAPTER ELEVEN

Stern Exhortation

S tern exhortation is a form of proclamation that offers moral instruc- tion or correction of a sort more common in the preaching of pre- vious eras. It is a heightened form of teaching that tends to be in the imperative voice, demanding change and urging immediate action. To some people, stern exhortation sounds only like *must, should,* and *have to,* and they experience it as paternalistic and condescending or author- itarian and offensive. It sounds like a critical parent keeping unruly off- spring in check. In other ages or cultures where authority is honored and not regarded with suspicion, demands and warnings can be received as reliable wisdom, as words spoken in love for the good of the people involved. In the present time and culture, stern exhortation might still be welcome if people have faith that the word really is from God and not just the preacher. In any case stern exhortation functions theologically as trouble because normally it casts people on their own resources to change.

We will distinguish between two kinds of exhortation, one that is nur- turing, which functions to proclaim the gospel (see chapter 14), and the present kind that comes as a stern word of God. Stern exhortation of this sort comes close to the root meaning of the Greek noun *parainesis* (verb *paraineo*), or warning that means caution, admonishment, or rebuke of the sort used in public affairs, debates, or situations of some urgency. It is impassioned, yet tends to be impersonal and public, has little warmth, and is usually made by someone in authority; within the church context it is made by or on behalf of God. It dictates advice on practical matters of ethical living and Christian behavior. M. B. Thompson finds some degree of scholarly agreement on characteristics of *parainesis* in Paul's letters: (1) it expresses conventional wisdom, (2) it is of a general nature and is easily applied, (3) it is often presented as a reminder about something familiar, (4) it is typically demonstrated in lives of particular people, and (5) it is generally offered by someone who has more experience than the listeners.[1] Its goal is to persuade and promote action, not to preserve things as they are.

When we think of this kind of exhortation, we may associate it with the kind of teacher that Paul had in mind in Galatians 3:24, "The law was our disciplinarian [*paidogogos*] until Christ came, so that we might be justified by faith." Passages of stern exhortation often appear at the conclusions of some of Paul's letters and come mixed with teaching in various locations, such as in Romans 12:1–15:13; Galatians 5:1–6:10; Ephesians 4:1–6:20; Colossians 3:1–4:6; and 1 Thessalonians 4:1–5:22. In the Epistles, exhortation might include a simple imperative statement, similes, contrasts, illustrations, proverbs, extended comparisons between two possibilities, lists of social virtues and vices, and reciprocal duties in various relationships.[2] The following passage from Ephesians 4:29–5:2 stands as a good example:

> Let no evil talk come out of your mouths, but only what is useful for building up, as there is need, so that your words may give grace to those who hear. And do not grieve the Holy Spirit of God, with which you were marked with a seal for the day of redemption. Put away from you all bitterness and wrath and anger and wrangling and slander, together with all malice, and be kind to one another, tenderhearted, forgiving one another, as God in Christ has forgiven you. Therefore be imitators of God, as beloved children, and live in love, as Christ loved us and gave himself up for us, a fragrant offering and sacrifice to God.

This kind of proclamation is akin to Luther's law as "hammer of judgment."[3] It is also akin to Calvin's first (though not principal) use of the law that he said was law in its "punitive function": "it warns, informs, convicts, and lastly condemns, every man of his own unrighteousness." Calvin compares it to the mirror in 1 Corinthians 13:12, "now we see in a mirror, dimly," for it "discloses our sinfulness, leading us to implore divine help."[4] The more clearly the law reveals God's righteousness, "the more it uncovers our iniquity."[5] The effect on unbelievers is to cause terror for their obstinacy of heart; believers, by contrast, "come to realize that they stand and are upheld by God's hand alone; that, naked and empty-handed, they flee to his mercy, repose entirely in it, hide deep within it, and seize upon it alone for righteousness and merit."[6]

In earlier centuries the exhortative sermon was a common form of sermon that has since disappeared, at least by name. Phillips Brooks spoke of it as a sermon that summons people to live "a good life" and addresses the "conscience and the heart."[7] In our day perhaps the closest parallels are topical sermons on subjects of salvation, morality, family values, the life of faith, and social justice. Because our age may be oversensitive to authority, even modest forms of moral or spiritual instruction can seem to have the hard edge that this kind of exhortation often implies. Exhortation of this stern sort needs to be used with caution and out of a position of well-established trust.

Exhortation in Practice

Exhort against Bad Behavior

Augustine offers many examples of exhortation concerning what people should not believe: "Let no-one, therefore, believe that the Son of God was changed or transformed into the Son of man."[8] Augustine also exhorts concerning behavior to avoid, such as is practiced on New Year's Day: "On this day the Gentiles celebrate their festival with worldly joy of the flesh, with the sound of most vain and filthy songs, with banquets and shameless dances."[9] Here is an exhortation concerning further pagan practices he abhors, all said in the name of Jesus Christ:

> Let nothing happen that is odious to God—iniquitous games, shameless amusements. . . . Listen: you are Christians, you are the members of Christ—think of what you are, consider at what great price you have been purchased.
>   . . . On the Nativity of John, that is, six months ago, for there are that many months between Herald and the Judge—Christians copying a superstitious pagan rite, went to the sea and there bathed themselves. I was absent at the time, but as I learned, the presbyters, thoroughly aroused by the matter of Christian conduct involved, disciplined certain parties as the Church's norms require. There was grumbling and some said: "What was so extraordinary about this that we should be taken to task for it? Had we been warned ahead of time, we would not have done it. Had those same presbyters warned us before, we would not have done it."
>   Your bishop is forewarning you. I warn you. I state this publicly, I make this an official declaration. Hear your bishop commanding you! Hear your bishop admonishing you! Hear your bishop pleading with you! Hear your bishop adjuring you. I adjure you in the name of Him who was born this day. I adjure you, I make this your responsibility—let no-one do it![10]

Suggestions for Creative Adaptation

Often there are times a preacher must speak against certain types of behavior, and occasionally in order to communicate the importance of the subject, a heightened style is needed beyond teaching. On this occasion, Augustine was addressing actions he considered immoral, and the seriousness is indicated by the strength of his response. However one may agree with Augustine, it may be difficult to imagine a circumstance in which such strong warning would be broadcast to an entire congregation today. It might be the same kind of action that would provoke condemnation (see chapter 9). Or it might be in preaching to a youth group that had acted poorly, perhaps endangering someone's life.

This kind of reproof stops short of condemnation. Unlike with lament, there is still time to act, but it must be quick. This example of stern exhortation is proclamation in that Augustine invokes the name of God ("Him who was born this day"), and the commandment is understood as not Augustine's alone. The greatest caution is needed not to misrepresent God. Still, to the degree that any correction from the pulpit functions or is heard as God speaking, it serves as proclamation.

Exhort Good Behavior

A general homiletical guideline is to preach for something, not against something. John Chrysostom in the early church exhorted his congregation to good behavior in the following superb example that has sufficient vitality and relevance to sound almost contemporary:

> Let us do everything we do in such a way as to move each one who sees us to glorify God, for it is written, "If you do anything, do all for the glory of God."
> What do I mean? If you ever wish to associate with someone, make sure that you do not give your attention to those who enjoy health and wealth and fame as the world sees it, but take care of those in affliction, those in critical circumstances, those in prison, those who are utterly deserted and enjoy no consolation. Put a high value on associating with these; for from them you shall receive much profit, you will be a better lover of true wisdom, and you will "do all for the glory of God." And if you must visit someone, prefer to pay this honor to orphans, widows, and those in want rather than to those who enjoy reputation and fame. God Himself has said: "I am the father of orphans and the protector of widows." And again: "Judge for the fatherless, defend the widow. Then come let us talk, saith the Lord."[11]

In the same way Hildegard of Bingen (1098–1179) warned gathered clergy. In this case she adopts the persona of God and speaks as God:

> Oh my dear sons, who feed my flocks. . . . I have placed you like the sun and other luminaries that you may give light to men through the fire of teaching, shining in good report and offering burning hearts. . . . But you are prostrate and do not sustain the Church. You flee to the cavern of your delight and because of the tedium of riches and the avarice of other vanities you do not fill those under you, nor allow them to seek teaching from you. [Later, in her own voice, she warns against the Albigensians:] While they remain with you, you cannot be safe. The Church mourns and wails over their wickedness while her sons are polluted by their iniquity. Therefore cast them from yourselves, lest the community and city perish.[12]

Suggestions for Creative Adaptation

The clarity with which Chrysostom recommends Christian association with those who are disadvantaged is exemplary. Hildegard displays similar moral clarity in dealing with ordered clergy. Some preachers today seem reluctant to speak directly about moral behavior except in the most general ways for various possible reasons: the desire to avoid controversy, the divisive power of issues like homosexuality, the complexity of many ethical issues, or the desire on the part of many congregations to have a simplistic answer. The result has been an age in the church that struggles with issues of leadership. It may be no coincidence that Pentecostal churches show consistent growth, for typically they both nurture faith and do not hesitate to tell their people what to do, for good or ill.

On the other hand, all preachers have the opportunity to speak of core values and beliefs. They may do so with the kind of clarity shown by Chrysostom that may drive some away, but may also draw others. Such preaching assists congregational conversations and may motivate congregational action on issues—all of which shapes what Stanley Hauerwas calls communities of character. It might be interesting for preachers, perhaps working with members of the congregation, to maintain a list of moral issues in the community as a way to be intentional about raising them. Some issues need entire sermons or study programs, and others, such as with whom we associate, are ideally geared to a portion of a sermon.

Hildegard's device of speaking on behalf of God to critique what she sees may seem bold to us, yet perhaps we do no less each time we preach in God's name. Are there some instances in the life of a congregation in which such speech might be appropriate and even advised?

Exhort about Relationship to God

The following exhortation is taken from a sermon by the Puritan John Howe (1630–1705). It almost needs to be read aloud in order to catch its import:

> Demean yourselves with that care, caution, and dutifulness that become a state of reconciliation. Realize that your present peace and friendship with God is not original and continued from thence, but hath been interrupted and broken; that your peace is not that of constantly innocent persons. You stand not in this good and happy state because you never offended, but as being reconciled, and who therefore were once enemies. And when you were brought to know in your day, which you have enjoyed, the things belonging to your peace, you were made to feel the smart and taste the bitterness of your having been alienated and enemies in your minds by wicked works. When the terrors of God surrounded you and his arrows stuck fast in you, did you not then find trouble and sorrow? Were you not in a fearful expectation of wrath and fiery indignation to consume and burn you up as adversaries? Would you not then have given all the world for a peaceful word or look, for any glimmering of hope of peace? How wary and afraid

should you be of a new breach! How you should study acceptable deportments, and to walk worthy of God unto all well-pleasing! How strictly careful should you be to keep faith with him, and abide steadfast in his covenant![13]

Stern exhortation is closely related to condemnation, as is apparent from this example in a traditional hellfire-and-brimstone sermon by George Whitefield in the 1700s:

God help you, young people, to put your foot on this ladder, don't climb wrong: the devil has got a ladder, but it reaches down to hell; all the devil's children go down, not up; the bottom of the devil's ladder reaches to the depths of the damned, the top of it reaches to the earth; and when death comes, then up comes the devil's ladder to let you climb down. For God's sake, come away from the devil's ladder; climb, climb, dear young men. . . . Young women, put your feet upon this ladder; God lets one ladder down from heaven, and the devil brings another up from hell. O, say you, I would climb up God's ladder, I think it is right, but I shall be laughed at; do you think to go to heaven without being laughed at? The Lord Jesus Christ help you to climb to heaven; come, climb till you get out of the hearing of their laughter. O trust not to your own righteousness, your vows, and good resolutions. . . . It is a shame the children of God don't climb faster; you may talk what you please, but God's people's lukewarmness is more provoking to him than all the sins of the nation.[14]

Suggestions for Creative Adaptation

The first example above by John Howe is a creative reminder to the congregation that they have been redeemed from something. It could easily be preached in almost any church today, with adjustments mainly in language. Essentially it is a summons to remember where you might have been if God had not come into your life. It can be developed as a reminder that at no point in one's life journey was God ever separate; remember who you are and whose you are.

Concerning Whitefield's example, there are some congregations in which hellfire and brimstone still work, even as there are others that resist the subject as a form of manipulating by fear. Horace Bushnell was among the first to write against such practices, arguing the importance of people being nurtured into the faith through gradual training in the family-like setting of a loving congregation (*Christian Nurture*, 1847). In adapting stern exhortation for today, one imagines talk that is stern, yet firm, perhaps as is found in spiritual direction, "Do not do that." In receiving spiritual direction, one submits to the wisdom of a spiritual director, and one practices what Margaret Guenther calls "holy listening."[15] (Such counseling relationships also involve mentoring, yet that friendship dimension relates more to the subform of nurturing exhortation that will be discussed later.) Eugene Peterson calls for pastors to leave behind concerns about self-image and administrative and economic success and return to three basic acts crucial for pastoral ministry: praying, reading Scripture, and giving spiritual direction.[16]

It would be interesting to hear Whitefield's exhortation revised in different ways: one revision could summon people to be who God calls them to be, not to get distracted by what is popular, most immediate, loudest, or brightest. The image of a ladder, stairs, a path, or a street could still be used. Such a warning can be heard as loving, depending on how it is said; hearers may be grateful that the preacher cared enough to speak to them directly about their situation.

Proclaim the Gospel through Exhortation

The danger with stern exhortation on its own is what we have seen before: it places the burden on listeners to carry out their faithful duties. Luther said such appeal can only slay by making the listener aware of how far apart from God he or she may be; it does nothing to alleviate the despair or to empower change. J. J. G. Kippen in Pitcairngreen, Scotland, in the 1870s demonstrates how even through exhortation, the gospel may be proclaimed:

> There is set before you the means whereby you may enter into fellowship with God, may cease to walk in the darkness, may begin to walk in the Light. O, do not despise the means; do not refuse to walk in the way! Come and confess your sins. Keep no longer silent. Pour out your heart before God. Tell Him everything. Hide nothing from Him. Make no excuses for yourselves. Let Him know the very worst. Be open with Him. Make Him your confidant. Cast away from you all hypocrisy, and deceit, and guile. Be frank, and straightforward, and true. Make full acknowledgement of all your transgressions. What else does He require from you? Listen to His own words which He speaks to each of you:—"Only acknowledge thine iniquity, that thou hast transgressed against the Lord thy God, and hast not obeyed my voice." He is waiting, that He may be gracious unto you. He is ready to multiply forgivenesses towards you. He is longing to make you clean, and pure, and well-pleasing in His sight. O, will you not let Him have His way with you? Why will you any longer thwart and hinder His gracious work in your souls? Turn ye, turn ye; why will ye die? Cease to strive against Him. Cease to resist His Spirit. Humble yourselves under the mighty hand of God. Submit yourselves to His righteousness. Yield to His ordinance. Obey His voice. Only thus can you be truly blessed. If you refuse, you forsake your own mercy; you hate your own souls; you are in love with death. God granted you forgiveness of sins and cleansing from all unrighteousness in Christ Jesus; and He causes proclamation of this gift to be made to you in the Gospel of His grace.[17]

Suggestions for Creative Adaptation

Some preachers might be content simply to teach the importance of turning to God. Kippen goes further by proclaiming. He pleads and reassures, nudges and coaxes, reprimands and rewards. As a result he communicates a God who is like a parent with a child learning to ride a bike, urgently caring for that child's welfare. In adapting the above passage we might feel more comfortable removing the threats of death and turning them into promises of life. The question for each of us is, What can we learn from stern exhortation? It can be a good way above teaching to communicate the law. For all of the negative stereotypes some people may have of exhortation, it can also be a way to communicate love when handled with sensitivity. Some things need serious, immediate, urgent address. Knowing when and how to use it can be the mark of an excellent leader and preacher.

Genres of Proclamation of the Gospel

We have explored trouble genres of proclamation, namely, *condemnation, lament,* and *stern exhortation.* For the most part they awaken people to sin, evil, or wrongdoing and demand change in a particular direction. In Ebeling's terms, these genres bring certainty of wrongdoing and the need for change. By contrast, the genres of proclamation of the gospel help bring certainty of salvation: *testimony, prayer, nurturing exhortation, proclamatory statements, doxology,* and *celebration.* They demonstrate Brunner's "faith-awakening, faith-furthering, faith-wooing address." While the trouble genres largely cast people on their own resources, the gospel genres provide the ample resources of a gracious and beneficent God. Both are needed: the one condemns sin, and the other names what God does in relation to it. Together they are the gospel; we are both sinners and saved. They provide a setting in which one may hear saving words of address from God. Since the gospel genres represent the most fulsome proclamation of the gospel, in them the identity and works of Jesus Christ are made manifest and God's promises are fulfilled.

We have seen an emotional and spiritual progression from condemnation to lament (both of which say, in effect, something terrible has happened) to stern exhortation (which says there is still time to change). We continue that same progression now as we move through the gospel genres from testimony through to celebration.

CHAPTER TWELVE
Testimony

Testimony is confession or witness and speaks of the faithfulness and steadfast nature of God. Testimony is the practice of speaking truthfully about one's faith. The testimony given may be the preacher's own or spoken on behalf of someone in the Bible or contemporary world, or on behalf of a group, for example, the congregation as a whole. Lament is spoken in anticipation of deliverance. Testimony, by contrast, is spoken in recollection of it. The two mirror each other, and testimony about suffering can be called lament. In our use of it, testimony usually concerns God and God's faithfulness. Thomas Hoyt Jr. says, "In testimony, people speak truthfully about what they have experienced and seen, offering it to the community for the edification of all."[1] He compares it to a law court in which evidence is given, received, and evaluated: "It is a deeply shared practice—one that is possible only in a community that recognizes that falsehood is strong, but that yearns to know what is true and good."[2]

Testimony in the Bible is the primary means of legal proof, reinforced by the ninth commandment against giving false witness. God also gives testimony. The Old Testament refers to the laws of the Torah as divine testimonies (*'eda*) and to the Ten Commandments, the ark, and the tables of the Law as testimony (*'edut*).[3] In the New Testament the Holy Spirit gives testimony (*martyria*) to Jesus Christ in Acts 5:32 and John 15:26-27, as does the Father (John 5:37). Many people give witness throughout John in particular, in the gospel accounts of the resurrection, and in Acts. Testimony includes much of Acts and parts of the Epistles. Paul speaks specifically of "the testimony of Christ" and gives thanks that it has been strengthened (1 Corinthians 1:6). In the New Testament, testimony is linked to the life, death, and resurrection of Jesus Christ (Acts 10:39; 3:15; 1:22; 1 Corinthians 15:5-8).[4]

Countering Resistance to Testimony

Testimony is one of those words associated with preaching that can have negative connotations for different reasons. It may imply heavy-handed personal witnessing that treats people as objects for evangelism, or that seems manipulative or disrespectful. My father modeled respectful testimony. I used to get irritated as a child that Dad would always talk to people. We knew exactly what we were looking for in a store, we could get it and go, and yet he would ask a clerk some question or engage in conversation. He would not go out of his way to tell people that he was a minister, but from time to time, he would find a way of saying something positive about God, "It is a grand day that God made," or in relation to some sad story in the news, "I think God must be disappointed." People did not have to respond in like fashion (they often did), but Dad planted a seed out of his joy for life.

John M. Buchanan, former moderator of the Presbyterian Church (U.S.A.), was against testimony for another reason. He was taught the importance of avoiding in the pulpit the use of personal pronouns, personal stories, or statements beginning with "I believe." Such focus pulls attention from God to the preacher and the preacher's experience. All of this was challenged when he attended a workshop offered by a noted preacher, who invited each participant to stand up and offer a testimony of where the Holy Spirit had been perceived to be at work. At issue was the fact that we preachers need to let people know *that* we believe. Though Buchanan felt uncomfortable, he came away "more and more convinced that behind and beneath the preaching vocation is the call to testimony."[5] James Fodor says testimony has "a twofold movement: a centrifugal impulse which distinguishes the self from the world and from other people, but also a centripetal thrust which 'pours language back into the world' and thus binds us to one another."[6] In Fodor's terms, Buchanan knew about the centrifugal thrust of religious testimony as something that affords identity and divides people, but he needed to learn its centripetal, community-building dimensions.

Thomas G. Long tries to counter negative associations with testimony in his *Testimony: Talking Ourselves into Being Christian*:

> A common misunderstanding is to think that talking about faith means getting our belief system all worked out in advance before we open our mouths. . . . To the contrary, saying things out loud is part of how we come to believe. We talk our way *toward* belief, talk our way from tentative belief through doubt to firmer belief, talk our way toward believing more fully, more clearly, more deeply.[7]

He compares the act to two people speaking of their love and in so doing discovering it more completely. He encourages testimony as not mere dogmatic assertion, but reflection that allows for doubt and longs for a fuller witness to the truth of God in the midst of life.

Testimony in Daily Life

Faithful testimony is personal witness appropriate to a moment and arising out of experience. It may be very simple. It need not be original, though it must be authentic, like the classic praise testimony in some African American churches: "Thank you, God, for waking me up this morning: for putting shoes on my feet, clothes on my back, and food on my table. Thank you, God, for health and strength and the activities of my limbs. Thank you that I awoke this morning clothed in my right mind."[8] Many African American gospel songs and spirituals are testimonials, including the African American anthem, James Weldon Johnson's "Lift Every Voice and Sing." This is true in other communities, for example in the many hymns of Fanny Crosby ("All the Way My Savior Leads Me") and other hymn writers. Testimony arises out of Christian experience and finds expression in acts of compassion, in songs, in preaching, and in celebration of the sacrament. In the latter, Hoyt says, "We offer testimony to one another and to God that we are bound to one another and to Christians of every time and place."[9]

Sometimes people perform exemplary acts in terms of loving God and neighbor, and their lives become seen as testimony. A grandmother takes presents to her grandchildren each time she visits. They thus acquire not only various children's books, each devoted to one person in the Bible, but they also begin to acquire faith through her reading to them. A man quietly goes about outreach, coordinating neighboring churches to start a women's shelter, to staff a family shelter at mealtimes, and to provide aid to peasant farmers overseas. As enacted forms of testimony, they witness to the role of God in individual and communal life.

Testimony in Sermons

What about testimony in preaching? In one way of thinking, everything that a preacher does in a sermon is a witness to faith: choosing a text, interpreting and applying it, telling stories from contemporary life, reaching out to those in need, and sending forth in mission. Ancient rhetoric taught as much; the preacher's ethos or character is discerned through everything that is said.[10] In a more technical way of thinking, testimonies are personal narratives of experience of God. People have occasionally poked fun at the stereotypical "three points and a poem," yet the poem often served an unacknowledged purpose as testimony. Anna Carter Florence says in *Preaching as Testimony*: "A sermon in the testimony tradition is not an autobiography but a very particular kind of proclamation: the preacher tells what she has seen and heard in the biblical text and in life, and then confesses what she believes about it. . . . There is no proof for testimony other than the engagement of a witness. . . . One can only believe it or reject it."[11]

The word that David J. Lose prefers is *confession*. He uses it to describe the nature of Christian speech about one's deepest convictions in a postmodern context: "Christianity exists solely by confession, the conviction and assertion of revealed truth apart from any appeal to another criterion; we live, that is, always by faith alone."[12] The purpose of confession within the sermon is to say fresh words that "actualize the text and offer it to the community to be appropriated through the power of the Holy Spirit."[13] Lose identifies features of confession that resonate with New Testament understandings of testimony:

- Confession involves perceiving God's work most clearly revealed in the cross and resurrection, and finding Christ in situations that resemble both, especially places of weakness and brokenness rather than what the world takes to be places of strength or glory.[14]
- It implies invitational rhetoric that offers but does not impose an alternative worldview and creates a "relationship of mutual regard and reciprocity"; it invites the hearer to appropriate "the Christian identity and pattern of meaning offered" without demanding a particular response.[15]
- Confession offers a communal identity as "followers of the crucified and risen Lord rendered in the New Testament."[16] What God has accomplished in the cross and resurrection is "not principally to persuade us of something, but in response to our desperate need";[17] thus preachers might opt for confession and witness as opposed to argument and persuasion.
- Sermons as confession offer, first, "patterns for making meaning of the world (participation)"; second, critical space and distance (distanciation); and third, the opportunity through the Holy Spirit to enter Christian identity for themselves (appropriation).[18]

A sermon on Romans 8:28 ("We know that all things work together for good for those who love God") might therefore proceed, first, by questioning how this statement is true for those who suffer, probing several unsatisfactory possibilities; second, by considering the passage through the lens of other biblical texts and the preacher's experience; and third, by appropriating Paul's confession as one's own.[19] Lose's three-stage movement has a natural affinity with the movement of narrative from conflict to resolution, or the movement of thesis-antithesis-synthesis, or the movement of law to gospel. For him confession leads to confession, or reaffirmation of faith.

Confession or testimony is a purpose of the entire sermon, that is, to bring forward biblical and contemporary witness to God in a manner that invites faith. As a subform of preaching, testimony is (1) words reflecting experience of conversion or other encounters with God that may include doubt or apparent absence of God but that ultimately attest God's saving faithfulness, (2) words that offer the experience of various people, the preacher, or God and that are addressed to people or God, (3) words affirming the words and actions of the triune God in history, especially in the cross and resurrection, (4) words of the above sorts that go beyond teaching and are spoken with intensity of feeling and passionate belief, and (5) noncoercive words designed to invite listeners to cruciform living at the dawn of a new age.

Testimony in Practice

Put Testimony in the Mouth of Jesus

The Bible offers example of testimony from God. There is nothing to prevent us from using testimony as John Knox did in the mid-1500s, placing it in the mouth of Jesus Christ, in this case in response to the first temptation offered him by Satan to change stones into bread (Matthew 4:1-7). Once again, one may need to read this aloud to facilitate comprehension:

> The very life of man consists in God, and in His promises pronounced by His own mouth. . . . And although all creatures in earth forsake him, yet shall not his bodily life perish till the time appointed by God approach. [The testimony of Christ begins here, but Knox does not make this clear until the second paragraph below:]
> "For God has means to feed, preserve, and maintain, unknown to man's reason, and contrary to the common course of nature. He fed His people Israel in the desert forty years without the provision of man. He preserved Jonah in the whale's belly; and maintained and kept the bodies of the three children in the furnace of fire. Reason and the natural man could have seen nothing in these cases but destruction and death, and could have judged nothing but that God had cast away the care of these, His creatures, and yet His providence was most vigilant toward them in the extremity of their dangers from which He did so deliver them, and in the midst of them did so assist them, that His glory, which is His mercy and goodness, did more appear and shine after their troubles than it could have done if they had fallen in them. And therefore I measure not the truth and favor of God by having or by lacking of bodily necessities, but by the promise which He has made to me. As He Himself is immutable, so is His word and promise constant, which I believe, and to which I will adhere, and so cleave, whatever can come to the body outwardly."

In this answer of Christ we may perceive what weapons are to be used against our adversary the devil, and how we may confute his arguments.[20]

Suggestions for Creative Adaptation

In addition to being a fine example of testimony, Jesus' words here are also a superb summary of the doctrine of God's providence. Presumably any of the key doctrines of the faith could be shaped as testimony, whether placed in the mouth of Christ or someone else.

The words attributed here to Christ are not words that he literally said in the Bible, but they are words consistent with what he said and presumably does say through the Holy Spirit in any age. His words anticipate his death and resurrection ("to which I will adhere, and so cleave, whatever can come to the body outwardly"). Testimony appropriately speaks of the heart of the faith; thus in practice similar ways can be sought to link to it. As with other proclamation subforms, the links can also be provided later in the same sermon.

By way of critique, this sermon does not identify that Christ is speaking until after he has finished his testimony. Whenever there is the possibility of listener confusion, there is the danger of miscommunication. In actual delivery Knox might well have said something beforehand to alert the hearers. Or perhaps his hearers initially thought these words of testimony were his own, as in many ways they also were.

Offer Contrasting Testimonies

Preaching can offer models of testimony for hearers to practice, and Calvin does so first critiquing the testimony given by some and then more substantially offering the right kind of testimony to give, the one an improvement on the other:

> In order to profit better by this passage, let us weigh well what Job says. "Although what remains here," he says, "may be worn away after my skin, yet shall I see my God." This is not believing in God only because he causes the earth to produce corn and wine, as we see many brutish persons who have no taste or feeling that there is a God in heaven unless he feeds them and fills their bellies. When they are asked, "Who is God?" they answer, "He is the one who nourishes us." It is true that we surely must understand the goodness and the power of our God in all the benefits which he bestows upon us, but we must not stop there. For, as I have already said, our faith must rise above all that can be seen in this world.
>
> And so, let us not say, "I believe in God, because he sustains me, because he gives me health, because he nourishes me." But let us say, "I believe in God, since already he has given me some taste of his goodness and of his

power when he cares for this body which is only corruption. In that I see that he declares himself Father, in that I subsist by the power of his Spirit.

"But I believe in him alone, since he calls me to heaven, since he did not create me like a bull or an ass to live here some space of time, but he has formed me in his image in order that I may hope in his kingdom to be partaker of the glory of his Son. I believe that daily he invites me there, in order that I may not doubt that when my body shall be cast into the sepulcher, that it will be there, as it were, annihilated, nevertheless it will be restored at the last day. And that meanwhile my soul shall be in safekeeping and secure, when after death God will have me in his protection, and that even then I shall contemplate better than I do now the life which has been acquired for us through the blood of our Lord Jesus Christ."[21]

Suggestions for Creative Adaptation

This passage catches fire even on the page. The term *plain style* is often associated with the Puritans and Calvin. Calvin himself looked for means whereby to increase the interest of dense material in this sermon on a tough subject, why bad things happen to good people. He puts his testimony in the form of a conversation, mirroring conversation in his text from Job. As noted earlier, preachers can look to the form of their biblical texts to help shape sermon passages arising out of it.

Calvin's passion and pace increase in the latter half of the above excerpt. His proclamation becomes more fulsome, as indicated by his use of parallel structures, long sentences made up of short clauses that contribute to a breathless quality, and urgent tone. All of this also adds interest to his material. In composing proclamation of any sort, it is good to pay attention to sound, perhaps speaking the sermon as one writes it.

Calvin intentionally models testimony for his people, frequently saying, "I believe. . . ." It is not enough, he says, to say God is good in relation to physical things; we must testify out of our faith and speak to matters of the soul. He uses words that any one of the congregation might say, in his time or ours, because they form an effective summary of the faith. They proclaim the heart of the gospel.

Suggest Testimony that Others Might Give

Henry Ward Beecher (1813–87) preached the following sermon on "I was spared" (Ezekiel 9:8) in which he offers a sample testimony for someone to say, as a way to encourage its practice:

I do not believe there is an old woman in earth, living in the most obscure cot in England, and sitting this very night in the dark garret, with her candle gone out, without means to buy another—I do not believe that old woman would be kept out of heaven five minutes unless God had something for her to do on earth; and I do not think that yon gray-headed man now would be preserved here unless there was somewhat for him to do. Tell it out, tell it out, thou aged man; tell the story of that preserving grace which has kept thee up till now. Tell to thy children and to thy children's children what a God he is whom thou hast trusted. Stand up as a hoary patriarch and tell how he delivered thee in six troubles, and in seven suffered no evil to touch thee, and bear to coming generations thy faithful witness that his word is true, and that his promise cannot fail. Lean on thy staff, and say ere thou diest in the midst of thy family, "Not one good thing hath failed of all that the Lord God hath promised." Let thy ripe days bring forth a mellow testimony to his love; and as thou hast more and more advanced in years, so be thou more and more advanced in knowledge and in confirmed assurance of the immutability of his counsel, the truthfulness of his oath, the preciousness of his blood, and the sureness of the salvation of all those who put their trust in him. Then shall we know that thou art spared for a high and noble purpose indeed. Thou say it with tears of gratitude, and we will listen with smiles of joy—"I was left."[22]

Suggestions for Creative Adaptation

In some ways this whole passage is Beecher's testimony, yet by speaking for the "aged man," he adds interest and makes plain that he models what others might say. Some preachers today might be reluctant to speak with such confidence concerning the situation of the woman or the man he names here, yet he does what proclamation does; he speaks with confidence out of his own faith without proof, and he brings certainty to those seeking it. Preachers today need to find their levels of comfort, their range of styles, yet at the same time be challenged to move beyond their comfort zones. What may stop us from speaking confidently about God's purposes for all?

Speak of Coming to Faith

One stereotype of testimony is stories of conversion. They nonetheless can have considerable power. Here is the personal testimonial of Charles Finney (1792–1875) about his decision to accept Jesus Christ, which came in the midst of one of his sermons:

Many persons . . . seem not to believe what God says, but keep saying, *If, if, if* there only were any salvation for me—*if* there were only an atonement provided for the pardon of my sins. This was one of the last things that was cleared up in my own mind before I fully committed my soul to trust God. . . . I was on my way to my office, when the question came to my mind—

What are you waiting for? You need not get up such an ado. All is done already. You have only to consent to the proposition—give your heart right up to it at once—this is all. Just so it is. All Christians and sinners ought to understand that the whole plan is complete—that the whole of Christ—His character, His work, His atoning death, and His ever-living intercession— belong to each and every man, and need only to be accepted. There is a full ocean of it. *There* it is. You may just as well take it or not. It is as if you stood on the shore of an ocean of soft, pure water, famishing with thirst; you are welcome to drink, and you need not fear lest you exhaust that ocean, or starve anybody else by drinking yourself. You need not feel that you are not made free to that ocean of waters; you are invited and pressed to drink— yea, to drink abundantly! This ocean supplies all your need. You do not need to have in yourself the attributes of Jesus Christ, for His attributes have become practically yours for all possible use.[23]

Conversion stories can also be about others. Dwight Lyman Moody (1837–99), a founder of the YMCA and the Moody Bible Institute, was col- loquial in his manner of preaching and employed many stories. He tells a lengthy story of a woman out West who came to him after a prayer meet- ing and pleaded with him to ask her husband, a judge, to come to Christ. Moody reluctantly agreed and, rather than argue with the judge, who deemed him a fool, only asked him to communicate with him when he came to Christ. A year and a half later the judge came to him and told of his wife going off to a prayer meeting one night, how his thoughts turned to God, and how he found himself in prayer. Moody relates the story in the judge's words:

"I said, 'O God, teach me.' And as I prayed, I don't understand it, but it began to get very dark, and my heart got very heavy. I was afraid to tell my wife when she came to bed and I pretended to be asleep. She kneeled down beside that bed and I knew she was praying for me. I kept crying, 'O God, save me; O God, take away this burden,' but it grew darker, and the load grew heavier and heavier. All the way to my office I kept crying, 'O God, take away this load of guilt.' I gave my clerks a holiday, and just closed my office and locked the door. I fell down on my face: I cried in agony to the Lord, 'O Lord, for Christ's sake, take away this guilt.' I don't know how it was, but it began to grow very light. I said, I wonder if this isn't what they call conversion. I think I will go and ask the minister if I am not converted. I met my wife at the door and said, 'My dear, I've been converted.' She looked in amazement. 'Oh it's a fact, I've been converted!' We went into the drawing-room and knelt down by the sofa and prayed to God to bless us." The old Judge said to me, the tears trickling down his cheeks, "Mr. Moody, I've enjoyed life more in the last three months than in all the years of my life put together." If there is an infidel here—if there is a skeptical one here, ask God to give wisdom to come now. Let us reason together, and if you become acquainted with God the day will not go before you receive light from Him.[24]

Each of the above styles tends toward the grand in passion and energy. Here is a testimony in the moderate style. Episcopal priest Fleming Rutledge demonstrates in a beautiful way that testimonies of coming to faith do not have to involve dramatic conversion in order to be powerful:

> When I was a child in Franklin, Virginia, my aunt, Mary Virginia, lived nearby. There is very little to tell about her in worldly terms. Unlike my father (her brother) she left me very little trace in the history of our town. She did not leave me any money or silver or jewelry. This is what she left me: she left me Jesus. That was her legacy, which explains why I love her memory so much. It gladdens me this morning to remember how she used to call Jesus "the Master" as she told me stories about him. I always associate the term with her. It is nice to think how clear she was about what it meant. For her, and for the little girl at her knee half a century ago, there could be no doubt: Jesus was not a master; he was *the* Master.[25]

Suggestions for Creative Adaptation

Testimony of faith experience and of people coming to faith is popular in much preaching through the ages, in hagiography or the stories of saints, in the lives of denominational leaders or pioneers of movements, and in the lives of ordinary church members. Some stories have lasting significance in being about the authors of certain testimonial hymns, like John Newton, author of "Amazing Grace," whose prayer for mercy in the throes of a storm at sea marked the beginning of his faith; or Sarah F. Adams, whose "Nearer, My God, to Thee" came to her while lying awake in the middle of the night; or Horatio Gates Spafford, who wrote "It Is Well with My Soul" after financial ruin and in faithful response to hearing of the deaths of his children at sea. In the Methodist tradition, Sunday evening services were often devoted to testimonials as a way "to equip the saints for the work of ministry, for building up the body of Christ" (Ephesians 4:12).

Conversion stories of both the dramatic and the nondramatic variety are obvious testimonies to use. The most famous is Paul, who told of his conversion, notably in Galatians 1:11-24. Philippians 3:4-17 does not identify a particular moment of conversion but nonetheless stresses a complete change of life, and an ongoing process of being transformed in Christ's death and resurrection (3:10-11). In numerous places Paul uses accounts of his suffering to "boast" in giving praise to God, at greatest length in 2 Corinthians 11:16–12:10.

Other ages used conversion stories effectively—perhaps they were better evangelists—even as some preachers overused them. On the negative side, these stories may communicate that the only way to faith is through sudden, dramatic experience, which some denominations maintain in pointing to a specific moment of being born again. These days, when some people come to church with no background in it, stories of preachers being converted may be incorrectly heard to imply that a call to faith is the same thing as a call to ordered ministry.

The stories of Beecher and Moody's judge can be retold today. They need a little freshening as simple as, "I came upon an old story that still has power." Rutledge's beautiful story is important, first, because it is the story of a woman (too often omitted in history) and, second, because it is the testimony that anyone might give in recalling a key person in the faith journey. The purpose of her telling this story was to bring attention not to herself but to God, and to bring to the minds of her congregation those who were instrumental in leading them to Christ. To hear her aunt speak of Jesus as "the Master" is intimate. Preachers might be more intentional about soliciting stories from the congregation of how people came to faith or were nurtured in it.

Give Testimony to God's Authorship of Particular Events

Testimony can also be less direct, reading God into stories when the key person may not have been aware of God. This powerful testimony was preached by Hugh Reed, an outstanding preacher in Toronto. He gives it in the moderate style of narrative:

Allan (not his real name) came to me at my previous church in Hamilton, wanting to be baptized. He was a child (or victim) of the "me decade" and felt compelled to leave home and family to find himself and, of course, lost himself, becoming a stranger to himself and the world, wandering the streets of East Vancouver trapped in a world of drugs. One night he managed to get off the street for a night in one of the shelters. He crashed into the bunk, staring up at the ceiling, listening to the groans, and trying not to be overcome by the odours of the strangers in the bunks around him. He didn't know where he was, he didn't know who he was, but he wanted it to be over with and he considered how he might take his own life.

He was shaken out of his thoughts when someone came in and called out a name from another world.

"Is Allan Roberts here?"

That had been his name once but he hadn't heard it for some time. He hardly knew Allan Roberts anymore. It couldn't be him being called.

The caller persisted, "Is there anybody named Allan Roberts here?"

No one else answered so Allan took a risk, "I'm Allan Roberts (or used to be)."

"Your mother's on the phone."

My mother, no, you've made a mistake. I don't know where I am, how could my mother know where I am?

"If you're Allan Roberts, your mother's on the phone."

Unsure what to expect, he went to the desk in the hall and took the receiver. "Allan," it was his mother, "it's time for you to come home."

"Mom, I don't know where I am, I have no money, you don't know what I'm like. I can't go home."

"It's time for you to come home. There's a Salvation Army officer who's coming to you with a plane ticket. He's going to take you to the airport to get you home."

She couldn't trust him to send him the money or the ticket; he'd use it to buy drugs. She hadn't known where he was, she just called every shelter and hostel for months until she found him.

He went home and, supported and loved by his mother, who had never ceased to know him though he had forgotten himself, and influenced and inspired by the faith that had sustained his mother's hope and love, he began attending church services and one day he came to my office seeking to be baptized. I had the additional pleasure of later marrying Allan and then baptizing his first child.

He did not find his own way to my office. . . . A path, not of his own making, [was] made by the love that found him, that knew him better than he knew himself, and invited him to "follow me."[26]

Suggestions for Creative Adaptation

Some stories need to be retold just as they are, and this may be one of them. It is about a particular event in someone's life. One could do similar things with stories from the news, even at the national level, in which one perceives the action of God. To have the story function as testimony, one needs to do as Reed has done: God's role in the story needs to be clearly identified; otherwise Reed's story is primarily a testimony not to God but to motherhood, coincidence, or whatever. Simply by adding to the story that it was Jesus Christ who called Allan with the words *follow me* secures the story as an action of God, the same God whom we know in faith, who seeks the lost and brings them home, even via the cross.

Be Candid about One's Faith

The great Lutheran preacher Joseph Sittler (1904–87) once confessed from the pulpit that his faith was not as robust as that of some people, comparing himself to Moses looking into the promised land:

As your preacher this morning, it is only honest to say that I have never known fully that kind of life within the full, warm power of that faith for whose declaration I am an ordained minister. . . . [But] is the opulence of the grace of God to be measured by my inventory? Is the great catholic faith of nineteen centuries to be reduced to my interior dimensions? Are the arching lines of the gracious possible to be pulled down to the little spurts of my personal compass? Is the great heart of the reality of God to speak in only the broken accent that I can follow after? No. That ought not to be. Therefore, one is proper and right when he sometimes talks of things he doesn't know all about. In obedience to the bigness of the story which transcends his own apprehension, one may do this.[27]

H. Beecher Hicks observes that we are all in bondage to certain responsibilities and identifies his garments of ordination as his chains in the sermon "The Preacher's Predicament":

> I'm walking in my chains. I'm not what I ought to be.
>   I'm not what I'm going to be, but thank God, I'm not what
>   I used to be.
> I'm walking in my chains, but I walk by faith and not by sight.
> I'm walking in my chains. But I still believe that "The steps of
>   a good man are ordered by the Lord: and he delighteth in his
>   way" (Psalm 37:23).
> I'm walking in my chains, but I believe John was right: "If the
>   Son therefore shall make you free, ye shall be free indeed"
>   (John 8:36).
> I'm walking in my chains, but I still believe then Lord is the
>   Spirit: and where the spirit of the Lord is, there is liberty
>   (2 Corinthians 3:17).
> I'm walking in my chains, and if I stumble or if I fall, God
>   promised to send angels to bear me up in their hands lest I
>   dash my foot against a stone (Psalm 91:12).
> I'm walking in my chains, and I'm walking up the rough side
>   of the mountain, and I'm doing my best to make it in.[28]

Suggestions for Creative Adaptation

To what degree is personal self-disclosure appropriate in a preacher's testimony? The guidelines here are the same as apply to other stories about oneself: distinguish between public stories and stories that are private and belong in a counseling session. Avoid stories that put oneself in too positive a light and seem boastful or proud (like the Pharisee's words against the publican). In other words, don't make yourself the hero of a story. Is it acceptable to testify to something that God has done in one's life and attribute it to an anonymous someone else in order not to appear to be the hero?

Possibly, if one has already told a story about oneself and one needs to keep self-references to a minimum. Generally, however, if told effectively, testimony makes God the hero, not the preacher. Also avoid those stories that cast into question the character or office of the preacher; for instance, there is no room in most pulpits for a preacher who no longer believes in the power of prayer.

Self-disclosure and vulnerability are important. Sittler discloses that others seem to have greater faith than his own, and Hicks says that at times he feels chained to the responsibilities of his calling. Many members of the congregation would respond well to such testimony because it reflects their experience and invites engagement with both the preacher and faith. Both testimonies invite faith. Sittler testifies that he relies on the "bigness of the story" that transcends his experience, and Hicks speaks of the liberty he has found in following the Son of God. They both offer the right kind of balance between vulnerability and confidence, weakness and strong faith, cross and resurrection. These testimonies could easily be quoted directly in a sermon. Both use a heightened style, yet Hicks uses a collage of Bible verses to give structure. Preachers might ponder the Bible verses they might use to frame and assist their testimonies.

Give Testimony through Conversation with God

Testimony may also be addressed to God, as in the following Christmas sermon by James A. Forbes of Riverside Church in New York:

When I was writing this sermon, it was as if Jesus came to me and said, "You're talking about me as the Hero of Bethlehem. Jim, what do I mean to *you*? Not what shall you preach to the people—what do I mean to you?" And I found myself answering him, "Jesus, I'm not just preaching about you. You're my ideal. I don't know anybody in the world or beyond the world who challenges me as you do. Jesus, I'm impressed by your integrity. I am impressed with your power, your vision, your love, your peace, your discipline, your courage, your faithfulness; and in the moments when I'm not watching myself, I find myself thinking, 'To be like Jesus—oh, how I long to be like him!'"

I said, "Jesus, not only are you my ideal, but you are my deliverer. There have been so many times when in the midst of my struggles between hope and fear you've come to me and released me from my guilt about things that I have done. You've come to me, and you've lifted me—how many times!—out of depression. You've helped me overcome long periods of meaninglessness, and when I'm scared, you come to me and say, 'Be not afraid; lo, I am with you.'"

I said to Jesus, "Jesus, not only are you my ideal, not only are you my deliverer, but you're my Lord. I'm willing to bet my life that you are Lord of history—that the way the whole, created scheme of things turns out will hinge on what you do. Jesus, you're my Lord because I'm willing to take my cues from you. I'm willing to take orders from you. I'm willing to receive encouragement from you. I'm willing to participate with you in this cosmic battle between the kingdoms. Jesus, I have confidence in you; my hope rests in you. You are my hero; you are my leader. And I'm going to stick with you."

Christmas is going to leave us behind. But if Jesus goes ahead of us, if Jesus leads us, we'll make it all right.[29]

Suggestions for Creative Adaptation

Testimony thus far has been addressed to the church. Another kind of testimony is addressed to God and typically involves confession of faith, doubt, or sin. The narrator alone may speak, as in nearly all of the testimonial psalms; or both the narrator and God, as in Psalm 81, "I hear a voice I had not known: / 'I relieved your shoulder of the burden'" (vv. 5c-6; a literary device also found in Isaiah 40–52). Even when biblical testimony is addressed to God, the narrator intends it to be overheard, and this is the case with Forbes. He uses conversation, yet speaks for all listeners and in effect invites all into the conversation.

Though the scenario Forbes paints is fictitious in point of fact ("it was as if Jesus came to me"), it is nonetheless a true portrait of his faith and confidence in Jesus Christ, and of the gospel in general. He does not use this testimony to obtain acceptance of the doctrines he espouses, but uses it invitationally to disclose his faith ("I'm willing to bet my life that you are Lord of history"). This stance gives permission to demur. He is not saying, believe exactly the way I believe, and of course, this invitational stance is an obvious strength of testimony in our postmodern era.

A preacher today could simply quote Forbes or adapt his words so that they become one's own (with appropriate citation in the notes), or one could compose a new testimony using his method. Forbes used three aspects of Jesus' nature to structure his testimony: my ideal, deliverer, and Lord. Few people could listen to him and not have their faith kindled by the Spirit.

Closing Remarks

The preacher has several options concerning testimony. It can be offered in a sermon by a Bible character (e.g., "Ruth says . . ."), a contemporary person ("A teenager says . . ."), an entire congregation ("We say . . ."), even a nation ("The country says . . ."), or God. Testimony can be words that people actually said, or words we attribute to people who give due honor to the gospel. Such modeling helps strengthen the faith of all Christians.

A further challenge for preachers concerning testimony might be this: every time God is mentioned, at least consider adding an adjectival phrase in praise of God, for example, "God, whose love knows no beginning or end, will uphold you." Even two or three small additions of this sort in a sermon can give important witness.

CHAPTER THIRTEEN
Prayer

Prayer is speech addressed to God. As a subform of the sermon, prayer marks a time when the preacher shifts from addressing the people to speak to God. It may take place at any time in the sermon. Unlike prayer in the worship service itself, there is no call to pray. The prayer just starts, and thus in practice it is often the preacher's prayer overheard. It is part of the sermon fabric and not separate in any way, and there is no amen to mark its close. It is like a dramatic aside in theater, and the address simply shifts back to the people. The act of calling upon God in this manner is a way to offer thanks or petition for help, yet it is also a way to proclaim the gospel. Though addressed to God, it proclaims several things about God: the identity of Jesus Christ and the Holy Spirit, the creating and saving nature of God, the names of God, and the actions of God in history—God is vitally concerned about human need, God may be counted on, whatever the need, and God is a partner in this preaching venture. Prayer is an elevated form of teaching. Even as prayer has content that says something, so too the subform itself, the act of praying, says something. Within the sermon it witnesses that the preacher believes in God, it shows what the preacher believes, and it proclaims God's presence as the recipient of the prayer even in this moment of preaching. More than this, prayer gives voice to the Spirit. If we follow Paul in Romans 8:26, the Spirit "intercedes" for us and teaches us "how to pray as we ought."

Prayer as a subform may occur anyplace in the sermon, early or late, except at the very beginning or end, where it would be considered outside the sermon itself. It is not to be confused with a prayer of invocation or illumination common in many churches before the reading of Scripture or the sermon, in which one asks God to bless the reading of the word and the receiving of it. Nor is it to be confused with an ascription of glory or doxology that may immediately follow the sermon.

Prayer in itself has several genres that may appear in the sermon: invocation (a call upon God with earnest desire for wisdom, help, or mercy), confession, thanksgiving, intercession or petition for others, and praise. Biblical prayers contain complaint, condemnation, or imprecation (as in many of the psalms of lament), affirmations about the character and faith of those who pray, nonverbal elements (as in the Spirit's "sighs too deep for words" of Romans 8:26), and glossolalia (1 Corinthians 14:14-15). The Epistles sometimes contain prayer, as in the prayer of thanksgiving early in both Romans (1:8-15) and Colossians (1:9-12); and at two places in Ephesians (1:17-19; 3:14-21). Prayers also inevitably teach, and sermonic prayer, like any other, can instruct about communicating with God: it can recall what Jesus did in prayer, taught about it, and affirmed about its effect.

In the history of preaching, prayer is a distinctive subform, though it is less common than the other subforms we name here. Nonetheless, it has potential for creative proclamation.

Prayer in Practice

Use Prayer as a Way to Glorify God in the Sermon

Augustine is partway through his sermon when he turns to offer a brief prayer:

> The Lord Jesus willed to be man for our sakes. Do not disdain His mercy. Wisdom came to dwell upon earth. *In the beginning was the Word, and the Word was with God, and the Word was God.* [The prayer begins:]
> O Food and Bread of the angels! From Thee do the angels have their fill, by Thee are they satisfied, and they are not surfeited. From Thee they have life; from Thee they have wisdom; from Thee they have happiness. Where is it that Thou art for my sake? In a little hovel, in swaddling clothes in a manger. And on account of whom?
> The Ruler of the stars nurses at a mother's breasts, He who feeds the angels![1]

Suggestions for Creative Adaptation

By turning to speak directly to God in Christ, Augustine communicates the intimacy of his relationship with him and of Christ's relationship to the people in the act of preaching. The prayer briefly lifts up two names of Christ, Food and Bread of the angels, and Augustine briefly develops their significance. As already noted, in contemporary preaching we do not make enough use of the many names of God and Jesus (numerous websites are devoted to listing them), all of which can help to communicate and praise God.

Place a Prayer of Illumination in the Midst of a Sermon

French bishop Jean-Pierre Camus (d. 1652) preached a sermon on the death of a colleague, and partway through, perhaps seven minutes into the sermon, he offered a particularly eloquent prayer that we would call a prayer of illumination, the sort of prayer that in some traditions today would precede either the reading of Scripture or the sermon itself. In this sermon he prays this after he has already discussed his text, namely, "His lamps are entirely fire and flames (Song of Songs 8:6)," and after he has held up the life of the deceased as an example of God's light:

Ah, dear friends, would that I could give forth such light and such ardor!—I, who am forever deficient in warmth and lacking in beams of clarity!

O Eternal Father, Father of all light, even light without shadow, you who are the very essence of flame and the all-consuming fire—you who make your presence known in burning bushes, in radiant mountains, in fiery furnaces—enlighten my darkness, fill with your warmth the coldness of my nature!—but let me be not like the sun which while heating all else stands too distant to know its own warmth, not like a torch giving light to others while remaining in darkness to itself, not like a lute which can fill all ears with harmony yet cannot hear itself! Grant rather that the words of fire which you speak to others through my mouth may equally bring enlightenment and warmth to my inmost being, that as a torch-bearer bringing light to others I may likewise enlighten myself. May true warmth be kindled in me by the fervor of this meditation.

O Son Divine, O Admirable Jesus, who came to bring new fire to the earth, who fanned so devoutly the feeble fires of human hearts that you never ceased to sigh in your labors even unto death on the Cross, impart to me the merest spark of your sacred fire that I may kindle the hearts of all before whom I speak today.

O Holy Spirit, living source of light and of love, of fire and of Charity, grant that your spiritual anointing may pour life into this discourse on fire and on Charity. Shine forth your light upon our senses and spread your love throughout our hearts.[2]

Following this prayer, the sermon continued for more than an hour.

Is it too wild a notion for our time that we might offer a prayer of illumination in the midst of a sermon? Perhaps, yet one advantage of hearing examples from preaching history is that our imaginations are stretched about what might be possible. Such a prayer might seem too self-focused, in asking for illumination only for the preacher, or it might be exactly the kind of prayer that all of the gathered people should put on their lips as the preacher offers it. In adapting it for our time we might change *I* and *my* to *we* and *our*. In addition to speaking to God, this prayer teaches the congregation concerning the nature of the preaching event, that one expects it to be divinely inspired, a word from God to the gathered community. This prayer also proclaims who God is in the three persons of the Trinity. Were we to offer such a prayer, we might consider doing what Camus did; he structured it around the imagery of his biblical text.

Put a Prayer on the Lips of the People

John-Baptist Massillon, one of the great French preachers of the early 1700s, preached a sermon that lasted at least two hours. In the last third, several brief invocations are used, usually at the end of lengthy paragraphs:

> If it is thus, who, O my God! will be entitled to salvation?
> . . . Thou alone, O my God! knowest who belong to thee.
> . . . O God! where are thy chosen? And what a portion remains to thy share!
> . . . What do I know, O my God? I dare not with a fixed eye regard the depths of thy judgments and justice.[3]

As part of a rousing climax in the final paragraphs, Massillon inserts a longer prayer that he asks his congregants to say to themselves:

> Then, my dear hearer, if you wish to be of the small number of true Israelites, say, in the secrecy of your heart, [the prayer begins:] It is thou alone, O my God! whom we ought to adore. I wish not to have connection with a people who know thee not; I will have no other law than thy holy law; the gods which this foolish multitude adores are not gods: they are the work of the hands of men; they will perish with them: thou alone, O my God! art immortal; and thou alone deservest to be adored. The customs of Babylon have no connection with the holy laws of Jerusalem. I will continue to worship thee with that small number of the children of Abraham, which still, in the midst of an infidel nation, composes thy people; with them I will turn all my desires toward the holy Zion. The singularity of my manners will be regarded as a weakness; but blessed weakness, O my God! which will give me strength to resist the torrent of customs, and the seduction of example. Thou wilt be my God in the midst of Babylon, as thou wilt one day be in Jerusalem.
>
> Ah! the time of the captivity will at last expire; thou wilt call to thy remembrance Abraham and David; thou wilt deliver thy people; thou wilt transport us to the holy city; then wilt thou alone reign over Israel and over the nations that know thee not. All being destroyed; all the empires of the earth; all the monuments of human pride annihilated, and thou alone remaining eternal, we then shall know that thou art the Lord of hosts, and the only God to be adored. [The prayer has ended.]
>
> Behold the fruit which you ought to reap from this discourse; live apart; think without ceasing.[4]

Suggestions for Creative Adaptation

Massillon's prayer moves the sermon to an emotional and doxological pitch, inspired by the Spirit. The prayer is part of the sermon itself, not added to the end. The various invocations that a preacher may use can communicate God's intimate involvement with the preaching event: if God can be addressed in its midst, God is indeed present, and both the preacher and the congregation are accountable before God in the preaching moment. Additional purposes are served by Massillon's invocation: he uses it to sketch the kind of life that one ought to live and the promises of God concerning the end times.

Massillon's words are geared to the needs of his congregation and times. He preaches on Jesus' words about the many people with leprosy in Israel who were not cleansed when Naaman the Syrian was cleansed (Luke 4:27). If preachers were to adapt what he does, they might ask, To what kind of prayer does my text or sermon lead me? Might it be effective to include this prayer as part of the sermon, something that one places on the lips of the people as Massillon does?

Allow Prayer to Include Other Genres

The following prayer by Henry Ward Beecher around the 1870s arises out of and includes stern exhortation:

> Oh! careless sinner, mad sinner, thou who art dashing thyself now downward to destruction, why wilt thou play the fool at this rate? . . . Be wise, I pray thee. Oh, Lord, make the sinner wise; hush his madness for awhile; let him be sober and hear the voice of reason; let him be still and hear the voice of conscience; let him be obedient and hear the voice of Scripture. "Thus says the Lord, because I will do this, consider thy ways." "Prepare to meet thy God." "Oh, Israel, set thine house in order, for thou shalt die and not live." "Believe on the Lord Jesus Christ and thou shalt be saved." I do feel I have a message for someone tonight.[5]

Suggestions for Creative Adaptation

This type of prayerful pleading with a sinner—some people might feel it is threatening—was more typical in an earlier age when the minister's authority (and every other kind of church authority) was less challenged than it is in many places today. Similar prayer might still be used, though one's congregation may offer some parameters about what will be the most effective ways to address seekers and the hard of heart. This prayer could be very effective serving as a model for corporate change in the church, a plea for God's help to remove complacency concerning violence, economic injustice, or racial isolation, for example.

Adapt a Famous Creed, Prayer, or
Hymn to Serve as a Prayer

In a sermon published in 1881 Washington Gladden, a founder of the Social Gospel movement, turned Jesus' prayer, "Thy kingdom come" (Matthew 6:10 KJV), into contemporary proclamation:

"Thy Kingdom come!" the strong of faith were crying; and a Presence unseen by men stood among the prisoners in the dungeons that were festering dens of disease and vileness, and laid its gentle hand upon these hapless children of the evil, and lifted the weight of hate and scorn that made their lot so desperate, and sought to lead them forth to ways of purity.

"Thy Kingdom come!" God's children cried; and the victims of insanity saw a beam of hope through the mental darkness in which they were walking, and found themselves no longer chained and scourged like criminals, but gently led and kindly treated.

"Thy Kingdom come!" was the voice of millions who groaned in slavery, and of millions more who remembered their brethren in bonds as bound with them; and one by one the fetters have snapped asunder,—the strong shackles of the Roman law, the wounding cords of feudal villenage, the degrading toils of British slavery, the prescriptive manacles of Russian serfdom,—until even in our own land, and in our own day—

Our eyes have seen the glory of the coming of the Lord, as he comes proclaiming liberty throughout the land to all the inhabitants thereof.

"Thy Kingdom come!" the children of light were pleading; and the hierarchies that sought to confine the thought of men were baffled and paralyzed, and the Bible was unchained, and the ways that lead to the mercy-seat were opened to the feet of all penitent believers.[6]

Suggestions for Creative Adaptation

In this case three words of the Lord's Prayer are put on the lips of various groups of people as a means to call for social justice and liberty now. The prayer becomes a refrain for the congregation to take with them into the world, "Thy Kingdom come!" The passage ends by extolling the value of these prayers in effecting the coming of God's realm. Prayer is answered. Preachers need to imagine the result of prayers in their prayers as Gladden has done; he shows what the kingdom will look like in relation to the worst human suffering of his time.

The Holy Spirit teaches us to pray (John 14:26; Romans 8:26-27), and holy fire is communicated through this prayer, as through the entire sermon, giving the people the faith and wisdom to call for God's help anew. Such prayer in the sermon is proclamation; God speaks it in demonstration of the Spirit.

Preach an Entire Sermon as a Prayer

Walter J. Burghardt, S.J., at the height of the Vietnam War in 1969, preached an entire sermon as a prayer at a special Mass for peace at St. Patrick's Cathedral in New York City. Here is his opening:

> Lord, we come before you a motley lot. We are wonderfully and dreadfully different. Some of us are violent in our convictions; others could not hurt a fly. Some of us have years behind us; the lives of others lie ahead. Some of us are knowledgeable, others quite ignorant. Some of us are happy people; others have forgotten how to laugh. Some of us have money; others must pinch and squeeze, beg and borrow. Most of us are white; only a few, I'm afraid, are black or yellow or brown. Some of us are settled, have it made; others are restless, trying to make it. Some of us have killed; others have seen death only on TV.
>
> Some of us are awfully sure—about the war, about its morality or immorality, about ROTC and Dow Chemical, about American idealism or imperialism, about napalm and defoliation; others are confused, uncertain, torn this way and that, even anxious.[7]

Here is his concluding paragraph:

> That is why, Lord, in much hope and some fear, I am asking the men and women in front of me to take a first step toward peace. I am asking each to clasp the hand of the person next to him or her, the person on each side—whoever that person is, whatever he or she looks like—without even looking. I want them, by this act of faith and trust and love, to cry out to you that we do want peace, that we want to begin it here and now, that we see in each human being a brother or sister and the image of your Christ, that our hearts are open to them as never before, that we are ashamed and weep for our crimes against them. And I am asking them to sit like that, hands clasped, for one minute . . . at peace.[8]

Suggestions for Creative Adaptation

Prayer is an unusual and daring approach for an entire sermon, yet desperate times require fervent prayer. Nearly every paragraph has a reminder that Burghardt addresses God. Presumably the hearers are not just listening and responding to him; many are making his words their own in the manner of prayer. There is a danger that such use of prayer may seem manipulative, which is why he takes exceptional care to include and acknowledge in the opening minutes nearly every perspective on war that might be held in the diverse gathering of people before him, that all may feel free to enter his words. He offers no judgments on people with perspectives that may differ from his own; he simply urges all to follow Christ's way of peace.

Use Prayer to Emphasize God's Victory over Trouble

C. L. Franklin, the father of soul singer Aretha Franklin, used this prayer in the midst of a joyous celebration in the latter third of a sermon:

> O Lord.
> You know when I think about
> the world that we live in,
> when I think about
> how frustrated many of us are,
> when I think about how
> neurotic we've become,
> when I think about
> how tension-filled
> many of our lives are,
> when I think about
> how afraid of life
> so many of us are,
> why,
> I think about what Jesus said,
> to those fearing
> and doubting disciples.
> "Peace be unto you."
> Great God.[9]

Trinette V. McCray slips into invocation and prayer in a natural way in the second paragraph below of a sermon preached to ministers:

> As we are forming ourselves as ministers of the gospel, it behooves us to take a moment to allow God's light from God's lighthouse to shine upon us and come into our hearts and into our souls, and to shine into the deepest corners of our existence, which we keep hidden from others but can't keep hidden from the Lord. [The prayer begins:]
>
> Shine on, Lord. Shine your light into our closets, shine into our cupboards, and if you find anything that shouldn't be, O Lord, call it to our attention and let your Holy Spirit call it from our lips. We want to be right. We want to be saved. We want to be whole. [The prayer ends.]
>
> We have to watch out because we are walking in ordered steps.[10]

Suggestions for Creative Adaptation

Prayer as a subform of preaching is prayer inserted into the midst of another conversation. Warren H. Stewart Sr. says,

---

It is not unusual to experience a black preacher having a first-person conversation with God about his or her calling to the ministry on Mt. Horeb in front of a burning bush or concerning his or her retreat to the desert because no one is standing up for Jehovah amidst the confrontations with the prophets of Baal or dealing with a courageous testimony before the Nebuchadnezzars of society who have warned all believers in Jehovah to be still or be killed or describing a clandestine confession before the Master somewhere on the outskirts of Jerusalem at midnight.[11]

Prayer can readily be placed on the characters in any biblical text as a way to add both interest and proclamation.

Christians might do well to implement prayer as a part of any conversation, as a form of witness that lets others outside the faith overhear how believers talk to God. Sermons can model the practice.

CHAPTER FOURTEEN
Nurturing Exhortation

W e now come to a form of exhortation that belongs specifically to gospel proclamation, namely, nurturing exhortation or encouragement. It may involve admonishment or petition, yet unlike stern exhortation (chapter 11), it has the warmth, comfort, and love associated with God as a nurturing parent, Savior, Counselor, and friend. This kind of exhortation in history tends to be for the entire community of faith. It is for those who already believe and are in the journey for the long haul, which may be part of the reason it is less stern and has less of the already-too-late urgency that marks condemnation and it's-not-too-late-but-hurry urgency of stern exhortation. At its best, nurturing exhortation does what it talks about. It both urges change and lovingly bestows the means. It cannot be conceived separate from the action of God through the Holy Spirit, who is the source of all love.

What distinguishes nurturing exhortation from teaching? Exhortation of this sort is an emotionally charged form of expression designed not to inform but to change how the listener behaves or is disposed toward things. Again, solid teaching must precede it, as C. H. Spurgeon explained:

> There must be instruction, otherwise the exhortation to believe is manifestly ridiculous, and must in practice be abortive. . . . Exhortations, entreaties, and beseechings, if not accompanied with sound instruction, are like firing off powder without shot. You may shout, and weep, and plead, but you cannot lead men to believe what they have not heard, nor to receive a truth which has never been set before them.[1]

There is no absolute distinction between teaching and any of the forms of proclamation. In subforms we can speak only of a dominant form and function. However, the main difference is that nurturing exhortation *does* what it refers to; it offers the help from God that teaching only talks *about*.

Nurturing Exhortation in the New Testament

Stern exhortation and nurturing exhortation are not lexically separate in the New Testament, yet there is foundation for a distinction there. As we have seen, *parainesis* has as its meaning "stern warning, admonishment," or "rebuke," and it is used in public affairs, debates, or situations that call for some urgency. It is imperative with little warmth, is impersonal and public, and is usually made by someone in authority.

The other more common New Testament word for *exhortation*, *paraklēsis* (verb *parakaleō*) means "admonition, petition, encouragement, urging, comfort," or "request." Both words urge parties to act, but *paraklēsis* assumes a close relationship between parties. Where *parainesis* is imperative and directive, *paraklēsis* is subjunctive and suggestive. It suggests intimacy and implies the need for an urgent decision in relation to some blessing. *Paraklēsis* carries no specific theological meaning, but it is associated with gospel and an invited response "to the proclamation of salvation."[2] It tends to be ascribed to God and God's agents,[3] and appropriate response is typically expressed in mutuality and community.[4] One commentator says, "The paracletic chain of concern extends from God (in Christ; 2 Cor 5:20), through the proclaimer, to the people . . . and causes ever anew the acceptance and propagation of the exhortation."[5]

Paraklēsis has the same root as the English word *Paraclete* (*Paraklētos*) or Holy Spirit, and in the New Testament means "helper, comforter, advocate," or "legal advisor." The term is used in 1 John 2:1 to describe Jesus Christ interceding to the Father on behalf of his followers, and in John's gospel as a title for the Holy Spirit, the Advocate (e.g., 14:16, 26). Nurturing exhortation is inseparable from the action of the Holy Spirit.

Nurturing exhortation is associated with "the *consolation* of Israel" (Luke 2:25, my italics on all vv. in this paragraph); with "the God of steadfastness and *encouragement*," who enables harmonious living (Romans 15:4-5); with the "God, who *consoles* the downcast" (2 Corinthians 7:6-7); with "*encouragement* in Christ" (Philippians 2:1); and with God making an "*appeal* through us" as "ambassadors for Christ" (2 Corinthians 5:20).

Exhortation and Calvin's Uses of the Law

Calvin helps make a further distinction. Stern exhortation is related to his first use of the law. Nurture may be compared to Calvin's third or principal use of the law. Calvin has three uses of law. First is law in its punitive function that warns, teaches, convicts, condemns, and corrects. Second is civil law that protects and deters. Third is excitement to obedience; "by frequent meditation upon it [one may] be aroused to obedience, be strengthened in it, and be drawn back from the slippery path of transgression."[6] Calvin explains the third use in relation to David,

The prophet [David] proclaims the great usefulness of the law: the Lord instructs by their reading of it those whom he inwardly instills with a readiness to obey. *He lays hold not only of the precepts, but the accompanying promise of grace, which alone sweetens what is bitter.* For what would be less loveable than the law if, with importuning and threatening alone, it troubled souls through fear, and distressed them through fright? David especially shows that *in the law he apprehended the Mediator, without whom there is no delight or sweetness.*[7]

The principal and third use of the law applies specifically to those who have already accepted Jesus Christ.[8] It is not to frighten but to equip. It is not an impossible burden but a demand accompanied by the very means of accomplishing it, the "sweetness" and "promise of grace" and an inward "readiness to obey."[9] In and through this law David meets his God. As one commentator has said, this use of the law is "an indicator of the character and activity *of God.*"[10]

Calvin's third use is law that humans must obey, but it is gospel in a larger sense typically overlooked—it is always present alongside grace. The third use of the law cannot be conceived apart from grace. *The third use is the law together with its fulfillment, who is Jesus Christ.* Paul speaks to this when he says of the obedience of the Philippians, "It is God who is at work in you, enabling you both to will and to work for his good pleasure" (Philippians 2:13). Luther also speaks of Christ as the sweetness that comes with the law: "Hunger is the best cook. As the earth thirsts for rain, so the Law makes the troubled heart thirst for Christ. To such hearts Christ tastes the sweetest; to him he is joy, comfort and life."[11] Still, Luther was concerned (prophetically, it would appear) that the third use of the law would be conceived apart from grace, and hence that it would fall back into works righteousness, which is the reason he rejected it.

Nurturing exhortation functions as Calvin's third use of the law in being law, yet it is law accompanied by its accomplishment, law united with grace and power, law in the presence of Jesus Christ through the power of the Holy Spirit. The third use of the law is proclamation of the gospel in that through it, the identity and activity of God are made known in Christ. It both highlights and enacts in the Spirit the help a person receives in obedient living. It proclaims by encouraging, informing, nurturing, supporting, and reminding people of who they are in Jesus Christ. It leaves listeners not dependent upon their own strength, but with a sense of mission in which Christ is a constant companion who gives them his powers. The direction given and the ability to meet it in Christ are one.

Johannes Thomas says the same thing of *paraklēsis*; it is in tension with law "because in God's economy of salvation, his saving mercy itself has become the norm of action. Thus the exhortation to serving love is the concrete application of the gospel."[12]

He says that in the pastoral letters *parakaleo* "is a word that brings about repentance . . . and a new attitude . . . is always in accordance with doctrine . . . and . . . is in harmony with the office bearer who has been called to comfort."[13]

A good example of what this sounds like is Paul's words in 2 Corinthians 8:5-9:

> They gave themselves first to the Lord and, by the will of God, to us, so that we might urge Titus that, as he had already made a beginning, so he should also complete this generous undertaking among you. Now as you excel in everything—in faith, in speech, in knowledge, in utmost eagerness, and in our love for you—so we want you to excel also in this generous undertaking. I do not say this as a command, but I am testing the genuineness of your love against the earnestness of others. For you know the generous act of our Lord Jesus Christ, that though he was rich, yet for your sakes he became poor, so that by his poverty you might become rich.

In practice, nurturing exhortation commonly comes toward the end of a sermon and in line with a mentoring stance; the people are spoken to or treated as "friends." In terms of my Four Pages of a sermon, which move from law to gospel or trouble to grace, Pages One and Two are trouble in the biblical text and our world, and Pages Three and Four are grace in the biblical text and our world. Stern exhortation is closely related to law and mission, hence is most fitting in the first half on Page Two. Nurturing exhortation is closely related to both gospel and mission, and is thus typically found on Page Four. However, mission in this location at the end of the sermon is already altered by the gospel that previously has been proclaimed. Mission is no longer a command but an invitation because in doing what is required by the law, one is met by one's Lord and Savior; one's faith and strength are renewed. Thus mission is something one longs for and is excited to engage in and through the Spirit. It is mainly good news.

Nurturing Exhortation in Practice

Exhort Christian Virtues

Augustine is an older man when he uses nurturing exhortation to encourage people to be loving in his sermon "On Charity." The flames of this passage leap off the page:

> [Charity] endures in adversity, is moderate in prosperity; brave under harsh sufferings, cheerful in good works; utterly reliable in temptation, utterly

openhanded in hospitality; as happy as can be among brothers and sisters, as patient as you can get among the false ones. Acceptable in Abel through his sacrifice, safe in Noah through the flood, absolutely faithful in the wanderings of Abraham, as meek as meek can be in Moses amid insults, so mild and gentle in David's trials and tribulations. In the three young men it innocently awaits the kindly fires; in the Maccabees it bravely endures the ferocious fires. Chaste in Susanna toward her husband, in Anna after her husband, in Mary apart from her husband. Free in Paul for rebuking, humble in Peter for listening and yielding. Human in Christians for confessing, divine in Christ for pardoning. . . . [Augustine here quotes 1 Corinthians 12:31–13:8.]

What a great thing this charity is! The soul of the scriptures, the force of prophecy, the saving power of the sacraments, the fruit of faith, the wealth of the poor, the life of the dying. What could be more magnanimous than to die for the godless, what more kindly than to love one's enemies? It is the one thing that is not cast down by another's good fortune, because it is not jealous. It is the one thing that is not pricked by a bad conscience, because it does not act boastfully. It is steady and unshaken amid reproaches, it is well disposed in the face of hatred; calm in the face of anger, innocent in the midst of intrigues, groaning in the midst of iniquity, breathing again in the presence of truth. What could be braver than charity, not for paying back insults, but for not caring about them? What could be more faithful, not for vanity, but for eternity?[14]

Gregory the Great uses nurturing exhortation in preaching on the value of hope and repentance. He exhorts the congregation to Christian living by holding up four people from the Bible as examples of people who received divine help in their trouble:

I look at Peter, at the thief, at Zaccheus, at Mary and I see in them nothing else but examples put before our eyes of hope and repentance. Perhaps someone has fallen away from the faith: let him look on Peter, who wept bitterly for his fainthearted denial. (Matt. 26:75.) Perhaps someone else has been enflamed with malice and cruelty against his neighbor: let him look on the thief, who even at the moment of death attained the reward of life by repenting. (Luke 23:43.) Perhaps another, enflamed by avarice, has plundered a stranger's goods: let him look at Zaccheus, who if he had stolen anything from anyone restored it fourfold. (Luke 19:8.) Perhaps another yet, being enkindled with the fire of lust, has lost the purity of his body: let him look on Mary, who purged away the love of her body by the fire of divine love. (Luke 7:47.)

See how almighty God puts before our eyes at every turn those whom we ought to imitate; he provides at every turn examples of his mercy. . . . God freely forgets that we have been guilty; he is ready to count our repentance as innocence. If we have become dirtied after the water of salvation, let us be born again from our tears. . . . Our Redeemer will solace our fleeting sorrows with eternal joy, he who lives and reigns with the Father in the unity of the Holy Spirit, God for ever and ever. Amen.[15]

Suggestions for Creative Adaptation

Both of the above passages come at the end of the sermons that have already plainly preached the gospel. These passages echo and reinforce it by way of identifying mission.

Augustine uses the word *charity* instead of *love*. He cites "God is charity" (1 John 4:8, 16 KJV) and points to God as the source of all charity, empowering the congregation to daily acts. Short phrases, parallel structures, and repeating words contribute to an energy that he uses to encourage and excite his people. Gregory focuses on other virtues, hope and repentance, and plainly offers both by the end. Our age might do well to recover from previous centuries something of the practice of preaching the virtues, exhorting people in nurturing ways to practice them.

Both preachers use a catalogue of biblical characters to help structure their exhortations, Augustine uses Abel, Noah, Moses, the three young men, the Maccabees, Susanna, Anna, Mary, Paul, and Peter. Gregory uses Peter, the thief, Zaccheus, and Mary, and he claims God's role both in setting before them these examples of the biblical people and in bestowing grace through them. In using so many examples these preachers offer different biblical perspectives, different people with whom to identify and find encouragement. It is an excellent way of dealing with characters in one's biblical text and connecting with the larger biblical story.

Exhort Communal Identity and Social Justice

John Winthrop's famous 1630 sermon was written and preached as he traveled to the New World aboard the ship *Arbella*, headed for the Massachusetts Bay Colony. It contains a fine example of nurturing exhortation that follows upon an initial warning of a "shipwreck" if they fail to follow God:

> Now the only way to avoid this shipwreck and to provide for our posterity is to follow the Counsel of Micah, to do Justly, to love mercy, to walk humbly with our God (Micah 6:8), for this end, we must be knit together in this work as one man, we must entertain each other in brotherly Affection, we must be willing to abridge our selves of our superfluities, for the supply of others' necessities, we must uphold a familiar Commerce together in all meekness, gentleness, patience and liberality, we must delight in each other, make others' Conditions our own, rejoice together, mourn together, labor, and suffer together, always having before our eyes our Commission and

Community in the work, our Community as members of the same body, so shall we keep the unity of the spirit in the bond of peace (Eph. 4:3), the Lord will be our God and delight to dwell among us, as his own people and will command a blessing upon us in all our ways, so that we shall see much more of his wisdom, power, goodness, and truth than formerly we have been acquainted with, we shall find that the God of Israel is among us, when ten of us shall be able to resist a thousand of our enemies, when he shall make us a praise and glory, that men shall say of succeeding plantations: the Lord make it like that of New England: for we must consider that we shall be as a City upon a Hill, the eyes of all people are upon us.[16]

The following sermon comes again from the French preacher Jean-Baptiste Massillon (1663–1742):

If each of you were, according to the advice of the apostle, to appropriate a certain portion of your wealth toward the subsistence of the poor . . . , then should we quickly see the number of the afflicted to diminish: we should soon see renewed in the church that peace, that happiness, and that cheerful equality which reigned among the first Christians: we should no longer behold with sorrow that monstrous disproportion, which, elevating the one, places him on the pinnacle of prosperity and opulence, while the other crawls on the ground, and groans in the gulf of poverty and affliction: no longer should there be any unhappy except the impious among us; no secret miseries except those which sin operates in the soul; no tears except those of penitence; no sighs but for heaven; no poor, but those blessed disciples of the gospel, who renounce all to follow their master. Our cities would be the abode of innocence and compassion; religion, a commerce of charity; the earth, the image of heaven, where, in different degrees of glory, each is equally happy; and the enemies of faith would again, as formerly, be forced to render glory to God, and to confess that there is something of the divine in a religion which is capable of uniting men together in a manner so new.

But, in what error here consists, is, that, in the practice, nobody considers charity as one of the most essential obligations of Christianity.[17]

Suggestions for Creative Adaptation

Winthrop's concluding passage about the "City upon a Hill" is the most quoted of his writing. He sets before his Puritan companions a vision of what it means to be a community of Christ ("our Community as members of the same body"), reinforcing what he has said earlier in the sermon that the well-off had a holy duty to care for the poor.

Massillon gives a similar passionate vision of social justice based on John 6:1-14, the feeding of the five thousand, in which Jesus distributes the bread to those gathered. Massillon laments the disparity between rich and poor and the impression of God it presents to the world.

Even in postmodern times, preachers do well to urge visions of unity, especially in the face of dire circumstances like the terrorist attacks of 9/11. The encouragement of the gospel toward communal response is important to remember. Winthrop's example of leadership might encourage preachers to contemplate what issues go unaddressed in their churches and settings, what kind of vision does the church offer to the local or larger community, what kind of a caring place does it want to be, and what kind of a testimony to who God is does it want to offer? What image of the community might be appropriate to exhort?

Winthrop's metaphor of a shipwreck is powerful (especially if one is actually preaching on a ship at sea, as he is). The entire passage is even longer than cited above. It is one sentence and may well be a candidate for the longest sentence in an English sermon. The point for us is not the period but what the punctuation marks help to signal: the breath units, the pace, and the emotion behind the words. This passage stands in contrast to the rest of the sermon, giving testimony to a passion in preaching not commonly associated with Puritans.

Exhort to Communicate the Power of God

Horace Bushnell was convinced that preachers should preach about God not in abstract ways, but as power for salvation:

> If, then, we are to succeed [in the effort to complete our Christian life] we must succeed in God's way, and take the method he himself has chosen. The main difficulty with us is to entertain a thought so high as that he is concerned to have Christ formed in us. . . .
>
> Or if you have looked despairingly upon this work, believe in God, and your despair will give way to courage and hope. Doubtless your sins are strong and you are weak, but Christ is here, and Christ is not weak. Had you looked upon the vast abyss of chaos, without form and void and covered with the pall of darkness, you might well have despaired. . . . But when you behold the divine Spirit hovering over it, and the divine Word by whom the worlds were made descending into it, to form it into shapes that dwell in the eternal mind, then surely there is hope even for chaos. So also in the wilder chaos of sin that reigns within you. There is nothing, in fact, that you can undertake with so great hopefulness and assurance as a victory over yourselves, if only you can believe in God. It is nothing then but to have Christ formed in you, and that is a work to be done not as much by you as by him.
>
> Still, there is something for you to do. And here we may sum up all in one comprehensive rule, viz., that you are to present yourselves to Christ in just that way that will most facilitate his power over you and in you.[18]

Suggestions for Creative Adaptation

In 1847 Horace Bushnell wrote his radical book *Christian Nurture*, in which he advocated educating children for the faith through nurture, not through emphasis on dramatic conversion experience. It is no surprise, therefore, that in his preaching we find Spirit-inspired examples of nurturing exhortation. What can be instructive is his emphasis on not preaching God as ideas, moral principles, or doctrines, but preaching Christ as the power of God in believers' lives.[19] Preachers might adapt Bushnell, finding their own ways to make his point, urging people to rely on the power of God and thereby experience a relationship with Jesus Christ.

Build Up the Value of Each Individual

One of the great preachers in the first half of the 1900s was George Campbell Morgan, who spent much of his vocation as minister of Westminster Chapel in London. The following exhortation is the final paragraph in the sermon "The Power of the Gospel":

> I would like my last note in this address to be an appeal to any man who is face-to-face with this problem [of not believing in this gospel]. My brother, God believes in you, and that in spite of all the worst there is in you. God knows the worst in you, better than you know it yourself. Yet he believes in you; and because he believes in your possibility, he has provided righteousness in and through the Son of his love, and by the mystery of his passion. I want you to respond to God's faith in you by putting your faith in him and demonstrating your faith in him by beginning with the next thing in obedience. You also will find that the gospel is the power of God; not theory, nor inference, but a power, that coming into the life, realizes within the life and experience all the things of holiness and of righteousness and of high and eternal beauty.[20]

San Francisco preacher Valerie Brown-Troutt preached a fine sermon on Hadassah (Esther), addressing the situation of people who lack parents or who have had bad things happen to them. Here are her last two points:

> 4) Believe you have a purpose in life. God does not create junk, people do. God did not create you for nothing. You matter and were born with a purpose of God. Everyone has value and God-given purpose. Hadassah became the savior of her people! Say this right now: God created me. God is my heavenly parent. I do have a purpose! I was given life to live in this world for good. The world will be a better place because I am alive. I will fulfill my God-given purpose.

5) Believe the opportunities we have are more important than the ones we wish we had. We can trust God to weave together the events of life for our best, even though we may not be able to see the overall pattern. Hadassah did not know why her biological parents had to die. I don't know and cannot really tell you why anyone's biological parents are dead. But I can tell you that God cares and is looking to bless your lives.[21]

Suggestions for Creative Adaptation

It is hard to imagine a congregation that would not catch fire with such loving proclamation as these preachers demonstrate. Morgan speaks God's love in Christ directly into the lives of doubters before him, and he makes use of Bushnell's principle: he speaks of God not as abstraction but as the power to save. Bushnell provides an excellent example of Calvin's principal use of the law that comes accompanied by the grace to fulfill it.

The device used by Brown-Troutt can be an effective way to involve the listeners: half of the sermon is devoted to a list of five principles that may offer courage; each point is exhortation in the sense of implying *epiclesis*, the bestowal of the Spirit, for each is nurturing and invokes God's help. She also invites the congregation to repeat a short phrase to ensure their involvement.

When a preacher chooses exhortation to build people up, the focus needs to stay on God as the provider because in so doing, one offers the ongoing resources of God—one offers God—to the individual, not just praise and encouragement. Moreover, no one does praiseworthy acts without God's assistance. In the process of adaptation, preachers might want to make the link to the gospel even more evident here by drawing on the cross and resurrection. Alternatively, nurturing exhortation can feed into or lead from explicit treatment of the gospel elsewhere in the sermon.

It is also hard to overestimate the importance of preachers offering nurturing exhortation of this sort. It is not just for the doubting or self-doubting. It is for everyone listening, for we all go through such periods in life. What a difference it makes that the preacher believes and cares enough to reach out in this way, for that person can be a true pastor.

Both excerpts are written in moderate style. Preachers might experiment in style, making sure to be true to themselves so as to ensure authenticity. More passion does not mean being less authentic, but to be sure, one might seek out a trusted coach, perhaps someone with a speech, drama, or music background, to help rehearse new styles.

Improvise on Other People's Exhortations

One of my graduate students, Basil E. Coward, has spoken of the importance of improvisation and has noted it in published sermons.

Charles G. Adams was probably not the first person to make the kind of series that he has used throughout his ministry and that we find here:

Bad religion takes life. Good religion gives life.
Bad religion destroys folk. Good religion liberates folk.
Bad religion talks about national defense. Good religion talks about national purpose.
Bad religion divides folks. Good religion unifies folks.
Bad religion makes you hate folks. Good religion makes you love every-body.
Bad religion segregates. Good religion integrates.
Bad religion stays in church. Good religion breaks loose in the world.
Bad religion hangs around the altar. Good religion walks down the Jericho Road.[22]

Clarence James uses the same paradigm of bad and good religion to make his series:

Bad religion makes churches museums of pious saints. Good religion makes churches hospitals for sick sinners.
Bad religion wants a full church. Good religion wants a pure church. . . .
Bad religion stays inside the church waiting to be seen and thought well of. Good religion ventures out on the Jericho road seeking to save wounded humanity. . . .
Bad religion is class conscious and color struck, brags about how many big-time members we got, how many doctors, lawyers, professors, and business owners. Good religion is not a club that looks at class . . . "Whosoever will, let them come."[23]

Another instance of improvisation on a common paradigm is found in Teresa Fry Brown, who calls on hearers to "just preach":

Just preach—until the lonely feel loved, the homeless have homes, and the naked are clothed.
Just preach—until everyone everywhere knows that Jesus is love and God is alive.
Just preach—until the wicked cease from troubling and the weary are at rest.
Just preach—believing that the Lord will make the way.
Just preach—until everyone knows that Satan is a liar.
Just preach—letting nothing and nobody turn you around.
Just preach—with the courage of your convictions.
Just preach—speaking the truth in love.
Just preach—always faithful to the text.
Just preach—living out the Word.
Just preach—without apology or manipulation.

Just preach—until Pentecost is every day.
Just preach.[24]

Vashti M. McKenzie ends her sermon this way:

Palm-tree preachers will be needed to preach the gospel of the living God.
Preach until cold hearts are warmed.
Preach until sinners are saved.
Preach until joy breaks out.
Preach until hatred subsides and love arrives.
Preach until the gates of hell shake off their hinges.
Preach until sickness gives up.
Preach until limbs strengthen.
Preach until cancer goes into remission.
Preach, palm-tree preacher! Preach!
If they won't let you preach in church, preach on the sidewalk.
If they won't let you preach on the sidewalk, preach in the bathroom.
If they won't let you preach in the bathroom, preach in the bedroom.
If you've got two people, preach.
If you've got seven people, preach.
If you've got seventy people, preach.
If you've got seven thousand, preach.
But for God's sake, preach![25]

Suggestions for Creative Adaptation

Each of the four examples above is nurturing exhortation: the first two exhort good religion; the second two, the importance of preaching. The latter paradigm could be used by anyone, but it may have particular importance for women preachers whose voices often have been silenced.

There is value in seeing how different preachers use the same paradigm. They can be models in our improvisation practices. Many preachers are reluctant to borrow in this way, yet it is to be encouraged, as we will explore later in chapter 19. One might say in the bulletin, "A portion of today's sermon dealing with____was inspired by____."

Each of the above is known as a set piece. Set pieces are passages that can be used in nearly any sermon and may be repeated many times over the course of one's preaching life. It can be one of a memorized group that can be drawn upon at will in preaching on nearly any text or theme. The preachers who are best at speaking at the spur of the moment are the ones who have prepared most beforehand. As Mark Twain is reported to have said, "It takes about three weeks to prepare a really good extemporaneous speech."

Exhort Seekers: Introduce People to God

Fleming Rutledge often uses nurturing exhortation at the end of her sermons, and in this one, on "I believe; help my unbelief!" (Mark 9:24), she confronts listeners with the living Christ:

> Dear people of God, through the retelling of this story, Jesus Christ the Lord has arranged a meeting between himself and you. It is out of my hands. It is in his hands. He is not waiting for you to figure it all out. He is not lying back observing to see if you have enough faith. He is not withholding his approval pending your successful application. He has come forward to meet you, in word and sacrament. The only person with perfect faith is Jesus Christ. When he says, "All things are possible to him who believes," there is a sense in which he speaks first of himself. It is by *his* faith, *his* faithfulness, that we receive our own faith. There is no foundation more certain than that. . . .
>
> Are you a believer or an unbeliever? No matter how troubling your doubts may be, no matter how inadequate you may feel compared to others, no matter how often you may feel that you are just going through the motions, you would not be here this morning if you did not have some germ of faith, however small. That is the Holy Spirit of Christ already at work in you. It is enough. Trust the Lord of faith to make it grow. We need never say again, "I wish I had more faith." Instead, we have the infinite privilege of praying, "Lord, I believe; help thou mine unbelief," knowing that in the fullness of time he will speak the word that will banish the enemy forever. Amen.[26]

Suggestions for Creative Adaptation

Rutledge uses exhortation here as a means to proclaim the gospel and to call people to respond with their lives to the word. The flame one experiences in this passage is like the Christ candle in some churches that burns strong and steady. Elsewhere in this sermon she recites Edmund Steimle's advice to preachers not to preach about faith: "If you want your child to make friends with the child down the street, you can talk to her about friendship till you're blue in the face and it gets you nowhere. What you can do is arrange a meeting where friendship might occur. Or it might not. It is no longer in your hands."[27] She does what Steimle recommends; she introduces people to their Savior in an intimate and loving way. Her exhortation performs the gospel that she speaks about.

In adaptation, one might pay particular attention to how she accomplishes this meeting. She shows us Jesus, mentions his hands, names where he may be found, in the sacraments, and lets us hear him speak his own encouragement, "All things are possible to him who believes." She then leads even the most doubting person, the one with the least faith, into Jesus' care.

Concluding Remarks

Nurturing exhortation is largely encouragement to greater faith or better living. It is not just the preacher who offers this, for it is associated with God's power and help already at work in the hearers even in the moment the words are uttered. In encouraging faith, the Spirit acts to bestow it. The speaking of it is also its realization in Christ. Such nurture is meant to build up the entire community, and it is offered with an intimacy that may reach and touch each person listening. Exhortation of this sort serves mission in that every sermon should have some desired outcome by way of congregational response, and that response is Spirit-led.

CHAPTER FIFTEEN
Proclamatory Statements

P roclamatory statements consist of words of love and grace spoken by God or in the name of God directly to the community of faith. They are short pronouncements or sentences that represent what lies at the core of the gospel. As a subform of preaching, these statements are bundled, coming as multiple declarations in the same passage. They are human-directed, God-uttered speech used in a variety of ways that have the eventful quality of revelation, encounter, and meeting one's Savior. They are an unconditional declaration of good news from God, and as Paul says, they are "the power of God for salvation to everyone who has faith" (Romans 1:16). They are words that do things, performing what they speak about, as in Isaiah 55:11:

> So shall my word be that goes out from my mouth;
> it shall not return to me empty,
> but it shall accomplish that which I purpose,
> and succeed in the thing for which I sent it.

Such speech represents for God's word an immediacy of enactment, as is signaled by Jesus' words, "Today this scripture has been fulfilled in your hearing" (Luke 4:21).

David Lose calls such speech ultimate speech, ultimate language: "A Christian sermon not only needs such moments of declaration, of ultimate speech, but the sermon's center of gravity is located in them."[1] With proclamatory statements, the sermon "grounds its authority in the God who speaks through the texts, and declares that God's promise has, in fact, already been fulfilled in Jesus Christ and so utters it as a present reality for his hearers."[2]

This is the kind of speech discussed earlier, notably at the end of chapter 7. In relation to Forde and Jensen it is first-to-second person, present-tense address. In fact, most Lutheran homiletical discussion of proclamation is limited to individual sentences and does not venture into sustained genres of proclamation. Proclamatory sentences conceived as bundled units may be in direct quotation of Bible texts, paraphrases of those texts, or summary statements of the faith that the preacher composes or adapts from elsewhere and applies to God. The preacher speaks them with a certain degree of intimacy:

1. Some biblical texts contain proclamatory sentences, like Luke 2:10-11, "Do not be afraid; for see—I am bringing you good news of great joy for all the people: to you is born this day in the city of David a Savior, who is the Messiah, the Lord"; or John 11:25-26, "I am the resurrection and the life. Those who believe in me, even though they die, will live, and everyone who lives and believes in me will never die." Such statements are often used as opening sentences in a worship service or as assurances of pardon, and may be found or adapted anywhere in the Bible:

I will be your God, and you will be my people.
I will remember your sins no more.
I love you.
I came for you.
I died for you.
I died your death for you.
In your baptism I claim you.
I will not let you go.
I forgive your sins.
Go and sin no more.
I will wipe away every tear from your eyes.
You are my new creation.
Peace I give to you.
Not as the world gives do I give.
Come to me, all of you that are weary and heavy laden, and I will give you rest.
Take heart! Do not be afraid! Your faith has made you well.
The water I give you is a spring of water gushing up to eternal life.
I am your Shepherd.
Everything that I have is yours.
Let not your hearts be troubled; neither let them be afraid.
Well done, my good and faithful servant.
Whatever you bind on earth will be bound in heaven; and whatever you loose in heaven will be loosed in heaven.
I set you free.
I go to prepare a place for you.
Where two or three are gathered in my name, there I am.
I am with you to the end of the age.
This is my body, broken for you.
This is my blood, poured out for you.

2. The words that one puts into God's mouth can be adaptations of entire texts. For example, the words of many psalms function as testimony, but for emphasis they can be turned into proclamatory sentences,

should one so wish, such that it is no longer the psalmist but Jesus Christ who speaks them directly to us. Thus the Twenty-third Psalm becomes:

> I am your Shepherd, you shall not want.
> I make you to lie down in green pastures; I lead you beside still waters; I restore your soul.
> I lead you in paths of righteousness for my name's sake.
> Yea, though you walk through the valley of the shadow of death, you will fear no evil: for I am with you; my rod and my staff they comfort you.
> I prepare a table before you in the presence of your enemies: I anoint your head with oil; your cup runneth over.
> Surely goodness and mercy shall follow you all the days of your life, and you will dwell in the house of the Lord forever.

A similar alteration may be done with Psalm 139:7-12, or any number of texts, and we again hear the voice of the Good Shepherd speaking proclamatory sentences directed to us. When Christ specifically speaks them to us, we hear them spoken through the filter of the cross and resurrection. For example, the promise "if you make your bed in Sheol, I am there" is fulfilled in Christ's descent into hell:

> Where can you go from my spirit,
>   Or where can you flee from my presence?
> If you ascend to heaven, I am there;
>   if you make your bed in Sheol, I am there.
> If you take the wings of the morning
>   and settle at the farthest limits of the sea,
> even there my hand shall lead you,
>   and my right hand shall hold you fast.
> If you say, "Surely the darkness shall cover me,
>   and the light around me become night,"
> even the darkness is not dark to me;
>   the night is as bright as the day,
>   for darkness is as light to me.

The psalmist's original "Where can I go from your spirit?" has become Christ's "Where can you go from my spirit?" which, for Christians at least, is a natural and fair reading, one that a good preacher will often strive eventually to reach in a sermon without necessarily claiming that the original psalm was speaking of Christ. This functions as an application of the text. In this shift, one has a good example of what Forde means by "doing a text" or what we mean by "doing the gospel" to the people. In truth it is not we who do the doing, for God performs the saving act.

3. The words put into God's mouth can also be words that a preacher hears God say to the specific situation at hand from various places in the Bible. These might sound like,

My table is never too small; there is room for everyone.
   Eat of this bread. There is enough here for all the nations, and it will sustain you to eternal life.
   If you have been rejected, I did not push you away.
   If you are worried about your child in prison, do you not know that I am as present there as anywhere else?

Gospel Considerations

Proclamatory statements are usually first-to-second person, present-tense forms of address that do God's salving acts. Do they have to be first to second person? Ideally yes. There are exceptions:

1. Many indirect statements about God nonetheless can be heard as personal address. John 3:16, "God so loved the world that he gave his only Son," functions in this manner if the hearer hears in it God's "I love you." The same is true of many other core teachings, such as Jesus is Lord (= I am your Lord), Christ is raised from the dead (= I give you my life), and so forth. Since the preacher stands in some way as God's spokesperson, when the preacher proclaims statements like these, tender souls in faith often make the right connection, that God is speaking directly to them.
2. Similarly, words may be addressed to the entire community, yet individuals may experience them to be spoken just for them. Again, direct connection between the individual and God is significant, and the Spirit may establish this at will.
3. Alternatively, teaching claims *about* God's activity in or behind biblical texts may stand as proclamation in some instances. The claim, "Jesus heals the blind man" (Mark 10:46-50), necessarily becomes at some point in the sermon, "Jesus heals today" (= "I am healing you"), otherwise why preach? "God brings Israel to the promised land" becomes the proclamation, "I bring you home."

Of course, God can take any words and use them for proclamation. It is the preacher's duty to assist God in bringing the message home in this manner, from abstract truth to personal encounter. Proclamation is thus simply the sweet sound of the gospel heard as personal address.

At issue with all of the forms of proclamation is the degree to which they in fact express the gospel. The speaker is key. The proclamation at the end of Matthew, "I am with you always," depends on Jesus to be the speaker, not some stalker. The other key is the identity of Jesus beyond the name. He could be anyone, perhaps Wonder Woman or Rambo or some superhero. His name may mean little to some hearers. He is just another Beyoncé Knowles or Matt Damon until he stands before them crucified and risen. The person in the pew must have a clue about who Jesus is in relation to the gospel before such statements can function as proclamation. In other words, proclamatory statements gain their authority in the Spirit when his identity is established: he is the Jesus of history who humbled himself on the cross and rose from the dead to give us life. Only by such confession do proclamatory sentences glow with divine fire that can be received by all who are present.

Proclamatory Statements in Practice

Adapt Words from the Culture to Serve as Proclamatory Statements

Most scholars believe that Paul adapted material from the wider culture when he wrote 1 Corinthians 13, yet in doing so he made it a commentary on Christ, or Christ a commentary on it. A further example of adapting literature to serve proclamation is from the 1300s. *Fasciculus Morum*, a handbook for preachers, quotes these words from Ovid's *Metamorphoses* and encourages preachers to read them "spiritually" in terms of Christ's passion:

> Behold my wounds, which traces are of ancient fight:
> What'er thou hast, I gained it with my blood.
> Behold my wounds, my painful plight.
> All the wealth you own I won in fight.
> I am sorely wounded, behold my skin.
> Dear life, for my love let me now come in.[3]

The author of *Fasciculus Morum*, at the end of the same section, composes his own proclamatory sentences:

> "But truly Christ cancelled this servitude totally when he left his whole body for us on the cross as a charter. For Christ says, 'I am on the cross for you. Why sin? Cease for my sake! Cease, and I give you grace; confess, and I spare your pain.'"[4]

Suggestions for Creative Adaptation

The early and medieval church frequently practiced syncretism, borrowing elements from non-Christian sources and blending them into

Christian understanding and practice. They allowed, for instance, that God had spoken prophetically in the great poets and philosophers of previous ages, or at least that their words at times pointed to the truth of Christ. For them an obvious example was in the fourth of Virgil's *Eclogues* where the story is told of the birth of a boy sent down from heaven who shall bring a reign of peace and put the serpent to death.[5]

We do not need to attribute revelation to cultural sources in order to apply those sources in proclamation to revelation. We could quote a speech from a novel or a movie, provide its context, and say, "In the words of that woman to her son we can hear Christ speaking to each one of us." Words might also be adapted from a song like the hymn "In the Garden," "And he walks with me, . . . and he tells me I am his own," or from a popular song about romance, taking words of love or longing and placing them on God's lips. In other words, the whole culture is fair game, provided that wisdom and discretion are used. Proclamatory statements are just that, sentences or statements; they do not need to be long and they do not need to be numerous, but they do need to be embedded in passages that assure the gospel in order to function as a defining subform in preaching.

Use Proclamatory Statements to Reach Out to the Least

John Wesley used proclamatory sentences to reach out to victims of alcohol among his listeners, people who were commonly refected:

> "Sinners of every other sort," said a venerable old clergyman, "have I frequently known converted to God. But an habitual drunkard I have never known converted." But I have known five hundred, perhaps five thousand. Ho! art thou one who readest these words? Then hear thou the words of the Lord! I have a message from God unto thee, O sinner! Thus saith the Lord, cast not away thy hope. I have not forgotten thee. He that tells thee, "there is no help," is a liar from the beginning. Look up! Behold the Lamb of God, who taketh away the sins of the world! This day is salvation come to thy soul; only see that thou despise not him that speaketh! Just now he saith unto thee, "Son, be of good cheer! Thy sins are forgiven thee!"[6]

John Dobie, a Glasgow preacher in the 1870s, preached a remarkable collection of proclamatory statements in relation to the crucifixion story. He ensures that no matter with whom listeners identify in the biblical story, not one is excluded from grace:

> "Master! surely you do not wish us . . . to offer mercy to the men who bore false witness against thee, and who insisted on thy condemnation and

crucifixion?" "Yes," says Christ, "offer mercy to one and all of them—make no exceptions! Go to the men who arrayed Me in mock royalty, and tell them that if they come to Me, I will array them in robes of linen, clean and white, in 'garments of wrought gold.' Go to the man who plaited the crown of thorns, and put it upon My head, tell him, that if he come to Me, I will put upon his head a crown of glory which shall never fade away. If you find the man who gave Me gall mingled with vinegar, to drink when My thirst was great, tell him, that if he come to Me, I will give him living water, and that the water which I will give him, shall be in him a well of water, springing up unto eternal life. Assure the man who subjected Me to the scourge, and with it tore My flesh, that if he come to Me, 'I will give him My flesh to eat,' and that he shall find 'My flesh to be meat indeed, and My blood drink indeed.' Say to the man who drove the spear to my heart, that I am willing to give him a place in that heart which he pierced, and to fold him to that bosom which he wounded, and that the blood he shed shall atone for the guilt of shedding it. Go even to Pilate, and tell him, that though he condemned Me, *despite My innocence*, I am not willing to condemn him *despite his guilt*, that I am willing to forgive and forget the past, to blot out his iniquity, and to assign him a position of honour and dignity in my kingdom."[7]

Former slave John Jasper put words in the mouth of Christ in the course of his preaching:

You must wait a little. The time is fast rolling on. Even now I hear my Savior saying to his Father, "Father, I can stay here no longer; I must get up this morning; I am going out to call my people from the field; they have been abused and laughed at and been made a scoffing long enough for my name's sake. I can stay no longer. My soul cries for my children. Gabriel, get down you[r] trumpet this morning; I want you to do some blowing. Blow gently and easy at first, but let my people hear your golden notes. They will come when I call."[8]

Suggestions for Creative Adaptation

The hearer would hear Wesley's words, "Cast not away thy hope. I have not forgotten thee," not just as Wesley speaking but as Jesus present in his risen power, offering real hope. In Wesley's day alcoholism was not yet understood as a disease; alcoholics were considered to be reprobates and were judged harshly. Wesley's Methodist organization would have been better equipped than most other institutions of his day to provide the community and spiritual support to help recovering addicts. Preachers might ask, Who in our own community is pushed to the fringes? Might it be good to address proclamatory sentences directly to them, just as Wesley did in his time?

Dobie's piece is compelling and moving because of (1) the beauty of his narrative prose, (2) the boldness and generosity of the words he puts into the mouth of Christ, and (3) the fire of imagination he uses in conceiving to whom Christ might speak. It is good to model for the community Christ speaking to many, whether through the biblical text or not.

In a similar manner John Jasper has Christ speak and ensures that all who are oppressed or abused discover their Savior speaking to them. The significance of this kind of divine personal address at the heart of the gospel cannot be overestimated, and preachers need to be daring in implementing it, not least from the biblical text.

Alter the Words of One's Text to Proclamatory Statements

Karl Barth preached on Leviticus 26:12, in which he takes each of the following three phrases in turn: "And I will walk among you, and will be your God, and you shall be my people." In this extract, he speaks to this process of altering the language of the text to the form of personal address:

> On [God's] authority I may and I must say to you, "Yes, you shall be my people!" Let us hear this assurance as well as the two preceding ones as God's word. Let us take it to heart, let us take it home, and maybe ponder it a while before we fall asleep tonight, "I will walk among you! I will be your God! You shall be my people!"
>
> I am at the end [of this sermon]. I tried to explain this Bible passage as the word of God fulfilled in Jesus Christ. Read and heard, understood and believed in this light, this word radiates infinite power. It then not only says, "I will walk among you," but, "I *walk* among you!" Not only "I will be your God," but "I *am* your God!" Not only "You shall be my people," but "You *are* my people!" Do you sense the power of this Word? The power of him in whom it is fulfilled and becomes a present reality?[9]

Suggestions for Creative Adaptation

Two things happen in the above passage: Barth isolates words spoken by God in his text, and he then makes them present tense and addressed to the people at hand. Arguably in our own texts, God may not literally speak, yet God always speaks to the discerning through the word. In order for a biblical text to function as gospel, it needs to testify to God. God needs to be found doing something in it or in the events behind it, acts that both condemn and free. In composing a sermon, once grace in the text has been located, the preacher can formulate it as a theme sentence, with God as the subject. From there it is not hard to convert this theme sentence into words that God actually says in the sermon as proclamatory gospel statements. Again, they are applications of the text to the gospel; the text leads to them but does not necessarily say them in itself.

Text	Theme Statement	Proclamatory Statement
Ruth 4: Ruth and Boaz	God restores the outcast.	In the name of Christ I restore you.
Isa. 6: Isaiah's call	God gives a new identity.	In the cross you are now mine.
Luke 11:33-36: Letting light shine	Christ lights our lives.	I give you eternal light.
Phil. 2: Christ's self-emptying	God exalts the lowly.	I raise you up with Christ.

A key in the process is to make gospel present tense, something that happens right now in the life of the hearer. Thus with the aid of the Spirit, the gospel is actualized in the life of the hearer.

Combine Proclamatory Statements with Other Genres of Proclamation

John Knox puts words into God's mouth, combining condemnation with various proclamatory statements:

> God speaks to His people; as if He should say, The tempest that shall come upon this whole nation shall be so terrible, that nothing but extermination shall appear to come upon the whole body. But thou My people, that hearest My word, believest the same, and tremblest at the threatenings of My prophets, now, when the world does insolently resist—let such, I say, enter within the secret chamber of My promises, let them contain themselves quietly there . . . and so shall they perceive that My indignation shall pass, and that such as depend upon Me shall be saved.[10]

The next example is from John Watson (Ian Maclaren), the Scottish short story author and preacher. He begins it as a lament for those who die too soon or with talents unrecognized, and he ends with wonderfully hopeful affirmation from Christ:

> [There are those] whose talents have been hid, not by their own doing, but by Providence. They realized their gift: they cherished it; they would have

used it; but for them there was no market. Providence, who gave them wings, placed them in a cage. Round us on every side are cramped, hindered, still-born lives—merchants who should have been painters, clerks who should have been poets, labourers who should have been philosophers. Their talent is known to a few friends; they die, and the talent is buried in their coffin. Jesus says NO. It has been sown for the harvest; it will come into the open and blossom in another land. These also are being trained—trained by waiting. They are the reserve of the race, kept behind the hill till God requires it. They will get their chance; they will come into their kingdom.[11]

In our own day Trinette V. McCray builds from lament to strong proclamation in one of her sermons:

I know what Peter felt like. I know what he felt like out there on the water [Matthew 14:28]. For the past several months, I've had some folks come to me with their winds. Discouraging winds, winds of despair, winds of hopelessness, winds of impossibilities. Winds, blowing winds. Winds, contrary winds, doubtful winds, lying winds, meddling winds, two-faced winds, stab-you-in-the-back winds, smiling-in-your-face-all-the-while-trying-to-take-your-place winds! We can't walk in the deep while we are paying attention to those winds! Jesus says to each of us, "I have ordered your steps. I will keep your feet. I will hold you up. I will still the waters. I will quiet the winds. I will fight your battles. I will keep you from falling." Jesus says, "Come."[12]

Desmond Tutu moves from teaching forgiveness to proclamatory statements at the end of one of his sermons:

To be partakers of the divine nature means we become more and more God-like, treating all with an even-handedness, even those we regard as evil. For you know, even the most evil, the Shipmans, the Saddam Husseins, Bin Ladens—we may not like it—but they remain God's children. This God, who lets God's sun shine on good and bad alike; who makes God's rain fall on all, for all, and we, who want to be God-like, are asked to forgive, even as God has forgiven us in Christ, forgive even that which we consider to be unforgivable.

To be like this God, who gives up on no-one, who loves us, not because we are loveable but that we become loveable only because God loves us, God loves us with a love that will not let us go, a love that loved us before we were created, a love that loves us now, a love that will love us forever, world without end. A love that says of each single one of us: "I love you, you are precious and special to me, I love you as if you were the only human being on earth, I love you and there is nothing you can do to make me love you more because I already love you perfectly."

How incredibly, wonderfully, it is that God says to you, to me: "There is nothing you can do to make me love you less. I take you, I take you very seriously, I take you—you—body and soul, you the visible and the invisible of you, I love you, I love you, I love you."[13]

Suggestions for Creative Adaptation

Each of the above samples moves from trouble to the gospel, which is the natural movement of the faith, from crucifixion to resurrection. One advantage in using this movement within a subform is that the effect of proclamatory statements is heightened by the juxtaposition of the two. Each of the above passages catches fire as the preacher experiences not just the truth of the words in speaking them, but also the joy they are bringing in the moment through the Spirit to needy hearers. Who will easily forget Maclaren's words of promise for those who have died too soon, or the words of assurance to the despairing that McCray puts on Jesus' lips, or the unconditional love powerfully expressed by Jesus in Tutu's sermon? They are as holy fire to us, burning with purity and healing power. Even as Paul carries "the marks of Jesus branded on [his] body" (Galatians 6:17), so too we carry the redeeming words of Jesus branded on our hearts.

Concluding Remarks

To proclaim is a daring act. Spoken in faith in the right setting, the words of proclamation are loving, tender, intimate, powerful words. Their justification, truth, and confirmation are found in relationship to the incarnation, cross, resurrection, ascension, and gift of the Spirit. Of course, any proclamation needs a foundation in solid teaching and should arise out of exposition of a particular text. Preachers thus often need to make a deliberate move from the biblical text at hand to the larger gospel story, connecting the text with Christ. In conceiving what kinds of sentences will work, we might ask, How many ways does God have to say, "I love you"?

Doxology

Doxology is a form of words that offers praise, glory, and honor to God. It moves people to praise and give glory. The Westminster Catechism (Shorter Catechism) says that the "chief end of man"—in other words, the purpose of life—is "to glorify God, and to enjoy him forever."[1] In a similar manner Paul instructs, "Rejoice always, pray without ceasing, give thanks in all circumstances; for this is the will of God in Christ Jesus for you" (1 Thessalonians 5:16-18). The early Christians are characterized by their acts of praise in Acts 2:47. The purpose of doxology in general lies in the fact that God alone is worthy of all thanks and praise. God alone is sovereign. Our postmodern age seems to resent God's sovereignty and tries to limit what God can and cannot do. Nonetheless, we say in faith that only by God's love is creation sustained and Israel delivered, and no more complete statement of that deliverance is found than in the cross.

Doxology in a sermon is proclamation, not just teaching. Its purpose is not primarily to communicate information, although like any of our subforms, it inevitably does this too, in particular about the identity and actions of God. The preacher utters doxological words (1) to honor God on behalf of the congregation and (2) to remind them of God's faithfulness and sustenance in ways that move them to praise. God enables our praise for our enrichment. When we praise God's faithfulness through the cross, God performs renewed trust in that faithfulness within listeners as "a demonstration of the Spirit and of power" (1 Corinthians 2:4). Not that we cause this, in the manner that a coin we put in a candy dispenser automatically produces a chocolate bar. Both Cain and Abel made offerings, both the Pharisee and the publican said prayers, yet all were not received. Still, Christ made an offering on behalf of all that was received. God is affected by our prayers and chooses to be faithful to the promises made in Christ: "I am with you always, to the end of the age" (Matthew 28:20).

Doxology contains movement in two directions. On the one hand, it is a human offering of praise to God; on the other hand, it proclaims to people what God has done and does. Both directions are evident in the inspiring doxology in Jude 24-25: "Now to him who is able to keep you from falling, and to make you stand without blemish in the presence of his glory with rejoicing, to the only God our Savior, through Jesus Christ our Lord, be glory, majesty, power, and authority, before all time and now and forever. Amen." The Bible also says that inanimate objects and creation itself contribute to God's praise,

> The heavens are telling the glory of God;
>> and the firmament proclaims his handiwork.
> Day to day pours forth speech,
>> and night to night declares knowledge.
> There is no speech, nor are there words;
>> their voice is not heard;
> yet their voice goes out through all the earth,
>> and their words to the end of the world. (Psalm 19:1-4)

The heavens, the seas, and the trees sing God's praise in 1 Chronicles 16:31-33. A time is coming when everyone will give praise to God (Philippians 2:9-11). These understandings support doxology.

Many psalms are doxologies (e.g., Psalms 29; 33; 98; 100; 103; 107; 135; 150). Two of the most common doxologies are not directly from the Bible: the *Gloria Patri* from the conclusion to the Athanasian Creed: "Glory be to the Father, and to the Son, and to the Holy Ghost. As it was in the beginning, is now, and ever shall be, world without end. Amen"; and variations on the last verse of "Awake, My Soul, and with the Sun," Thomas Ken's 1674 hymn:

> Praise God, from Whom all blessings flow;
> Praise God, all creatures here below;
> Praise God above, ye heavenly host;
> Praise Father, Son, and Holy Ghost.

Doxology has been a part of preaching since biblical times. As with other forms of proclamation, many expressions of doxology in the history of preaching are remarkable. It is unfortunate that such forms now tend to be found only in African American pulpits; they are biblical and are part of our common past. Some preachers may be reluctant to try doxology because it may sound borrowed. At issue is rediscovering authentic ways to give glory to God and to reclaim the practice of giving praise as a means of proclaiming the gospel.

Doxology in Practice

Use Parallelism and Contrast in Doxology

The following doxological passage is from a Christmas sermon of Augustine. Taken from his opening paragraph, it is a prime example of his use of his rhetorical principle of using contrasting elements and poetic parallelism:

My mouth will speak the praise of the Lord, of the Lord through whom all things have been made and who has been made in the midst of all things; who is the Revealer of His Father, the Creator of His mother; who is the Son of God through His Father without a mother, the Son of man through His mother without a father. He is great as the Day [i.e., God] of the angels, small in the day of men; the Word God before all time, the Word made flesh at a suitable time. Maker of the sun, He is made under the sun. Disposer of all ages in the bosom of the Father, He consecrates this day in the womb of His mother; in Him He remains, from her He goes forth. Creator of heaven and earth, He was born on earth under heaven. Unspeakably wise, He is wisely speechless; filling the world, He lies in a manger; Ruler of the stars, He nurses at His mother's bosom. He is both great in the nature of God and small in the form of a servant, but so that His greatness is not diminished by His smallness, nor His smallness overwhelmed by His greatness. For He did not desert His divine works when He took to Himself human members. Nor did He cease *to reach from end to end mightily, and to order all things sweetly,* [compare Wisdom 8:1] when, having put on the infirmity of the flesh, He was received into the Virgin's womb, not confined therein. Thus the food of wisdom was not taken away from the angels, and we were to taste how sweet is the Lord.[2]

In this next sermon, Thomas à Kempis lists attributes or actions of Jesus in the form of a doxology. This passage from the middle of a sermon is mostly one long sentence. It is easiest to read this antique translation if one at minimum alters the suffix *-est* to be *-s*, thus *loosenest* becomes *loosens*, *breakest* becomes *breaks*, and so on. If one does this, the fire of the passage bursts forth.

O most truly worthy and precious Tree of life, planted in the midst of the Church for the medicine of the soul! O Jesus of Nazareth, Thou that wast crucified for us! Thou loosenest the bands of sinners; freest the souls of saints; humblest the necks of the haughty; breakest down the power of the wicked; comfortest the faithful; puttest to flight the unbelievers; deliverest the pious; punishest the hardened; overthrowest the adversaries. Thou raisest up them that are fallen; Thou settest at liberty them that are oppressed; Thou smitest them that do hurt; Thou defendest them that are innocent; Thou lovest them that are true; Thou hatest them that are false; Thou despisest the carnal; Thou hast regard for the spiritual; Thou receivest them that come to Thee; Thou hidest them that take refuge in Thee. Them that call upon Thee, Thou hearest; them that visit Thee, Thou rejoicest; them that seek Thee, Thou helpest; them that cry to Thee, Thou strengthenest. Thou honorest them that honor Thee; Thou praisest them that praise Thee; Thou lovest them that love Thee; Thou glorifiest them that adore

Thee; Thou blessest them that bless Thee; Thou exaltest them that exalt Thee. On them that look to Thee Thou lookest; them that kiss Thee, Thou kissest; them that embrace Thee, Thou embracest; them that follow Thee, Thou leadest to heaven.[3]

Suggestions for Creative Adaptation

Were a preacher today to adapt Augustine and Thomas à Kempis, one would alter their antiquated language, but continue to use their contrasting elements and parallel structures. One surprising feature of Augustine's passage is the difficulty of its ideas relating to theological controversies in his time—today simpler concepts would be mandatory. Still, one listens because his words are said in musical, impassioned ways; it is almost as though Augustine says, "You need not understand all of this in order to be moved to join with me in giving praise to God." One joins with him in the same way one enters the beat with music. As in fast music, the rhythm and the energy are as important as the content. Thomas à Kempis addresses his doxology to Christ, and it becomes for the congregation an act of overhearing the preacher speak intimate words to his Lord. As such this doxology is also a prayer, yet it is for the sole purpose of praising God, not for the purpose of petition. In other words, subforms blend.

Use Doxology as Faith Summary

Melito of Sardis (d. ca. 180) is author of the second oldest surviving Christian homily outside the Bible. He uses doxology as an impassioned summary of the attributes of Christ:

He [Christ] arrived on earth from the heavens for the sake of the one who suffered. He clothed himself in the sufferer by means of a virgin's womb and came forth as a human being. He took to himself the sufferings of the sufferer by means of a body capable of suffering, and he destroyed the sufferings of the flesh. By a Spirit incapable of death he killed off death, the homicide.

This is the one who like a lamb was carried off and like a sheep was sacrificed. He redeemed us from slavery to the cosmos as from the land of Egypt and loosed us from slavery to the devil as from the hand of Pharaoh. And he sealed our souls with his own Spirit and the limbs of our body with his own blood. This is the one who covered death with shame and made a mourner of the devil, just as Moses did Pharaoh. This is the one who struck lawlessness a blow and made injustice childless, as Moses did Egypt. This is the one who rescued us from slavery into liberty, from darkness into light, from death into life, from a tyranny into an eternal kingdom (and made us a new priesthood, and a peculiar eternal people).

He is the Passover of our salvation. He is the one who in many folk bore many things. He is the one who was murdered [as was] the person of Abel, bound [as was] the person of Isaac, exiled [as was] the person of Jacob, sold [as was] the person of Joseph, exposed [as was] the person of Moses, sacrificed [as was] the person of the lamb, persecuted [as was] the person of David, dishonored [as was] the person of the prophets. This is the one who was made flesh in a virgin, hanged upon the wood, entombed in the earth, raised from the dead, lifted up to the heights of the heavens. He is the speechless lamb. He is the lamb who was slaughtered. He is the one born of Mary the beautiful ewe. He is the one who was taken from the flock and dragged to slaughter and killed at evening and buried at night, who was not crushed on the cross, was not dissolved into the earth, who rose from the dead and raised humanity from the grave below.[4]

Isaac Barrow (1630–77), known as one of the top orators of his time, also demonstrates doxology as a means to provide a review of the mighty acts of God in history and a summary of the gospel:

Let us consider, whose will it is, that requireth our compliance:
It is the will of him, whose will did found the earth, and rear the Heaven; whose will sustaineth all things in their existence and operation; whose will is the great law of the world, which universal nature in all its motions doth observe; which reigneth in Heaven, the blessed spirits adoring it, which swayeth in Hell itself, the cursed fiends trembling at it. And shall we alone (we pitiful worms crawling upon earth) presume to murmur, or dare kick against it?
It is the will of our Maker, who together with all our other faculties did create and confer on us the very power of willing; and shall we turn the work of his hands, the gift of his bounty against him?
It is the will of our Preserver, who together with all that we are, or have, continually doth uphold our very will itself; so that without employing any positive force, merely by letting us fall out of his hand, he can send us back to nothing: and shall our will clash with that, on which it so wholly dependeth; without which it cannot subsist one moment, or move one step forward in action?
It is the will of our sovereign Lord, who upon various indisputable accounts hath a just right to govern us, and an absolute power to dispose of us: ought we not therefore to say with old Eli, "It is the Lord, let him to me as it seemeth good to him"? Is it not extreme iniquity, is it not monstrous arrogance for us, in derogation to his will, to pretend giving law, or picking a station to ourselves? Do we not manifestly incur high treason against the King of Heaven by so invading his office, usurping his authority, snatching his scepter into our hands, and setting our wills in his throne?
It is the will of our Judge, from whose mouth our doom must proceed, awarding life or death, weal or woe unto us; and what sentence can we

expect, what favor can we pretend to, if we presumptuously shall offend, oppose that will, which is the supreme rule of justice, and sole foundation of mercy?

It is the will of our Redeemer, who hath bought us with an inestimable price, and with infinite pains hath rescued us from miserable captivity under most barbarous enemies, that obeying his will we might command our own, and serving him we might enjoy perfect freedom. And shall we, declining his call and conduct out of that unhappy state, bereave him of his purchase, frustrate his undertakings, and forfeit to ourselves the benefit of so great redemption?

It is the will of our best friend; who loveth us much better than we do love ourselves; who is concerned for our welfare, as his own dearest interest, and greatly delighteth therein; who by innumerable experiments hath demonstrated an excess of kindness to us; who in all his dealings with us purely doth aim at our good, never charging any duty on us, or dispensing any event to us, so much with intent to exercise his power over us, as to express his goodness toward us; who never doth afflict or grieve us more against our will, than against his own desire. . . .

It is the will of him who is most holy. . . .

It is the will of him who is perfectly just. . . .

It is the will of him who is infinitely wise. . . .

It is the will of him who is immensely good and benign. . . .

It is finally the will of him who is uncontrollably powerful.[5]

Suggestions for Creative Adaptation

Both excerpts are effective summaries of the gospel. Melito focuses on typological parallels between Old Testament stories and Jesus' life, and Barrow focuses on various attributes and actions of God. The closest that many churches come to his passage today is in some prayers that offer a narrative summary of the faith. Such summaries can be an effective means of both praising God and leading people to praise. Were the above models used today, they would need to be adapted, the imagery might be made even more concrete and the language more conversational, and it might need to be shorter for many congregational settings. That said, why not occasionally employ such passages of doxology, not least on key Sundays of the year?

Today we often fear that doctrine will be boring, academic, or removed from daily life. Earlier preachers lived in an age more sensitive to the beauty of language, and they were rhetorically trained in using it in ways that generated interest, intimacy, and passion. In each of the above examples, a single repeating phrase provides unity, "He is the one . . ." in Melito, and "It is the will of him . . ." in Barrow. Each paragraph focuses on a separate name or attribute of God. Each phrase describes a specific action of God. Doctrine here is not abstract or tightly argued; it is embedded in the summary of narrative events. The issue here should not be, Would Melito or Barrow preach today? but, What would I say about Christ or God if I was to offer fulsome authentic praise?

Use Old Testament Texts as a Resource for Language about Christ

Robert H. Muir, a Scottish preacher in the 1870s, preached a rousing doxology partway through his sermon, and in it he draws on several New and Old Testament texts (named and not named) to speak of Christ:

> Looking up to the Lord in whom I put my trust, I see Him in the heavens, the great High Priest of a continual mediatorship, bringing sinners nigh to God by the blood of His own sacrifice, by the merits of His own perfect obedience giving to the prayers of His people the odours of a sweet-smelling savour. I see Him "in His holy temple," as from a very sea of sanctifying grace, dispensing the holy issues of His great redemption work, pouring them forth for the washing of regeneration, and renewing of the Holy Ghost (Titus iii. 5). In His discriminating verdict as to clean and unclean, I see Him the Priest who "is our Judge." In His teaching by His word and Spirit, I see Him the Prophet who "is our Lawgiver." In the reign of His grace, I see Him exalted a Prince whose "throne is in the heavens." "The Lord is our Judge, the Lord is our Lawgiver, the Lord is our King, He will save us!" (Isa. xxxiii. 22). The person and work of the Lord our Saviour, as the Priest, the Prophet, the King of His covenant people, is thus the one engrossing object which fills the eye and the heart of the believing child of God. Everything gladdening, everything sanctifying, and all that is victorious in the power of the life of faith, springs, as from its fountain, in the person and fullness of "the Lord" Himself alone.[6]

Suggestions for Creative Adaptation

Muir preaches on Psalm 11:1-11, and his doxology is based on verse 4, "The LORD is in his holy temple, the LORD's throne is in heaven" (KJV). He does not feel constrained to draw on only his text but goes elsewhere, most obviously to Titus and Isaiah 6 and 33, with allusions to a host of others.

Although Muir preaches on the psalm, he has developed a set piece that could be used or adapted for inclusion in any sermon, should he choose to reuse it. It functions to give praise to God concerning who Christ is, and like the other doxologies we have seen, it goes beyond communicating knowledge to communicating salvation in the moment.

When we draw on or allude to a variety of texts in the above manner, we do so primarily with a view to effective praise today. We do not need to be concerned with whether the congregation will understand and appreciate the exact biblical sources of our language and imagery. We can use them simply for their beautiful language and their ability to please, delight, or move. In composing a doxology, one might list a few texts that one wants to draw upon and then experiment to see what praise arises from within them. Feel free to adapt your biblical sources with the same freedom that we encourage here in drawing on preachers.

Adapt a Biblical Text So That It Becomes Doxology

Fleming Rutledge offers a brief doxology in explaining the significance of Paul's definition of love in 1 Corinthians 13:

> It has been said that the meaning of the text will become clear if we substitute the name "Jesus" for the word "love": "*Jesus* is patient and kind, is not jealous; is not boastful or arrogant; is not rude, does not insist on his own way; is not irritable or resentful; does not rejoice at wrong, but rejoices in the truth. . . . *Jesus* bears all things, believes all things, hopes all things, endures all things."
>
> . . . Love does not lead to God; God in Jesus Christ leads us to love. Love does not arise out of the unaided human heart; God puts it there.[7]

Suggestions for Creative Adaptation

Rutledge constructs her doxology by taking Paul's words and substituting the name of Jesus for every word *love*. We suggested a similar exercise in the previous chapter in adapting Psalms 23 and 139 to become proclamatory statements. It might be good to experiment with different texts to see how they lend themselves to adaptation as doxologies. For example, a text like Proverbs 26:20-21 might be adapted doxologically as follows (the exact original wording is in regular font; the adaptations appear in italics):

> For lack of wood the fire goes out, and *yet where God is present, faith burns bright.*
>
> Where there is no whisperer, quarreling ceases; *thus God silences the whisperers and unites.*
>
> As charcoal is to hot embers and wood to fire, *so is God's word to our lives,*
>
> [as] a quarrelsome person [is] for kindling strife, *so is Christ's Spirit for bringing peace.*

Praise God through Praising Gifts of the Spirit

An example of praising God through praising the gifts of the Spirit is a sermon by William A. Johnson, who in the 1970s was pastor of Saint John Church—Baptist in Chicago:

> Ask that woman who had been troubled for years with a constant drain of blood. . . . She would tell you, FAITH MAKES THE DIFFERENCE.
>
> Ask that Canaanite woman who came to Jesus, crying. . . . "Truth, Lord, yet the dogs eat of the crumbs which fall from their masters' table." And to that Jesus replied, "O woman, great is thy faith: be it unto thee even as thou wilt" (Matthew 15:22, 26, 27, 28). She would tell you, FAITH MAKES THE DIFFERENCE.
>
> Or ask those two blind men sitting on the roadside, crying to Jesus, "Have mercy on us, O Lord, thou Son of David." "What will ye that I shall do unto you?" asked Jesus, and they replied, "Lord, that our eyes may be opened" (Matthew 20:30, 32, 33). And their eyes were opened. They would tell you, FAITH MAKES THE DIFFERENCE.
>
> Paul tells us in his letter to the Hebrews that it was faith that made Abel offer to God a better sacrifice than Cain's. . . .
>
> It was faith that made Noah hear God's warning about things in the future that he could not see. He obeyed and built an ark in which he and his family were saved.
>
> It was faith that made Abraham obey when God called him to go out into a country which God had promised him, leaving his own country without knowing where he was going. . . .
>
> Faith makes the difference between begging and praising, between crawling and leaping.
>
> No wonder the poet asked for:
> . . . a faith that will not shrink,
> Tho' pressed by ev'ry foe,
> That will not tremble on the brink
> Of any earthly woe.
> Are you troubled of mind? Faith is the answer!
> Are you burdened with sorrow? Faith is the answer!
> Are you crippled—lame—because of some sin? Faith is the answer![8]

Suggestions for Creative Adaptation

This passage of doxology praises God by praising numerous instances in which faith was rewarded. Doxology usually praises God directly, but doxology may also be offered to God indirectly by speaking of gifts of the Spirit, like faith, hope, or love. Here there is no doubt that God is the source of faith, and it is God who renews our faith in hearing this passage. The final three lines (above) utilize nurturing exhortation.

Convert Lists into Doxologies

Barbara C. Harris is an African American woman, the first woman bishop in the Episcopal Church in 1988. She adapts a doxology she has heard in using a list of biblical books to describe Jesus:

> And if you trace that word all the way through our "Source Book," the Bible, you will find that, according to one writer (and I have long-forgotten the source):
>
> In Genesis, he's the seed of the woman
> In Exodus, he's the Passover Lamb
> In Leviticus, he's the atoning sacrifice
> In Numbers, he's the smitten rock
> In Deuteronomy, he's the prophet
> In Joshua, he's the captain
> In Judges, he's the deliverer
> In Ruth, he's the kinsman
> In Kings, he's the ruler
> In Nehemiah, he's the restorer
> In Esther, he's the advocate
> In Job, he's the redeemer
> In Psalms, he's the shepherd
> In Proverbs, he's wisdom
> In Ecclesiastes, he's the goal
> In the Song of Solomon, he's the groom
> In the Prophets, he's the coming one
> In the Gospels he's the God made man
> In Acts, he's the risen one
> In the Epistles, he's the head of the church and
> In Revelation, he's the worthy one.
> If you are looking for a Savior, his name is Jesus—the one who was, the one who is to come, the one who is.[9]

Caesar A. W. Clark uses a list of adjectives to describe the power of God's word. When the sermon was proclaimed within his church, the congregation would join in as he indicates:

> But God's word is "amen."
> His word is absolutely reliable. [Well.]
> His word is absolutely dependable. [Well. Yes sir.]
> His word is absolutely unfailing. [Well.]
> His word is absolutely faithful. [Well.]
> His word is absolutely trustworthy. [Well.]
> His word is absolutely responsible. [Well.]
> His word is absolutely solid.

His word is absolutely sound.
His word is absolutely true. [Well. Come on up.][10]

Suggestions for Creative Adaptation

Harris uses her list of books of the Bible to emphasize the way they all point to the Savior. As a student noted, "She uses the whole counsel of God without fear of redundancy or being accused of simplicity."[11] We have already suggested in the chapter on prayer the advantage of drawing on lists of the names of God or Jesus. The same suggestion applies here for a way to compose doxology. One website lists alphabetically the following names and titles of Jesus, and here are the letters *A, B,* and *C*:

Advocate (1 John 2:1)
Almighty (Rev. 1:8; Mt. 28:18)
Alpha and Omega (Rev. 1:8; 22:13)
Amen (Rev. 3:14)
Apostle of our Profession (Heb. 3:1)
Atoning Sacrifice for our Sins (1 John 2:2)
Author of Life (Acts 3:15)
Author and Perfecter of our Faith (Heb. 12:2)
Author of Salvation (Heb. 2:10)
Beginning and End (Rev. 22:13)
Blessed and only Ruler (1 Tim. 6:15)
Bread of God (John 6:33)
Bread of Life (John 6:35; 6:48)
Bridegroom (Mt. 9:15)
Capstone (Acts 4:11; 1 Pet. 2:7)
Chief Cornerstone (Eph. 2:20)
Chief Shepherd (1 Pet. 5:4)
Christ (1 John 2:22)
Creator (John 1:3)[12]

Anyone who has never heard what doxology sounds like in an African American setting might watch *That's My King!* featuring Dr. S. M. Lockridge, who uses a list in a powerful way to describe the kingship of Jesus Christ.[13]

CHAPTER SEVENTEEN
Celebration

C elebration is rejoicing and thanksgiving and is a theological version of what rhetoric calls climax. Although it may appear at any time in the sermon, it most typically occurs at or near the end. It is a hybrid form of preaching that commonly draws upon any of the genres we have named (condemnation, lament, stern exhortation, testimony, prayer, nurturing exhortation, proclamatory statements, and doxology). It is primarily an expression of rejoicing in what God has given, offering thanks, and reveling in what we know in faith to be true. In some ways celebration is the summation of proclamation subforms, the final (or peak) word of the sermon, and the fullest expression of the gospel and response to it. Celebration is designed to remind people about what God has done for them in the past, is doing in the present, even in this worship service, and will be doing in the future, including the week ahead as they engage God's purposes for their lives. Their engagement starts now, with the assurance that in Christ, the powers of death are overcome. Henry Mitchell says a purpose of celebration is to get the congregation to act, for "people do what they celebrate."[1]

Celebration often provides an effective summary of the faith. It is related to personal testimony, though it is corporate in nature and its content, imagery, and memory extend all the way back to the Bible. It is a form of thanksgiving (*eucharistia*) or joyous utterance of gratitude, related also to the eucharistic prayer that is said at the Lord's Supper and often called the prayer of great thanksgiving. In fact, this prayer dates prior to Hypolitus of Rome, whose *Apostolic Tradition* (ca. 215) described early worship. Traditional great thanksgiving prayers have standard structural elements that are often hinted at in celebration, which by contrast is freely structured, including a trinitarian structure, various exchanges between the presiding minister (who in some traditions sings) and the people, remembrance (*anamnesis*) of the great acts of God in history and in the second person of the Trinity, and invoking of the presence and work of the Holy Spirit (*epiclesis*). Drawing attention to this similarity may point to some crossover influence, or it may simply indicate that celebration has at least muted expression in nearly every church.

At the same time, celebration is not a prayer per se; it expresses joy God-ward and its words are sometimes spoken in the character of God. Celebration is unlike doxology in that it does somewhat more than offer praise to God, remind people of God's praiseworthiness, and move them to praise: it encourages people to be glad, give thanks, step forward, join in, shout out, have hope, banish fear, and embody the joy of the gospel in their lives. It is like an extended Easter cry, "He is risen indeed." Celebration is also eschatological, looking to the future, in effect calling *maranatha*, "Come, Lord Jesus, come." Celebration is akin to singing: it invites participation by the congregation because of its effective reminder of what the people believe, its rhythm, and its gladness in the Spirit.

Like most of the other subforms, celebration brings what Ebeling longed for in preaching, certainty and joy. Celebration is found in every tradition. However, only within some African American traditions is it discussed and regularly practiced as a rhetorically sophisticated, theologically driven, and spiritually inspired subform of the sermon.

The roots of celebration are in the Bible, notably in the songs of Moses and Miriam at being saved from Egypt (Exodus 15); in the dancing of David before the Lord in bringing the ark to Jerusalem (2 Samuel 6); in psalms of rejoicing like Psalm 31; in the rejoicing at finding the lost sheep, lost coin, and prodigal son at the end of each of Jesus' three parables (Luke 15:6, 9, 32); and the rejoicing in heaven at the marriage of the Lamb (Revelation 19:7). Philippians 4:4 instructs, "Rejoice in the Lord always; again I will say, Rejoice"; 1 Thessalonians 5:16, 18 reads, "Rejoice always . . . give thanks in all circumstances; for this is the will of God in Christ Jesus for you"; and Ephesians 5:20 urges us to give "thanks to God the Father at all times and for everything in the name of our Lord Jesus Christ."

In numerous places in the Bible, God is both the source and the object of a believer's "joy" (Psalms 35:9; 43:4; Isaiah 61:10; Luke 1:47; Romans 5:11; Philippians 3:1; 4:4). Most of the New Testament words for rejoice or be glad (*chairō, sunchariō, agalliaō, euphrainō, kauchaomai*) are associated with the salvation or glory of God, in other words, with gospel.[2]

Reasons for celebration must first be established in teaching and other parts of the sermon. Celebration extols what is now possible with the help of the Spirit. It is designed to carry the congregation into the world in service of the gospel; thus typically it not only contains an invitation to rejoice, but it gets the people rejoicing. The Spirit accomplishes what the preacher's words invite by their content, energy, and direction. Rejoicing on the part of the preacher is infectious. It is the beginning of the people joining in the same and enacting their ministries in the week. In the best expressions of celebration the people become the message—they embody the word and become God's message to the world: "You are a letter of Christ" (2 Corinthians 3:3).

Celebration is marked in the same way as other forms of proclamation, that is, by increased pace, shorter phrases, various rhetorical devices, including repetition of key words, parallel sentence structure, musical rhythm, increased passion, inspired content, change from plain style (including whooping or humming in some African American traditions), greater intimacy, and most important, casting people on God's resources for whatever tasks God sets before them.

Celebration is not simply preaching with increased emotion; it is preaching with the fire of the Holy Spirit. Earlier we made a case against emotion for its own sake and upheld emotion as a theological issue, in which one is excited because of who God is and what God does. Celebration celebrates the divine. It is profoundly theological, and God is both its subject and the true source of its fire and power. The truths it upholds, the relationship it fosters with God and neighbor, what God does in and through it with saving power—all are worthy of excitement. Celebration is an effective integration of rhetoric's ethos, pathos, and logos, an embodiment of the gospel.

Paul wrote numerous passages of celebration, for instance, his account of the results of justification in Romans 5:1-5:

> Therefore, since we are justified by faith, we have peace with God through our Lord Jesus Christ, through whom we have obtained access to this grace in which we stand; and we boast in our hope of sharing the glory of God. And not only that, but we also boast in our sufferings, knowing that suffering produces endurance, and endurance produces character, and character produces hope, and hope does not disappoint us, because God's love has been poured into our hearts through the Holy Spirit that has been given to us.

Similarly his discussion of resurrection may be classified as celebration:

> What I am saying, brothers and sisters, is this: flesh and blood cannot inherit the kingdom of God, nor does the perishable inherit the imperishable. Listen, I will tell you a mystery! We will not all die, but we will all be changed, in a moment, in the twinkling of an eye, at the last trumpet. For the trumpet will sound, and the dead will be raised imperishable, and we will be changed. For this perishable body must put on imperishability, and this mortal body must put on immortality. When this perishable body puts on imperishability, and this mortal body puts on immortality, then the saying that is written will be fulfilled:
> "Death has been swallowed up in victory."
> "Where, O death, is your victory?
>   Where, O death, is your sting?"
>   The sting of death is sin, and the power of sin is the law. But thanks be to God, who gives us the victory through our Lord Jesus Christ. (1 Corinthians 15:50-57)

Might the Practice of Quoting Poems Once Have Functioned as Celebration?

A common feature in traditional sermons is the quotation of a poem or hymn at the end. Many celebrations also contain verses from hymns, songs, or poems. Is there a link? At some time in the history of preaching (evidence seems to suggest that it was in the last three centuries), it became common practice to quote a poem or hymn in closing, hence the stereotypical formula for sermons, three points and a poem. The Pauline corpus obviously provides several examples of quoted hymns (Ephesians 5:14; Philippians 2:6-11; Colossians 1:15-20; 1 Timothy 3:16; and possibly Romans 1:3-4) and poems (1 Corinthians 13; 15:32; Titus 1:12).[3] The practice was given added encouragement and modeling by John Wesley. His sermons were published as models for his followers to use. He cites poems and hymns frequently in the bodies of his sermons, and numerous ones have a verse of a hymn at or near the end.[4] His family, after all, was a family of poets. Most of the poems and hymns that he cites are from either his father, Samuel, an accomplished poet of the Stuart period, or his brother Charles, who wrote hundreds of hymns for the church.

One example of a hymn verse used as celebration by John Wesley appears at the close of his sermon "Human Life a Dream." He preached about the consequences of faith, hope, and love in the believing person to whom God reveals his Son. The sermon ends as follows:

> And how wonderfully do both faith and hope and love connect God with man, and time with eternity! In consideration of this, we may boldly say,—
>> Vanish then this world of shadows;
>> Pass the former things away!
>> Lord, appear! appear to glad us,
>> With the dawn of endless day!
>> O conclude this mortal story,
>> Throw this universe aside!
>> Come, eternal King of glory,
>> Now descend, and take thy bride![5]

Another of Wesley's sermons ends with the reading of a full hymn text of many verses that editor Albert Outler says is an authentic part of the sermon (that is, as opposed to something sung in the service or added in later publication for the benefit of the reader). Outler perhaps lacked any other genre with which to compare that full hymn when he identified it as the "equivalent of an ascription" of glory as happens at the end of sermons in many traditions.[6]

Hymn verses serve many of the purposes of celebration: to move people to rejoice, to communicate excitement to obedience, to focus on the gospel, to end on hope, and to signal a close by use of a contrasting rhetorical style and form. Celebration in African American practice is often compared with music and a kind of singing. When Wesley and others engaged in field preaching that reached thousands out of doors, they had to use their voices in ways that allowed them fully to project, and one of the best ways for that to happen is speaking in a manner that is close to song. Perhaps when Wesley got to the hymn verses at the end, he actually sang.

The effectiveness of hymns as celebration in practice in history can be a matter of discussion. Closely rhyming verses, if read aloud today, tend to sound less like celebration than sentimental greeting cards. Nonetheless, the practice of quoting hymns initially arose not just because it provided an easy way for a weary pastor to bring a sermon to a close; it also set the right theological tone and often summarized some dimension of the faith. It offered a rhetorical flourish at the end, something that even plain-style preachers like to employ as a means of signalling the end.

Celebration in Practice

Treat Celebration as a Hybrid Form

Of the sermon subforms we consider here, celebration to date is the only genre that has received wide attention, and that has been mainly in African American homiletics.[7] The various genres of proclamation have not been named. In a forthcoming volume, Luke Powery of Princeton Seminary identifies the importance of pairing celebration and lament.[8] Because celebration is rejoicing and thanksgiving, it is one of the most thorough expressions of the gospel.

Since celebration typically is thought to be of African American origin, as some of its elements in practice distinctly are, it is important here to show celebration's early roots in history. One of the earliest examples is at the end of a sermon by Melito of Sardis (d. ca. 180) in Asia Minor, a sermon that was recovered in its fragments in the 1930s and in most of its entirety in the 1950s:

> "So come, all families of human beings who are defiled by sins, and receive remission of sins. For I am your remission. I am the Passover of salvation. I am the Lamb sacrificed for your sake. I am your ransom. I am your life. I am your resurrection. I am your light. I am your salvation. I am your King. I lead you toward the heights of heaven. I will show you the eternal Father. I will raise you up with my right hand."

This is he who made the heavens and the earth, and formed humanity in the beginning, who is announced by the Law and the Prophets, who was enfleshed in a Virgin, who was hanged up on the Tree, who was buried in the earth, who was raised from the dead and went up into the heights of heaven, who is sitting on the right hand of the Father, who has the authority to judge and save all things, through whom the Father made the things which exist, from the beginning to all the ages. This one is "the Alpha and the Omega," this one is "the beginning and the end"—the beginning which cannot be explained and the end which cannot be grasped. This one is the Christ. This one is the King. This one is Jesus. This one is the Leader. This one is the Lord. This one is he who has risen from the dead. This one is he who sits on the right hand of the Father. He bears the Father and is borne by the Father. "To him be the glory and the power to the ends of the ages. Amen."[9]

The hybrid nature of celebration is seen here. Melito combines nurturing exhortation, proclamatory statements, and doxology.

Augustine uses nurturing exhortation and doxology in his celebration that occurs midway through a Christmas sermon (ca. 400):

Let us, then, celebrate the Lord's birthday with the full attendance and the enthusiasm that we should give it. Let men rejoice, let women rejoice. . . . For He was born without sin, that he who was with sin might be reborn.

Young men, you who lead chaste lives, who have chosen to follow Christ in a special manner, who do not seek marriage—rejoice! Not through marriage did He come to you, He in whom you have found your ideal. . . .

Rejoice, chaste virgins. A virgin has brought forth for you Him to whom you may espouse yourself without corruption. Neither in conceiving Him nor in giving birth to Him can you destroy what you love.

Rejoice, you who are just. It is the birthday of Him who justifies.

Rejoice, you who are weak and sick. It is the birthday of Him who makes well.

Rejoice, you who are in captivity. It is the birthday of the Redeemer.

Rejoice, you who are slaves. It is the birthday of the Master.

Rejoice, you who are free. It is the birthday of Him who makes free.

Rejoice, you Christians all. It is Christ's birthday.[10]

As a further indication of the extent of celebration in the early church, West and East, Latin and Greek, here is the final section from John Chrysostom's Paschal Homily (ca. 400), that is still read every Easter morning in every Orthodox parish:

Let no one bewail his poverty,
For the universal Kingdom has been revealed.
Let no one weep for his iniquities,
For pardon has shown forth from the grave.

Let no one fear death,
For the Saviour's death has set us free.
He that was held prisoner of it has annihilated it.

By descending into Hell, He made Hell captive.
He embittered it when it tasted of His flesh. . . .

It was embittered, for it was abolished.
It was embittered, for it was mocked.
It was embittered, for it was slain.
It was embittered, for it was overthrown.
It was embittered, for it was fettered in chains.
It took a body, and met God face to face.
It took earth, and encountered Heaven.
It took that which was seen, and fell upon the unseen.

O Death, where is thy sting?
O Hell, where is thy victory?

Christ is risen, and thou art overthrown!
Christ is risen, and the demons are fallen!
Christ is risen, and the angels rejoice!
Christ is risen, and life reigns!
Christ is risen, and not one dead remains in the grave.
For Christ, being risen from the dead,
Is become the first-fruits of those who have fallen asleep.

To Him be glory and dominion
Unto ages of ages.
Amen.[11]

Suggestions for Creative Adaptation

In addition to much African American preaching, some southern Pentecostal sermons model effective celebration, as is powerfully demonstrated in Robert Duvall's movie *The Apostle*. There is a danger in preachers imitating the delivery of preachers from other traditions. The subform itself can be imitated, but the delivery, style, and wording must be authentically one's own, appropriate to one's communities and cultures, adapted in ways that seem natural.

Inauthenticity comes from trying to sound like someone else, using words one would never use, or addressing a topic one would not engage. Still, most of us preachers do not use much of our full range. Preachers need permission from their congregations to experiment, to fail, and to grow. Even among our authors here we see considerable range of style and expression. Luther inserts stern exhortation into the middle of a celebrative passage, and typically in his sermons he moves back and forth between trouble and grace. Melito and Augustine use the grand style; Calvin comes closer to the moderate. Calvin here encourages gladness in his people via a difficult route, vengeance on God's enemies and the saving of the elect.

In our time preachers in some traditions may stick to one text in a sermon and shy away from quoting others in case the congregation cannot understand the textual allusions. Does it matter that they understand the source of all the words they hear? Is it not enough simply to use the beautiful language of Scripture regardless of what else may be drawn from it? Each of the above authors has woven a tapestry that has a variety of biblical allusions and texts.

Use Celebration in a Manner That Feels Comfortable

Both Luther and Calvin use celebration, though neither one seems to have prolonged passages. In this passage from Luther, celebration combines teaching, proclamatory statements, stern exhortation, doxology, and rejoicing. The passage is broken midway by a section of stern exhortation:

> When we know and consider that Christ came down from heaven and loved sinners in obedience to the Father, then there springs up in us a bold approach to and firm hope in Christ. We learn that Christ is the real epistle, the golden book, in which we read and learn how he always kept before him the will of the Father. So Christ is the "access to the Father" (Eph. 2:18) as St. Paul says. And John too bears witness that Christ said, "I am the way, and the truth, and the life" (John 14:6). "I am also the door" (John 10:7) and "no one comes to the Father but by me" (John 14:6). Now we see that there is no shorter way to the Father except that we love Christ, hope and trust in him, boldly look to him for everything good, learn to know and praise him. For then it will be impossible that we should have a miserable, frightened, dejected conscience; in Christ it will be heartened and refreshed. [Here Luther has several sentences of stern exhortation] . . . how kindly, sweetly, and lovingly Christ has dealt with people. For the Father commanded him to do so. This tastes sweet to the faithful soul and it gives all the glory, praise, and honor to the Father through the Son Christ Jesus. So God has nothing but the best and he offers it to us, weeds us, sustains us, and cares for us through his Son. That's the way our hearts are changed to follow Christ.[12]

Celebration is akin to Calvin's third use of the law, an excitement to obedience. His own use of celebration, as with Luther, can happen anywhere in the sermon. Here he combines teaching and doxology with rejoicing:

> St. Paul shows us that if we are of the number of the faithful, and we believe today the Gospel, we need not fear when Jesus Christ appears, nor be frightened by the majesty that will then be shining in Him. And how is this?
>
> For He will come (says he) to be glorified in His saints and to be admired in them. . . . What he said above of fire and flame, what he spoke of terror and dread, is not to discourage believers, that they should not desire the coming of our Lord Jesus Christ and raise their heads every time it is spoken to them. For He will come for their redemption. The doctrine that our Lord will come again joins together these two things, something that is common enough in Holy Scripture. He will come to take vengeance on His enemies, and He will come to deliver His own. He will come to be Savior of those who have served and honored Him, and to cast down and confound those who have hardened themselves against Him and His Word. Let us remember well then that this terrible description which is put here is not to frighten us but rather to make us glad that such is the love and grace of God toward us. Our Lord Jesus will come, indeed, with a dreadful power. And what for? To cast into the abyss all His enemies, to avenge the injuries, insults, and afflictions that we shall have endured.[13]

Suggestions for Creative Adaptation

Luther shows how one can use various Bible verses to help develop celebration. He understood that the way to do theology was to switch back and forth between law and gospel, and that is what he does in his sermons. In this one he breaks the celebration in two and uses it to sandwich a passage of stern exhortation. Luther does not want his listeners to make any mistake: grace is for the repentant and faithful, and law is to be heard especially by those who are stubborn in their sin. Today we can have broad understandings of trouble that apply law to all listeners. Concerning the intermixing of law and gospel, one wonders if it is not better to keep them more separate and allow each to be experienced in its own turn through sustained development? Otherwise the effect of gospel is a little like putting a bandage on a wound, applying it and removing it, applying it and removing it.

A similar comment may be made concerning Calvin. He does a fine job of building excitement in his listeners through his focus on the end times. He says he wants his listeners to be "glad" in "the love and grace of God toward us." He makes plain the identity of Jesus Christ. Still, by the end he takes away much of the gladness by his last sentence of condemnation upon the enemies. At least in our time it might be best to let celebration be celebration, and use condemnation in another place in the sermon.

Incorporate a Poem, Song, or
Hymn Verse in Celebration

A Scottish preacher in the 1870s, James Kerr, had a rousing celebration as his concluding paragraph and included in it quotation of a hymn verse:

> Let there be earnest prayer, and self-denying labour, to hasten the universal extension of Christ's kingdom. . . . The overthrow of all error and sin, and the universal triumph of truth and virtue, are promised to prayer and effort. The prospects of a speedy reformation are dark, very dark; but, as Judson said, when he thought of his meagre success in the mission field,—"The prospects are as bright as the promises of God." "As I live, saith the Lord, the whole earth shall be filled with My glory." [Isa. 66:18?] All the errors and iniquities of the wide earth shall pass away; and the glory of Christ shall fill all lands. The Broadchurchism of the Gospel shall be triumphant then. Christ in and over every heart; Christ in and over every household; Christ in and over His Church, then one; Christ in and over every association and community; Christ in and over every throne—all giving homage to Christ, all honoured by Christ, and Christ all in all. For—
> "All ends of the earth remember shall,
>   And turn the Lord unto;
> All kindreds of the nations,
>   To Him shall homage do."[14]

Suggestions for Creative Adaptation

We mentioned that nowadays the practice of hymn quoting at the end of a sermon can seem old-fashioned, not so much because three points and a poem may seem old, but because our age is not enamored of verses that may sound singsong. Predictable end rhyme schemes like *aa/bb/cc* or *abc/abc* can give a superficial feeling. However, when end rhyme is minimized and the words are powerful and the rhythm with which one speaks the verses is natural, the practice of using a hymn can still be effective, especially if it is part of a larger celebration and the practice is not overused.

Isaiah 66:18 seems to provide the direct inspiration for the overall celebration above, and the hymn verse picks up on its theme. If the hymn following the sermon is chosen with one's biblical text in mind, the verse one quotes could be from that hymn.

Much of the power of this celebration is derived from its eschatological focus; the preacher imagines how things will be when all are reconciled to God in Christ. Celebration has a prophetic quality to it when the preacher pictures God's dreams for creation.

Summarize the Gospel in Celebration

The Victorian poet and preacher Gerard Manley Hopkins (1844–89) grew up in the Anglican Church and later became a Jesuit priest. Here are the final words of a sermon that he preached early in his priesthood. This celebration contains nurturing exhortation, doxology, and rejoicing through an effective summary of the gospel:

> And though he bids us say we are unprofitable servants, yet he himself will say to each of us / Good and faithful servant, well done.
>
> And this man whose picture I have tried to draw for you, brethren, is your God. He was your maker in time past; hereafter he will be your judge. Make him your hero now. Take some time to think of him; praise him in your hearts. You can over your work on your road praise him, saying over and over again / Glory be to Christ's body; Glory to the body of the Word made flesh; Glory to the body suckled at the Blessed Virgin's breasts; Glory to Christ's body in its beauty; Glory to Christ's body in its weariness; Glory to Christ's body in its Passion, death and burial; Glory to Christ's body risen; Glory to Christ's body in the Blessed Sacrament; Glory to Christ's soul; Glory to his genius and wisdom; Glory to his unsearchable thoughts; Glory to his saving words; Glory to his sacred heart; Glory to its courage and manliness; Glory to its meekness and mercy; Glory to its every heartbeat, to its joys and sorrows, wishes, fears; Glory in all things to Jesus Christ God and man. If you try this when you can you will find your heart kindle and while you praise him he will praise you—a blessing etc.[15]

Suggestions for Creative Adaptation

Celebration at the end of a sermon is a way to bring together and unify the whole, where elements of the theme are picked up and reinforced. Because it is designed to move people to action, it is wise that gladness in the gospel be its basis. In fact, each of our above examples of celebration to varying degrees serves as a summary of the gospel. All of them point to what is possible with God, and with the help of the Spirit, they make it a reality in the moment.

In the present fiery example from Hopkins, the hearer is left with little doubt of what benefit will be found in practicing praise as the preacher recommends. God in Christ is the subject of the most celebrative sentences in both paragraphs; thus by the end the listener ideally feels moved beyond his or her circumstances and cast on the abundant resources of the Savior.

Allow Celebration to Have a Surplus of Meaning

Not every word of celebration needs to be absorbed by the listener, as in this example from former Atlanta preacher William Holmes Borders Sr.:

I imagine Paul spread himself before God saying, "I am your servant; you are my God. I am tortured and pained without end. I have done all I know. I have preached 'prayer.' I have preached 'power.' I have preached 'ability.' Now I am caught with a thorn in the flesh which I can't master. I prayed once. I prayed twice. This is a third time. I need a personal answer. When it stormed, you sent an angel. When I was in Philippi, you rocked the jail. When I was trapped, you let me down over the Macedonian wall. When I was headed for Damascus to raise hell, you blocked the traffic. When I was stoned, you saved me. I need a personal answer to my plea. You made my body. A master mechanic knows his product. I have the faith in God, and you have the power."

Paul expected God to come by land, and he came by sea. God does not always answer prayer the way we want, or expect, but rather his way. God answered Elijah with a raven. God answered Moses with manna from on high. God answered Jesus by increasing a fish sandwich to a supermarket in the wilderness. God answered Joshua at Jericho with tumbling walls. God answered our slave parents with Sherman's march from Atlanta to the sea. God answered Gideon with three hundred who lapped water. God answered Elijah by fire. God answered Isaiah with fire. God answered Noah in the flood with an ark. God answered Paul on a stormy sea with an angel. God answered Jesus on the stormy sea of Galilee with personal power when Jesus said, "Peace be still." God answered Stephen in a ditch being stoned to death. God answered Gandhi enabling him to give the Hindu salute of forgiveness as bullets of death killed his body. God answered Jesus as murderers ripped his body. God answers and not always the way you want or expect. Paul declares that after a third prayer God told him, "My grace is sufficient. . . ." (2 Corinthians 12:9 KJV.)[16]

Suggestions for Creative Adaptation

This celebration is brilliantly structured. It begins with an imagined prayer of testimony from Paul on the third occasion of his request that the "thorn in the flesh" be removed; it builds to a recital of the times God answered the prayers of many people; and it climaxes with God's specific answer to Paul. Even celebration can move by a kind of narrative plot.

Celebration like this is spoken in an excited manner, at a pace that is faster than one's norm, probably faster than most listeners would be able fully to absorb or comprehend, especially with all of the references, even if many of the people did know their Bibles. Celebration often contains more information than can be fully absorbed. There is an intentional surplus of meaning, and some of the meaning comes from the music and energy of the language. Content is vital, and pace, rhythm, and emphasis help to carry the day so that these words are set on fire in the Spirit and faith is renewed and vital.

Some meaning can afford to be lost in the above sample because while it communicates information, it also keeps the focus essentially on only one thought: God answers prayer. The speaker does not worry about tight correspondence to chronological or biblical order in listing the various characters of the Bible. What matters is what happened: God answered. In fact, one suspects that much preaching fails to soar precisely because preachers are too bound by excessive concern for order, history, logical links, and chronology rather than by exuberance to proclaim the gospel.

Use Celebration to Preach People into a Relationship with Christ

Bishop Vashti Murphy McKenzie has three distinct parts to her celebration in the latter part of her sermon on Peter healing the disabled beggar in Acts 3:1-10, three parts in an increasing movement of celebration. Because of space restrictions, only the end part is printed here:

> At the beginning of the text, the same man used to beg at the gate called Beautiful. At the end of the text, the power of God transformed his life. Some of us are like the lame man. Some of our churches and many of our ministries are like the lame man. We have everything we need to make it right. We have the intellect, the social standing, and the status. We have the equipment, structure, and success. We have skills and talent. We have attendees, givers, and members. We have everything we need to make it work, except we have no power. No power!
> What we need is the power of God released into our lives.
> What will happen to our churches if we do not speak the name of Jesus?
> What will happen to our preaching if we utter the words of God in Jesus' name and the power of God is released?
> What will happen to our singing if we sing in the name of Jesus—when the power of God is released into our anthems and in our hymns?
> What will happen in our prayer lives, praying in his name?
> What will happen in our marriages, our homes and families?
> What will happen in our children's lives if we give them what they need, the released power of God, instead of what they want, Nikes, and the like? When we gather ourselves together, signs and wonders will follow the preached word of God. [She moves on to her conclusion.][17]

Suggestions for Creative Adaptation

Celebration helps ensure that the gospel message is not received simply as abstract ideas or teaching, but as a relationship with Jesus Christ, as the power of the Holy Spirit to make a difference in life. McKenzie preaches in a call-and-response tradition; one knows that her questions would not be greeted with polite silence. If celebration is perceived to be not only an embodiment of the gospel on the preacher's part but also a manifestation of the Spirit who seeks to involve the listener, the participant is drawn into relationship with the divine. Celebration not only invites the listeners to become involved in the proclamation; it invites them to be that proclamation.

We have addressed the difference between emotion and emotionalism, but what about when the preacher's emotions, for whatever reason, give the lie to her or his words of celebration? Is it best to change the sermon at this point? Should the preacher act as though the celebration is real, in faith that the reality of grace will transcend his or her temporary emotional state?

These questions are worth pursuing. I recall walking through the Martin Luther King Jr. National Historic Site in Atlanta with Richard Lischer, author of *The Preacher King*,[18] and he commented that on the Sundays before King's major civil rights initiatives or sermons, his preaching was at times almost mumbled, as though he was laboring with his emotions and his righteous anger was building. Then a Sunday would come when his words were on fire.

Even in our own lives there are times when celebration may not seem possible for whatever reason. In such situations we are nonetheless called to preach the gospel, not something else, for it is the help that we and others need. Whether we preach the gospel ought not depend upon mood. When the Nicene Creed is read in church, not everyone can say with equal conviction all the words, and some folks in periods of doubt or illness may need to lean on the faith of the community to do their believing for them. Was there divine intent that the English word *preaching* would have the words *aching* and *reaching* within it?

When preachers are not able to celebrate, depending upon the occasion, they may need to preach a lament that makes only a strong turn to hope. Or perhaps on such a Sunday the preacher need only teach the gospel. Another possibility is to prepare words that could be preached in celebratory fashion, declaring the wonderful works of God with thanks, perhaps adapting a section from someone else's sermon (with citation). The words would represent what the preacher intellectually knows to be true even if she or he does not fully experience them at the moment. A preacher's expression on such a Sunday might be muted; not up to the excitement the words can inspire, they may have no more fire than a match might bring. Even someone lighting a match at night can be a tremendous comfort to someone in fear. Who knows? That match may kindle not only the congregation's faith, but also the preacher's in the very act of proclaiming. The fire that comes is not one's own nor is it at one's bidding; it is the delight of God to give.

Assessing

Proclamation

CHAPTER EIGHTEEN

The Effects of Genres of Proclamation

W e have considered nine forms of proclamation that have been most common in sermons over history: *condemnation, lament, stern exhortation, testimony, prayer, nurturing exhortation, proclamatory statements, doxology,* and *celebration.* We have considered examples of these genres in sermons from the early church to the present day. Where they have been located in the present, they are mostly in African American preaching. What has not been possible to demonstrate here has been the relative absence or decline of these subforms in most other traditions from roughly the early 1900s. How does one prove a decline or absence short of recommending that readers read widely in sermons of the last century to see for themselves? In any case, two facts attest to it: (1) preachers are generally uncertain as to what the word *proclamation* means, and (2) the notion of distinct genres of proclamation has sufficient novelty to suggest it is a practice not widely known.

Seminary students commonly will have studied form criticism in their biblical studies classes so they know something about genres. Using form criticism, students begin by identifying the conventional literary form/s within a biblical text. One can then try to work back to the intended meaning of that text by determining its setting in life (*Sitz im Leben*), how it functioned. For example, psalms were part of worship; law codes were part of court proceedings; laments were part of rituals of mourning; proverbs were used in instructing the young. Once the life setting is determined, one is better able to read texts.

What we have been doing in the preceding chapters with genres in sermons is similar. Form criticism in biblical studies is related to genre theory, but genre is the whole package (as we began to explore in the introduction to section 4): form, style, content, setting, purpose, presumptions, rhetorical effect, connections, and so forth.

Here we explore the effect of these genres. Because it is new to think of them, what difference do they make in how preachers might think of preaching?

What These Subforms Do

We can speak now with greater certainty about what our preaching subforms do. Using Augustine's term, they delight or persuade. With the help of the Spirit, they do what they say; they bring God to expression and give God voice. God may be experienced to speak in and through them, bestowing that of which they speak:

> So shall my word be that goes out from my mouth;
>> it shall not return to me empty,
> but it shall accomplish that which I purpose,
>> and succeed in the thing for which I sent it. (Isaiah 55:11)

In broad terms our subforms bestow trouble (law) or gospel. C. H. Spurgeon once said that "the miracles are the acted sermons of our Lord Jesus Christ,"[1] and we may say that the "doing of gospel" to the people is likewise a miracle: it is something that God does in and through the sermon. Jesus said to the disciples, "Whoever listens to you listens to me" (Luke 10:16). Even the trouble genres of proclamation serve the gospel when rightly conceived. True, they put the burden upon people to do something that they cannot do with only their own resources. However, trouble subforms not only communicate with certainty what is wrong; they make it a matter of urgency; they cry out for the grace that God actually delights in bestowing. Grace puts the burden on God, who has already accepted it in Christ Jesus. Grace in a biblical text may not fully be the gospel, but it is the doorway to it. The deeper one goes in preaching trouble, the higher one is potentially able to soar in preaching the gospel, and the greater the flame of God's love is enhanced for the listener.

Three significant effects of our subforms of proclamation remain in need of discussion: (1) genres and creativity, (2) genres and worlds they project, and (3) genres and sermon movement.

1. Genres Are Tools for Creativity

Genres are wonderful tools to assist the creative process. David Duff in literary studies defines *genre* as follows: "a recurring type or category of text, as defined by structural, thematic and/or functional criteria."[2] Genres allow speakers to say or do certain things because they provide models that say and do similar things. Genres enable listeners to understand by allowing them to categorize what they hear and thereby know how to interpret it. Genres also permit the wider culture to interact because genres are shared. The power of genre is obvious, for example, when audience members discover that a speaker is using comedy and is not serious, as they initially thought. Genre helps establish meaning.

Prior to the 1800s, genres were generally understood to be fixed in number, universal in application, and timeless. One could evaluate a poem from ancient Greece alongside a poem written in the present and use the same standards. The genres in Aristotle's world were limited in number to the "natural forms" of poetry: epic, lyric, and drama.[3] The Romantic poets rejected evaluation of literature according to form alone. Form, content, and function, they said, are interrelated. Friedrich Schlegel, the German Romantic poet and critic, wrote that "every poem is a genre unto itself,"[4] meaning that each poem operates by its own rules. By the mid-1900s the number of recognized genres had expanded, but genre became unpopular in literary studies because it was used primarily to limit or exclude—a poem or sermon might be judged bad if it did not fit existing recognized norms. Innovation was thereby discouraged.

Literary critics have now revived the unpopular idea of genre and stood it on its head. Genre is now reconceived in exciting ways: where genres were once fixed end products to which a writer aspired (e.g., a preacher might set out to write a three-point sermon), now genres are understood to have some fixed elements and also to be continually evolving, flexible, and a source of creative expression. Genres assist composition of new texts. Literary critic Tzvetan Todorov says, "Where do genres come from? Quite simply, from other genres. A new genre is always the transformation of an earlier one, or of several: by inversion, by displacement, by combination. . . . There has never been a literature without genres."[5] In other words, genres make communication possible; they are tools for the imagination. Preachers can use genres of proclamation to generate new expressions of witness to the gospel that otherwise might not be possible.

Preachers Have Freedom Using Genre

Earlier understandings of genre stressed purity and conformity as goals. Nowadays, genre is rarely considered to be pure, and genres are understood to participate in bigger systems. The author, the listeners, and the wider culture all unavoidably have notions of genre, even without knowing it, that enable them to communicate and understand when people are joking, issuing commands, ranting, or whatever. Genres interact with other genres and are changed by them (notably, we have seen that celebration is a hybrid genre).

Roman Jakobson spoke of a "dominant" genre as the "focusing component of a work of art: it rules, determines, and transforms the remaining components."[6] There are various dominant psalm genres, for instance, songs of ascent, songs of Zion, *Hallel* or hymns of praise, plus enthronement, royal, wisdom, lament, and praise psalms. Sermons similarly have dominant genres: propositional, narrative, expository, and so forth. There are also various minor genres in psalms, for instance, invocation, lament, imprecations or curses, confession of trust, report of deliverance, vow or shout of praise, and petition. These have their own forms, themes, and functions, or may share features with other genres. The minor genres of sermons include our subforms of proclamation.

In other words, preachers working on proclamation do not need to stick rigidly with one genre; they may combine genres or do whatever serves the needs of the gospel. To adapt Jesus' words in Mark 2:27, genres were made to serve people, not people to serve genres.

2. Genres Project Worlds

Genres are like public spaces (arenas, squares, theaters, art galleries); they foster certain kinds of communication. Embedded in each genre are certain norms, codes, and conventions of acceptable behavior that represent certain values, economic perspectives, and beliefs. Genres are patterns that repeat. They are not necessarily universal, for not all societies have epic poems, novels, or sermons for that matter. Each genre communicates certain perspectives on the world. Todorov says that the old approach to genre described only the end product when, by contrast, "we have to learn how to present genres as principles of dynamic production," as part of the creative process.[7] Like language itself, genres disclose the reality we experience. We do not simply

> look through pieces of text, as through a window, to an already constituted world outside it. . . . Far from being merely "stylistic" devices, genres create effects of reality and truth, authority and plausibility, which are central to the different ways the world is understood in the writing of history or of philosophy or of science, or in painting, or in everyday talk. These effects are not, however, fixed and stable, since texts—even the simplest and most formulaic—do not "belong" to genres but are, rather, uses of them; they refer not to "a" genre but to a field or economy of genres, and their complexity derives from that complexity of that relation.[8]

Theorists in literary studies like to think of new "texts as performances of genre rather than reproductions of a class to which they belong."[9]

Genres communicate worlds because they frame or reflect particular realities of place, time, and people. When we read Jesus' parable of the Good Samaritan, we are taken back into his world. Different genres communicate different worlds, though they may overlap significantly. Genres are lenses through which we view the world:

> The realities in and amongst which we live are not transparently conveyed to us but are mediated by systems of representation: by talk, by writing, by acting (in all senses of the word), by images, even by sound. Whereas [we] . . . tend to assume that reality is singular and external to the forms through

which we apprehend it, the notion of genre as "'frames' or 'fixes' on the world" implies the divisibility of the world and the formative power of these representational frames.[10]

Each genre frames or reflects reality in particular ways, allowing some things to be seen and obscuring others. Each genre molds experience into its own patterns. Each genre sends coded signals to listeners to hear in certain ways. Use of genres is thus not a neutral or an impartial practice. A speaker makes decisions about what genres to use because they have an effect on the hearers.

Proclamation subforms project worlds where God exists as sovereign, works miracles, and speaks saving words directly to humanity; where need is known and prayers are answered; and where faith, justice, and mercy find reward. Here humans are reconciled to God, and all things are made new in Jesus Christ. Right relationships are restored with God and neighbor. Action is key. The word does what it says; the subforms do in God's name what their names indicate: condemnation rejects, lament unites in sorrow, stern exhortation rebukes, testimony renders individual experience of the divine, prayer communicates divine will, nurturing exhortation encourages change, proclamatory statements declare God's love, doxology leads to praise, and celebration moves people to joyful, thankful mission. God is brought to voice. What God speaks is already begun in the Spirit; in utterance it comes into being. The worlds that these subforms project affect those who enter them because in and through them they meet their Savior and Lord. Preachers have reason to be passionate because in preaching the gospel they are offering faith. Faith makes a difference, change is possible, and promise is fulfilled.

Comparing the Worlds Projected by Teaching and by Proclamation

Teaching and proclamation project differing, though related, worlds. Teaching the gospel projects worlds that

1. are informational in purpose, not transformational;
2. focus on what people are to do (even with regard to God, it focuses on what people are to think and believe); and
3. talk *about* various topics, generally falling short of *doing* the word. Even when teaching is directly about the gospel, it implies, accept this, believe this, understand this, or do this. Teaching points to God, but it leaves one saying with Mary and Martha, "Lord, if you had been here, my brother would not have died" (John 11:21, 32).

Like proclamation, teaching may be composed of genres, but that is beyond our concern here, primarily because homiletics of the last fifty years unintentionally has concentrated so heavily on changing how we teach from the pulpit and the urgent need now is to find what has been lost.

Proclamation, in contrast to teaching, presents worlds in which

1. the gospel comes to the people as a summons of good news: "Jesus says, I died for you";
2. what God does now is highlighted: "The blind receive their sight, the lame walk, the lepers are cleansed, the deaf hear, the dead are raised, the poor have good news brought to them. And blessed is anyone who takes no offense at me" (Luke 7:22-23). We say what Mary and Martha were no doubt led to say, "Because you are here, my brother is alive";
3. listeners are introduced to God and cast on divine promises concerning life beyond death; and
4. listeners are introduced to God and cast on divine resources and power in the name of Jesus Christ.

Genres speak of norms. Our subforms inevitably teach as well as proclaim; thus seeking too fine or fixed a line between teaching and proclamation is futile. Moreover, while as humans we may draw a line between teaching *about* gospel and *bestowal* of its grace in proclamation, the Holy Spirit blows where God wills and at any moment can make even the stodgiest of teachings or the most damning of condemnations into a miraculous word of liberation and love.

3. Genres Provide Sermon Movement

Sermons need movement, and teaching must come before proclaiming. While proclamation of the gospel may happen at various places in the sermon, it represents the climax of the sermon because it centers on the gospel. To use the metaphor of theater, a sermon ideally has the effect of a two-act play: act 1, teaching; act 2, proclamation.

The model for this can be Luke 24. In act 1, the disciples journey with Jesus to Emmaus, and he teaches them: "Then he opened their minds to understand the scriptures, and he said to them, 'Thus it is written, that the Messiah is to suffer and to rise from the dead on the third day, and that repentance and forgiveness of sins is to be proclaimed in his name to all nations, beginning from Jerusalem'" (vv. 45-47). All of this is teaching. Act 2 takes place at the table when they recognize that they are in his presence; he is risen. In the giving of the bread they know him. The one who had been taught *about* is the same one giving himself as their salvation. Act 2 models proclamation, and they experience Jesus' love.

Søren Kierkegaard once used the metaphor of theater to describe worship. He reversed the common expectation of things. He said one assumes the minister is the actor on stage, the congregation is the audience, and God is the prompter. Instead one should think that the minister is the prompter offstage, God is the audience, and the congregation is the center of attention on stage:

> At the devotional address, God himself is present. In the most earnest sense, God is the critical theatergoer, who looks on to see how the lines are spoken and how they are listened to: hence here the customary audience is wanting. The speaker is then the prompter, and the listener stands openly before God. The listener, if I may say so, is the actor, who in all truth acts before God.[11]

Kierkegaard's image is richly suggestive of Christian life as drama.[12] Worship is about praising God, hearing God's word, and being empowered for ministry. Numerous authors have spoken of church doctrines in the manner of George Lindbeck's cultural linguistic model, as scripts to guide daily life.[13]

Kierkegaard's metaphor is good, but it is static and in need of modification. Many people do come into church with the expectation that the preacher is on stage, as it were. That model fits act 1 as teaching. However, when proclamation occurs, a shift takes place, and Kierkegaard's alternative metaphor kicks in. Now members of the congregation are center stage, and they are in the spotlight of God's love. Suddenly their lives are the focus, the issue, before God. The preacher is offstage as the prompter. In act 2, the congregation is in the spotlight on stage.

Acts 1 and 2 have parallels in the life of faith. The reasons that youth may leave the church can be many and complex, yet in my experience in youth ministry, they often leave because they do not have a living relationship with Jesus Christ. Through Sunday school and youth programs, they have achieved an act 1 level of faith: they know something about beliefs and faith practices. They intellectually understand important aspects of it. However, they leave without receiving an act 2 level of faith in which one appropriates those practices and beliefs as part of an ongoing daily relationship with one's Lord and Savior. The burden for these departures rests on all in the church, for all are called to proclaim the gospel.

The Preacher's Perspective

Acts 1 and 2 refer to the effect of proclamation on the listener. How may we speak of the movement of the sermon from the preacher's

---

perspective?[14] The gospel is itself a genre because in addition to having content, it has form and movement from crucifixion to resurrection, exodus to promised land, or trouble to grace. To be communicated adequately, something of this form and movement is needed in the movement of the sermon as a whole. A sermon that ends in condemnation cannot leave a lasting impression of love.

When sermons talk about trouble, they must talk either about the Bible or about the world today. The same thing is true of grace. Thus in thinking of what is possible in a sermon, we have generally four components: trouble in the biblical text, trouble in our world, grace in the biblical text, and grace in our world. These are no invention, just common sense. Preachers who never study theory still use them. These are basic grammatical elements of sermons. Theological effectiveness depends upon them.

They can also provide a rough normative pattern for sermon movement through the four elements. For practical purposes I have called them pages. Page One is trouble in the biblical text and is usually teaching; Page Two is trouble in our world and may include one of our trouble subforms of proclamation; Page Three is grace in the biblical text and is mainly teaching about the gospel; and Page Four is grace in our world leading to the climax of the sermon in one or more genres of gospel proclamation.[15]

The movement to proclamation is the movement to authentic faith and confession. David Lose says the sermon moves to "verbal testimony that 'Jesus is Lord.' In fact *faith finds its full actualization only in its articulation.*"[16] Lose is not interested in a postmodern homiletic per se but one "governed by the pattern of God's manifestation made most clear in the cross and resurrection of Jesus Christ."[17] Lose notes, "It is my contention that a Christian sermon not only needs such moments of declaration, of ultimate speech, but that the sermon's center of gravity is located in them, as in these moments the illocutionary intention of the sermonic confession is most clearly realized."[18] Generally proclamation comes not as a single moment isolated from other preaching moments but as moments embedded in genres of speech designed to bring about an experience of the gospel.

Doing the Gospel

Of course, people come to church with different expectations. People who just come to criticize say to God, "Show me." Those who desire instruction say, "Teach me." Those who have a question say, "Feed me." Those who seek union with God say, "Mold me." Those who need comfort say, "Hold me," and those who are wounded say, "Heal me." And yet beyond all of these cries is the one in most hearts: "O God, encounter us;

confirm our faith." In proclamation, these cries are met. People find themselves enrolled in the gospel story, what happened in the text happens to
them through the power of the Spirit, they catch fire in the Spirit, and
what happens in the gospel story becomes their experience. Hamlet's "all
the world's a stage" is realized: they are on stage performing in God's theater in the spotlight of God's love and power. Blind eyes are opened, deaf
ears are unstopped, hardened hearts are softened, and communities are
formed in the shape of the cross.

CHAPTER NINETEEN
Proclamation
An Outdated Practice or a New Beginning?

Although proclamation is common throughout the ages, it seems to be largely a lost art today. Where to go from here? What are preachers today to make of the genres of proclamation? Is proclamation an outdated practice that is best forgotten, a relic from eras in which both preaching and the gospel were understood differently? Or does proclamation present a way forward that holds promise for the church in crisis?

Michael Pasquarello III seems to speak in favor of proclamation:

> Perhaps nothing is more critical for shaping Christian identity and imagination in our time than the recovery of living remembrance, or commemorative doxology—a traditioned capacity for praise-filled thanksgiving. If this remembrance is lost, the church will be left without a sense of the biblical narrative or the proclamation of the living God, which is knowledge of God's speech and action by which Christian wisdom and character are sustained.[1]

The case we make here is that whatever other approaches the church might take in this postmodern age, the recovery of proclamation is central. Put more strongly, recovery of proclamation is recovery of the gospel. Until the gospel is proclaimed, it is not fully the gospel.

If proclamation is to be recovered, resistance to it will need to be addressed in significant areas of which we have not yet spoken: having an authentic voice in preaching, using authority well in preaching, and changing our attitudes toward imitation.

Having an Authentic Voice in Preaching

One of the biggest challenges to the recovery of proclamation is the fear that preachers rightly have of sounding inauthentic. Proclamation is distinctive. While its style may vary from moderate to grand, it is impassioned and inspired. The words are on fire. One does not speak them the way one normally mouths things in conversation, coolly and casually. Rather, in proclaiming, one speaks as one normally does when one is truly excited about something. Speech tends to be somewhat poetic, rhythmic, and energetic. It may communicate more feelings than a preacher normally shows. It may be more testimonial in the sense of revealing what the preacher truly believes and cares deeply about. Since most preachers rarely employ proclamation, to begin might seem risky. The reaction of the congregation is an issue—the preacher might need to teach them about proclamation in order to practice it. To try it, one would really have to believe in the merits of proclamation; one would need to long for a realization of the gospel; one would need to have faith it was God's will. If the gospel is not actualized in church through preaching of the word of God, where might it be?

Historical Reasons for the Loss of Proclamation

Understanding historical reasons for the loss of proclamation is important for its recovery. Kenneth Cmiel's *Democratic Eloquence* explains that at the beginning of the 1800s, educated people (in those days, men) were trained in Ciceronian eloquence. They translated Cicero from Latin, practiced him aloud in classrooms, and integrated every aspect of his rhetoric into their speech.[2] This led to what Edwin Griffin Parker first called "the golden age of American oratory"[3] with great speakers like Lyman Beecher, Phillips Brooks, and others. Gentlemen displayed Ciceronian eloquence as a mark of social class, power, education, and privilege. With the rise of both mass democracy and education, privileged ways of speaking were increasingly challenged by populist rhetoric.

Cmiel documents significant debates in the nineteenth century over topics such as the kind of language that was appropriate in public oratory, what constituted conversational English, newspaper rhetoric, standards of grammar, translations of the Bible, and even the kinds of words included in dictionaries. American English was gradually democratized, the speech of the common people was recognized, and technical language from the trades and sciences was broadly circulated in dictionaries. Gradually the ideal of speaking like a gentleman in a persuasive manner gave way to a new ideal fostered by the rising importance of science: speaking like an expert, speaking to facts, developing argument, using plain speech, and letting the facts speak for themselves. In the field of poetry, a parallel democratic movement took place from the 1850s when a revolt occurred against metered poetry toward free verse.[4]

By the turn of the twentieth century, traditional rhetoric was rarely heard in public spaces. The grand and even moderate styles of Cicero were generally abandoned in favor of the plain style. Rhetorician Robert S. Reid claims that the recovery of narrative ways of preaching in recent decades may be conceived as a recovery of the moderate style, even though in classical terms the moderate presents an argument and narrative does not.[5]

Reid says that a significant exception to the move to plain speech, not mentioned by Cmiel, was the African American community. Because they were denied access to public education, changes there made little impact. African American traditions were largely oral, and common oral practices continued. Arguments were commonly built using analogies, metaphors, narratives, and enthymemes, not the sequential chains of argument that came to be dominant in white preaching because of the growing need to sound like an expert. Persuasion remained a key purpose of speaking, and listeners were encouraged to enter the vision of life that the preacher offered. Moreover,

> preachers in this culture continued to emulate the kind of masterful persuasive speaking that occurred in the golden age of oratory in the middle of the 1800s. They were generally unafraid of issues of persuasion and, because they had no need to "let the facts speak for themselves" in the way that white experts tried to emulate, blacks continued to embrace the oral world of persuasion that modulates between the plain, the temperate and the Grand.[6]

African American preachers had received a tradition of proclamation common to all preachers that they went on to develop and refine. When the rest of the culture lost proclamation, African American communities did not. The moderate to grand styles continued to be employed whenever the preacher moved beyond teaching and sought both to praise God and to delight and persuade listeners in Christ.

Recovery of the Moderate to Grand Styles

The recovery of proclamation for the pulpit means recovery of what Augustine called the moderate and grand styles. The New Homiletic may have already begun that process with the recovery of narrative. One could argue that plain style is sufficient for our time, and if the culture itself evolves to embrace more fully the moderate and grand styles, as it might in time, the pulpit may then follow. Ecclesiastes implies that trends are like a pendulum; they eventually return, for "there is nothing new under the sun" (1:9) and "for everything there is a season" (3:1). Still, when one thinks of great speeches in the last century, one does not think of plain speeches. One thinks of rousing ones given by speakers who by training or instinct employed all of the styles well: for example, Ronald Reagan's address to the nation on the *Challenger* disaster, Barbara Jordon's keynote address to the Democratic Convention in 1976, John F. Kennedy's inaugural address, Martin Luther King's "I Have a Dream," Eleanor Roosevelt's "The Struggle for Human Rights," Winston Churchill's "Blood, Sweat, and Tears," or suffragette Anna Howard Shaw's "The Fundamental Principle of a Republic." We may not be accustomed to using moderate to grand styles, but we seem nonetheless to admire and best remember them. If we were being strictly biblical and allowing the Bible to shape our discourse, we would not opt for the plain to moderate styles alone; we would try to employ them all. Hence Augustine taught that the Bible teaches the rhetorical skills needed for the pulpit.

Being Authentic

How can preachers be authentic in using styles of public expression that may be new to them? First, there is no one ideal expression of each style, no one model to which everyone might aspire. Like genres, styles are rarely pure, and they admit other styles that complement or modify them. Preachers need to find expressions of the plain, moderate, and grand styles authentic to themselves. The classical ideal was that speakers modulate among all three styles, giving variance to tone, rhythm, pace, emphasis, content, and so forth.

Preachers may benefit by being coached in the use of a new style to ensure that it sounds natural. The coach makes a difference. A student experimented with the grand style at home and asked her mother to listen. Her mother said that she did not sound like herself, yet the class by contrast felt that she was perfectly natural. Upon closer analysis, it seemed that the mother may have reacted either to hearing her daughter be passionate in her expression or to hearing her daughter preach, since she was accustomed to neither. The class, on the other hand, did not have preconceptions about how this student should sound, except that she should project her voice and sound like the woman they knew, not someone trying to imitate someone else, and not putting on an unnatural preaching voice.

No pulpit speech is identical to what is used in conversation, yet in content, manner, and sound it must still appear conversational. The voice must reach the farthest corners of the room; gestures need to be large and intentional; the pace for plain speech and teaching generally may be slower than everyday conversation while the pace for the grand style may be slightly faster. All beginning preachers initially need to discover a natural voice for preaching, and the current challenge is simply to extend that exercise to find greater range in one's natural voice to accommodate other styles.

Using Authority Well in Preaching

A second issue that needs discussion if proclamation is to be recovered is authority in the pulpit. Does proclamation not claim too much authority for the preacher? Proclamation speaks on behalf of God. It declares thus and so. It is ultimate speech that one might say presumes ultimate authority. It requires boldness as an act of faith. Some people might thus conclude that the idea of proclamation belongs in a previous homiletical era. The thrust of Fred Craddock's *Overhearing the Gospel* was to highlight the value of overheard communication: adults hear the children's time better than they hear words addressed directly to them in the sermon. Is proclamation too direct? Another of his books, *As One Without Authority*, held up inductive preaching as a more gentle approach than deductive lecturing, less dominated by reason and the intellect and more fitting of the gospel. Numerous voices have encouraged a roundtable approach to preaching, a conversational style, and a tentative approach to truth claims. Homiletics today tends to focus on the congregation: who they are, how they hear, and what their needs may be. Might gains in these areas be lost if preachers were to reclaim authority, bring God to voice, and speak the gospel in confidence?

These concerns are legitimate. The call to recover the dual arts of teaching and proclamation is not a call to return to the past or to ways of authority that now seem excessive, oppressive, or predominantly male. It is a call to reassess the past in light of the gospel and to retrieve from it standards that can be refurbished as worthy guides in our time.

Homiletics may be said not to have paid enough attention to proper uses of pulpit authority. In our age we see increased calls for leadership because the church in various quarters lacks direction. Jackson W. Carroll responded to Craddock in his *As One with Authority: Reflective Leadership in Ministry*, stressing that authority is an unavoidable part of the office of ministry. He defined *authority* as follows:

> Authority is the right to exercise leadership in a particular group or institution based upon a combination of qualities, characteristics, or expertise that the leader has or that followers believe their leader has. To exercise authority involves influencing, directing, coordinating, or otherwise guiding the thought and behavior of persons or groups in ways that they consider legitimate. Within the Christian tradition, clergy have authority through ordination to proclaim the Word of God, to administer the sacraments, to exercise pastoral care and oversight, and to equip the laity for ministry.[7]

Several implications of his definition are helpful for preachers. Standards of how to exercise authority are not uniform or absolute and depend upon the community, the preacher, and the understanding of the divine mandate of the preaching office. Notions of call to ministry presume divine authority. Still, the community also gives authority, and the preacher seeks to earn and be worthy of it; accountability is two-way. Authority cannot be avoided, and most aspects of authority in ministry have expression even within the sermon (for example, as Forde said, preachers administer proclamation as a sacrament).

Authority is manipulation. There is no avoiding it. We manipulate just by speaking because we seek to influence those around us; thus it is more helpful to think of faithful and unfaithful manipulation. Our culture commonly judges authority to be misused if it is paternalistic and authoritarian, telling people what they must think, believe, and do. This was a critique of the old homiletic. At the other end of the spectrum, authority is misused by being neutral and offering lack of leadership, demonstrating an unwillingness to influence others, or bowing to whatever winds may blow. This is a critique leveled at some recent trends that leave sermons so open-ended that people are left not knowing what to believe. Somewhere between the extremes are faithful ways to use authority that fit cultural need and offer balance. They honor both the individual and the community, encourage questions, yet give guidance, and invite participation while proclaiming God's undying love.

Authority in Relation to God

What recent homiletics has said about authority in preaching mainly concerns listeners and has been mostly without regard to God's role in proclamation. The New Homiletic from the beginning has been about understanding the word as an event that encounters people, about relying on what the Bible says, about meeting the needs of people before the word, about learning how to preach in new ways, and about being sensitive to how language works. Fred Craddock encouraged inductive preaching as a way to prompt an encounter with God. Still, one could say that as the New Homiletic developed, it became apparent that God was more the assumed focus of its sermons than the actual, and what God says and does was not the intentional thrust of much homiletical instruction. Rather, what the biblical text says and does became the guiding principle, and if a text did not get to God, nothing ensured that the sermon got there. To the degree that this assessment is fair, proclamation as we discuss it here was not possible.

Discussion of the preacher's authority thus has been mostly limited to the preacher as teacher, and the push of late has been for more responsibility and mutuality. For example, Alice P. Matthews points to alternatives in her *Preaching That Speaks to Women*. She says that one can preach the Ten Commandments logically and legalistically, as impersonal rules, which tends to be a male approach, or one can preach them in terms of relationships, which tends to be a female approach. It considers "how others will be affected and what can be done to preserve or develop the relationships involved in the dilemma."[8] Thus the seemingly stern commandments become "wise ways of voluntarily staying in relationship with the One who had redeemed me from sin and death."[9] Some people listen for one kind of authority or the other in order to interpret what is said. Matthews maintains that if preaching on moral issues is to reach everyone, both approaches are needed.

Recovery of proclamation means that authority needs to be reconsidered on issues that have been sidelined recently, especially concerning the role of the divine and the role of the preacher as servant. Act 1 is teaching and the preacher is the actor on stage, the congregation is the audience, and God is prompter. When act 2 begins, the preacher goes offstage, God is the audience, and the congregation is on stage in the spotlight of God's love. The preacher's role becomes like that of Moses before the burning bush in the presence of the I AM (Exodus 3:14), one of reverent humility. Or the preacher stands with John the Baptist when he "rejoices greatly at the bridegroom's voice" and says, "My joy has been fulfilled. He must increase, but I must decrease" (John 3:29-30). In the movement of the preacher offstage, Christ's authority is foremost, and the preacher's role as servant is brought to its highest expression. The servanthood that marks all ministry now distinctly marks the authority of the preacher. It already comes with the checks and balances put in place by the church.

Proclamation requires boldness. It requires that preachers know themselves before God. Some people may argue that proclamation claims too much authority, truth is uttered with too much certainty, and dissent is stifled. True, people need to come to faith of their own volition, and dissent must be possible, yet preaching also must foster joyous faith and certain love. The preacher offers confession and witness. In and through it, Christ offers himself in word in a manner to what he does in the sacrament of the Lord's Supper. Time is given in the sermon for teaching when questions can and should be raised, but at some point faith needs to catch fire. What it looks and sounds like—who offers it—should become manifest.

The boldness required for proclamation should be no different from the boldness of any preacher in stepping into the pulpit, for the act in itself implies speaking for God. Some preachers in the New Homiletic seem falsely coy when they say they do not feel comfortable speaking for God.

That is exactly what preachers do, and people listen for God. Further, why should preachers feel comfortable doing such a daring act? Moreover, when preaching serves as an instrument of God, its authority is more invitational, empowering, and liberating than anything we humans might offer on our own. What God pronounces as freed is freed.

The preacher's authority is for the primary purpose of drawing attention to God: "Here is the one who saves." When pulpit authority is viewed this way, "there is no longer male and female" (Galatians 3:28). One does not dictate this is right and must be accepted, or else; rather, one lends one's voice to God in Christ for him to say, "I love you. Come to me. Be not afraid." When preaching rests on God's authority in this manner, listeners do not respond, "The preacher claims too much authority." Rather, in faith they hear God address them directly, and they say, "Thank you, Lord. You are my strength." The model for proclamation is not human authority, but what Paul says of God: "Love is patient; love is kind; love is not envious or boastful or arrogant or rude. It does not insist on its own way; it is not irritable or resentful; it does not rejoice in wrongdoing, but rejoices in the truth" (1 Corinthians 13:4-6).

Changing Our Attitudes toward Imitation

The recovery of proclamation requires that preachers be authentic using plain, moderate, and grand styles. To this we add that preachers need notions of God's authority in preaching, particularly for proclamation. A final issue in this recovery concerns changing common attitudes toward imitation. Preachers typically are negative about it; at the same time they are conflicted because they rely on imitation so much of the time.

Imitation in the Practice of Preaching

Preachers may think negatively of imitation with good reason. Illegal, cheap, counterfeit products imitate expensive originals and flood the marketplace. Internet resources are so readily available that one hears of preachers who no longer seek a fresh word of God from the Bible, who preach someone else's sermon as their own, including personal stories. Such practices give both preaching and imitation a bad name.

On the other hand, good and creative uses of imitation abound. Imitation is used whenever someone retells a story, borrows a phrase or image, or uses someone's angle on a text. Imitation is behind any paraphrase of a commentary, journal, or theology book. Every time preachers refer to some source, they imitate it in some way. Genre theory tells us this is normal, for every new piece of writing draws on earlier ones. Imitation is not being a slave to the past.

Originality in preaching is highly prized because one seeks a word of God for this particular congregation. Still, originality can be too highly prized. Strictly speaking, only God creates, and we humans imitate God by creatively rearranging what God gives. Proclamation probably cannot be recovered without imitation.

Imitation in the Academy

Preachers get conflicting attitudes from the academy toward imitation. On the one hand, it is encouraged as a way of establishing continuity with the past and learning from history. Scholars refer to what others have said. If one had to cite every influence in speaking, we would never get beyond footnotes. Ralph Waldo Emerson was aware of this:

> None escapes it. The originals are not original. There is imitation, model, and suggestion, to the very archangels, if we knew their history. The first book tyrannizes over the second. Read Tasso, and you think of Virgil; read Virgil, and you think of Homer; and Milton forces you to reflect how narrow are the limits of human invention. The "Paradise Lost" had never existed but for these precursors; and if we find . . . a book out of our horizon of thought and tradition, we are soon taught by new researches in its native country to discover its foregoers, and its latent, but real connection with our own Bibles.
>
> Read in Plato and you shall find Christian dogmas, and not only so, but stumble on our evangelical phrases. Hegel pre-exists in Proclus, and, long before, in Heraclitus and Parmenides.[10]

Derrida has a similar understanding that all texts are "double" in that they imitate or refer to something that came before[11] (he is partly responsible for the recent reassessment of genre).

The academy is also necessarily against plagiarism.[12] Is imitation, in fact, plagiarism? Plagiarism is knowingly representing as one's own any idea or expression of an idea. It is the exact copying of words as well as the borrowing of another person's thoughts, said in other words. Imitation can be plagiarism, but the key issue is not borrowing; it is borrowing without attribution, stealing intellectual property.

Legitimate imitation and borrowing involve giving credit where due. Thus when a preacher imitates a preaching subform from someone else, credit can be given in the sermon itself, in notes if the sermon is published, in the Sunday bulletin ("Part of this sermon was inspired by / adapted from . . ."), or in an oral discussion of the sermon. With these safeguards, imitation needs to be reclaimed as a creative and essential tool in the creative process.

A Countercultural Word Based in Theology

Proclamation is through the Spirit and thus challenges notions of intellectual ownership of ideas in preaching. Other cultures, like the First Nations in North America, had ideas that were communal; they valued stewardship of the land, not ownership, dominance, and control. Oral cultures in general pass on tradition through stories that belong to the whole community; the survival of future communities depends upon faithful repetition of the stories, even as each generation subtly adapts them for new times.[13]

James S. Stewart, the Scottish preacher, demonstrated a countercultural understanding of intellectual ownership in relation to his sermons. If legend is correct, when another great preacher, Peter Marshall, died, his wife gathered his sermon manuscripts and had them published, and one of those was a sermon originally written by Stewart. When asked if he was going to sue, he responded, "What, me sue another minister of the gospel? I should be honored that he found some use for my words." Stewart knew what many preachers know: the words that we preach may come from our mouths, but the Holy Spirit puts them there and one can hardly claim ownership. Preachers know this when they end their sermons with an ascription of glory, saying, "All thanks be to God," instead of, "All thanks be to me."

A servant model of authority acknowledges that the Holy Spirit is the true author of effective sermons. They are miracles wrought by God. A preacher conceives the words with divine help, yet the power and truth they demonstrate are God's, and their gift is to all humanity for the purpose of saving the world. From this perspective, one might say that inspired extracts from other people's sermons should be credited, to be sure, but also repeated, shared, and used broadly in the church through repetition, adaptation, and imitation. Like the gospel itself, this may seem too countercultural.

Proclamation and Creativity

Cleo LaRue says that in African American circles, young preachers find too hard the burden of coming up with fresh celebrations; they thus spend too much time on the end of the sermon and not enough on the body.[14] Some of this burden might be lifted if all preachers are given greater freedom to imitate. Instead of the word *imitate*, Michael

Taussig prefers the old Greek term *mimesis* that he claims as a creative art: "[It is] the faculty to copy, imitate, make models, explore difference, yield into and become Other. The wonder of mimesis lies in the copy drawing on the character and power of the original, to the point whereby the representation may even assume that character and that power."[15] When preachers imitate others, it is to be hoped that something of the character and power of the original passage comes through, for it isof God.

We may identify three stages of creativity for proclamation:

1. *Repetition.* In some instances preachers may largely repeat subforms from someone else's sermon (with appropriate citation), as long as one remains authentic to whom one is in terms of language, voice, and gestures. By occasionally just repeating what others have done, preachers come to understand particular genres and techniques, and are better able to compose for themselves. They may also gain confidence using rhythm, repetition, and more passionate expression than had been their norm.

2. *Adaptation.* Many models are from other ages and cultures. They need adaptation for one's own setting. The structure and many of the basic operating principles of the original remain intact, but improvisation can also be practiced. Adapting existing subforms affords creative expression and virtually guarantees the preacher a finished product for the Sunday sermon.

3. *Appropriation.* Gradually, as preachers become more accustomed to proclamation, they integrate, master, internalize, innovate, and express anew, thereby appropriating proclamation as part of their regular preaching repertoire. They grow skilled in dealing with words on fire.

For recovery of proclamation, we have named three changes that are needed that have to do with ensuring authentic voice, reclaiming divine authority in preaching, and using imitation as a creative practice. With these changes in place, proclamation can afford new opportunities for preachers to express their creativity and feed Christ's sheep.

CHAPTER TWENTY

Fulfilled in Your Hearing

If these chapters have done nothing else, they awaken us to the fact that preaching at its best both teaches and proclaims. We have made the case here that in order for preaching to be recovered as a dual art, teaching within the sermon needs to move beyond the essential historical and literary readings of a biblical text. It needs to get to how texts address matters of God and how we are to live as disciples empowered and equipped by the Spirit. In other words, the teaching needs to get to the gospel. This can mean that the identity of Jesus Christ and the meaning of his life, death, and resurrection need to be linked with the biblical text that is preached. For all of the advances in teaching in the pulpit in the last fifty or more years, arguably there is still a need for pulpit teaching to improve in relation to the gospel. When the cross is in focus, we have good reasons to claim that Christ comes to the hearers with renewing and transforming power.

In other words, sermons not only talk *about* things, that is, they teach, guided by the Spirit. They may also *do* things, that is, they offer the gospel. The Spirit directs and enlivens the words and offers Christ anew, not as ideas but as a relationship with the one who overturns the powers and principalities of this world. Salvation is given, and justice, mercy, and righteousness become possible. In every sermon there are *about* passages. In fact, most sermons today seem to be *about* sermons. For the health of the church we need to recover preaching as both *about* and *doing*. *Doing* sermons center on what God is accomplishing in Jesus Christ.

We have said that both teaching and proclamation rely on the Spirit. Teaching provides the theological, historical, and cultural information that people need (1) to understand who God is, has been, and will be, and (2) to know what our human role is before God in creation. Christian teaching is a gift of the Spirit (Romans 12:7; 1 Corinthians 12:8; Ephesians 4:11). The Spirit teaches. The disciples will be taught by the Spirit what to say before their opponents (Mark 13:11; Luke 12:12). Jesus says that the Advocate "will teach you everything, and remind you of all that I have said to you" (John 14:26) and "the Spirit of truth . . . will guide you into all the truth" (16:13). Paul says that the Spirit "intercedes" for us and teaches us "how to pray as we ought" (Romans 8:26). Inspired teaching enables us to read the Bible and to comprehend Jesus Christ; it helps us interpret society in light of the good news; it guides us in righteous living and instructs us in how to pray and live. It causes us to question and explore doubts, even as it leads to deeper faith. Still, the Spirit has other gifts that actually perform the good news.

We saw that some of the best insights about teaching in recent homiletics were anticipated by earlier preachers. We received practical guidance on how to teach effectively the Bible, theology, and social justice, and we saw the value of using principles such as compare and contrast, paradox, metaphor, and contradiction, principles deriving from the polar nature of language. As important, we saw how teaching may speak about many things, including God, but stop short of giving God to the people in a performance of the Spirit. Teaching helps people to learn, but it is not the doing of the gospel to those in need. Proclamation does that. Teaching analyzes the ailment and discusses the medicine, but proclamation gives it. Teaching can leave people uncertain about their relationship with God, and it ultimately casts them on their own resources to do whatever is needed. Teaching may spark like flint striking a rock, yet it offers no flame with which to set faith ablaze. Proclamation, by contrast, casts people on God's resources and offers certainty and joy. A saving relationship is given.

Proclamation of the gospel needs a prior foundation of teaching the gospel. The proclamation at Christmas, "Jesus Christ is born," is ineffective until a proper bed of teaching has been made in which the baby may lie, that communicates who he is, why he came, how he will die, and what all this means. The Easter proclamation, "Christ is risen," is important, though at the beginning of Easter worship, it may ring hollow for many. Those who did not attend the Good Friday service may not even have known that Jesus was dead. The responsive proclamation, "He is risen indeed," may thus be said with no more enthusiasm than saying, "Sally is up," or "The toast has risen." For proclamation to be proclamation, it needs preparation. By contrast, that same declaration at the end of the service may be expected to be fulsome, joyous, aflame with excitement, because teaching has been offered and the people have met their Lord in and through the word.

Neither teaching nor proclamation effectively stands on its own in the pulpit. Proclamation on its own is a lit wick with no candle, rhetoric without insight, passion without substance, enthusiasm without understanding. It is like someone going up to a total stranger and saying, "God loves you." The gospel may be humiliated and degraded. On the other hand, teaching on its own is a car tuned up for the trip with no money for gas; it is a traveler at a border with no passport; it is a concertgoer who has forgotten the tickets back home; it is a dinner party with no guests. Teaching without proclamation offers duty but no joy, possibility but no certainty, description but no encounter, and thus only partially equips for ministry. Teaching *about* God reflects proclamation. One cannot light a fire from a glowing reflection of a flame in a mirror. Teaching stops shy of holy fire. Instruction and information are given, sometimes passionately, but not salvation and the Spirit.

Teaching can exist without proclamation, even if it may fall short of God's intention for preaching, but proclamation cannot exist without teaching. Each is strengthened in the presence of the other. Teaching is stronger because it then offers God's help to follow through on its ethical and other implications. Proclamation becomes possible only with teaching because without kindling and wood in a fireplace, a flame cannot catch hold.

Proclamation includes various genres that support words at the core of the gospel and enable them to be heard. These genres have their own unity and are marked by a variety of features, like increased pace and balanced phrases. Of all the genres that the Bible contains, the ones most commonly found in preaching are those with close worship ties: *condemnation* and *stern exhortation* are akin to parts of prayers; to what was called the fencing of the table at Communion; to the renunciation of evil in adult baptism; and to the legal command in marriage services ("If anyone knows just cause . . ."). *Lament* is found in prayers and music. The gospel genres of proclamation also have their worship analogues: *testimony* (testimonials), *prayer* (prayers), *nurturing exhortation, proclamatory statements, doxology* (opening Scripture sentences, assurance of pardon, hymns and prayers, commissioning and benediction), and *celebration* (Eucharist). These genres communicate entire worlds that provide a context for salvation and liberation to be experienced. They bring God to voice. God's word is immediate enactment, instantaneous fire. Proclamatory language is performative in that it is doing, fulfilling, accomplishing, actualizing what is said. God is mediated in Christ through the Spirit.

A number of scholars have used distinctive terms to describe proclamation. Ebeling said proclamation brings joy and "double certainty" of both sin and salvation. Brunner called it "faith-awakening, faith-furthering, faith-wooing address." James S. Stewart said it is "God's life manifested and offered."[1] Gerhard Forde spoke of sacrament "doing the text to the people." David Lose called proclamation "ultimate speech" that communicates a truth that is beyond the preacher.[2] Here we have spoken of it as setting words on fire, remembering that as with Elijah's offering on Mount Carmel, God lights the fire (1 Kings 18:20-38), and "doing" the gospel to the people.

Proclamation communicates urgency partly through its moderate to grand style. What is spoken matters. God speaks, and the people are in the spotlight of God's love. They are enrolled in a script larger than their personal one, and the "performance" is now the drama of God's creation in which each person has an important role to play. In the move from act 1 to act 2 the hearer is transformed from observer to performer, from doubter to believer, from skeptic to recipient of God's grace. Faith is kindled anew. The preacher's authority gives over to God's authority. When this happens, we may say with Jesus, "This scripture has been fulfilled in your hearing" (Luke 4:21). Whenever we proclaim Jesus Christ in his true identity as is found in the cross and resurrection, a new creation is begun.

Questions Concerning the Practice of Proclamation

Several practical questions remain having to do with proclamation. The first of these is, *Does Jesus Christ have to be mentioned in every act of proclamation?* No. The gospel as God's saving action may be found anywhere in the Bible. Every sermon does not need to focus on Christ, and neither does every act of proclamation within a sermon. Nonetheless, the fullest expression of the gospel is in the life, death, resurrection, and ascension of Jesus Christ; thus normally the cross will be in focus. Christian faith presumably begins in the knowledge that Christ is alive now. Is it safe to say that Christ is implicit in every sermon that proclaims the gospel, even when he is not identified? The grace that defines gospel is always the grace of Christ—as trinitarian doctrine insists. The issue here is not whether Christ is present or not, for he has promised to be, but will listeners know he is present if he is not named? Will they know the identity of the one who encounters them?

Ought one to focus on Christ to the exclusion of other members of the Trinity? No. Trinitarian language is not least an amazing resource for preachers in that it gives various and diverse ways to sing God's praise. Moreover, we might claim that God is most fully known in trinitarian language. To be true to the faith we have received, we need to be able to speak of God as Father, Son, and Holy Spirit. One may generalize that the sermon is normally theocentric, that the gospel to which the sermon leads is normally christocentric, and that our encounter with God is through the Spirit.

How is proclamation to be delivered? Does it need to be memorized? Preaching without notes has been a goal of many preachers, and there are several books on this topic.[3] It is, however, a matter of individual decision and practice. Generally preaching without notes is highly overrated, for if one uses a manuscript properly, one is not reading or tied to the page. Most examples of celebration that we hear today in African American churches are memorized, yet one of the best African American preachers, Charles G. Adams (cited earlier), has always been a manuscript preacher. His celebrations are no less effective for having a page in front of him to which he refers.

How does proclamation of trouble relate to proclamation of the gospel in the sermon? Proclamation of trouble generally finds its place in the first half of the sermon, as is appropriate also with teaching about trouble. If it comes late in the sermon, the effect of the gospel is lessened. Gospel proclamation usually takes place in the second half of the sermon and most commonly wherever the climax occurs. By ensuring this, the biblical movement of the gospel from cross to resurrection is preserved and communicated in its power.

What does proclamation mean in terms of the New Homiletic? The New Homiletic as we have defined it here is about elements of broad consensus in recent decades. It remains important and its lessons stand, but they are primarily about teaching. Homiletics needs to be reconceived from the beginning of the preaching process such that God is at the center of the exegetical process and the gospel is the ensured outcome.[4] What is needed now in homiletics for proclamation of the gospel is a theological turn, building on the New Homiletic but going beyond it in substantial ways.

Beyond theological focus, are there other ways in which the dual arts of teaching and proclamation differ from the New Homiletic? One key difference concerns the Bible. The New Homiletic seems to encourage the notion that the purpose of preaching is to preach a text, or to have a text say and do now what a text said and did then, or even to have listeners experience the text in the same way as the original hearers did. It is also possible to argue that the purpose of preaching is to preach the gospel. Texts are indispensable tools in that service, and historical-critical and literary analysis is essential for textual interpretation to ensure they are heard to say what they do say. Still, when texts do not contain the gospel, as most do not the way they are cut, they need to be platforms from which one looks to the cross and the faith at large. In this manner both the gospel and the text are rendered anew in the power of the Spirit.

Proclamation does not assume that the gospel is present in a text. Thus if a text does not contain it, one uses the text as an essential window or lens to find it. For example, the parable of the Rich Fool in Luke 12:13-21 is a difficult text in which to find good news, *but one can find good news with it*. In the text, a man in the crowd wants Jesus to tell his rich brother to divide the family inheritance, and instead Jesus tells the man a parable. That Jesus does not respond directly to his request may indicate Jesus' disregard for the problems of wealth or his great concern for what is happening to this man's soul. To arrive at the gospel, a preacher might ask, What does the cross look like when one views it from this text? or What does this text look like in light of Christian worship and life? One could say that the rich fool relies on his own sufficiency, which the parable proves to be false. The good news here is that we need not rely on ourselves, but can rely instead on the grace of God in Christ. One could also say that people who most love wealth spurn the cross, yet Jesus accepts it for himself in order to save even those who make wealth or other things their priority. As Christians follow the cross, their lives become a new parable, this time of the rich wise person, who may be portrayed either as Christ or as someone who lays down her life for her neighbor or both. In preaching the gospel, almost as important as the biblical text are intertextual connections to other Bible texts, to the larger gospel story, and the degree to which together they render in faith the identity of Jesus Christ.

Is the passion of proclamation not a dangerous thing to encourage? Passion in the pulpit is dangerous if used to coerce, to persuade without good teaching, to entertain, or to present a false persona. Passion in itself ought not be the issue, however; the gospel is primary and whatever excitement may be appropriate to it. No one single way of expressing passion in the pulpit is the only correct model. What is right is what is natural to each preacher. The gifted preacher C. H. Spurgeon admired the power that lay in "clear arguments," but he also knew the importance of "emotional persuasion" or what he called "heart-argument—which is logic set on fire."[5] He explained it as follows:

> You must argue with them as a mother pleads with her boy that he will not grieve her, or as a fond sister entreats a brother to return to their father's home and seek reconciliation: argument must be quickened into persuasion by the living warmth of love. Cold logic has its force, but when made red-hot with affection the power of tender argument is inconceivable.[6]

In proclamation, it is not necessary that each person fully grasp every word, reference, or allusion. The flames dance where they will. Proclamation enables the preacher to witness with joy and energy, to assist in communicating God to the people, and to encourage the church to celebrate and be faithful.

Might proclamation not seem like a radical departure if it has not been practiced before? The congregation can be invited to be involved in the process. Preachers may find it helpful initially to preach about what proclamation is, have sessions to teach it, ask for sermon feedback, and encourage listeners themselves to offer it, perhaps by way of testimony.

Is proclamation just a matter of saying the right words? Proclamation is not formulaic or predictable in the manner that in some traditions the sermons commonly end with a reference to the table: proclamation is creative and has many genres. Proclamation is more than saying some key words; at its best it is heartfelt confessing and proclaiming Jesus Christ; more than intellectual address, it is embodied speech and personal witness. It is the utterance of the words that are authorized by the biblical text as it both illuminates the gospel and is illuminated by it. Such utterances are actualized, enlivened, and set ablaze by the Spirit. God speaks. Proclamation thus has the marks of a personal relationship and it is not just an argument with proclamation attached; it has intellectual, emotional, and powerful spiritual components.

How many subforms of proclamation might appear in one sermon? Subforms may vary in length, and they can be embedded in other subforms, so this question is difficult to answer. Perhaps there can be no fixed rules. If one agrees that up to one-half of a sermon should be devoted to trouble and one-half to God's action of grace and empowerment, a portion of each can be proclamation. It can happen several times in one sermon. Anything can be overused. Preachers have to find the right balance of teaching and proclamation, right for themselves, for their congregations, for the particular biblical text, and for the gospel.

Is proclamation too individualistic? The gospel is about more than saving individual souls. It is about shaping communities of faith as Christ's body in the world, equipped for acts of justice, mercy, and kindness. Proclamation is both to the individual and to the community, and in being the word that gives Christ, it forms community. By this word, God chooses to speak to the world. Without proclamation the church can still teach about the gospel, but the divine rules remain killing words sentencing death because we cannot on our own do what is required. Listeners may hear in teaching that hope is coming, but it never arrives and all promises are empty. As Brunner said, God meets us but "not as himself." In such preaching people are awakened to sin and the need to change, yet they still long for the unconditional love that transforms them into the new creation in Christ's image. No confession of Jesus as the Christ is evoked, and the church is not fully itself. Proclamation takes information *about* God and turns it into a word spoken *by* God, it turns impossible rules into doable roles, and it brings people into their true selves and community as God intended them to be.

Conclusion

Luke Timothy Johnson begins his book *The Real Jesus: The Misguided Quest for the Historical Jesus* with what may be the best opening line of any Christian book (apart from the Bible), "It makes a great deal of difference whether you believe someone is alive or dead." Perhaps novelist John Updike was getting at the same thing in his "Seven Stanzas at Easter":

Make no mistake: if He rose at all it was as His body;
   if the cells' dissolution did not reverse, the molecules reknit, the amino
      acids rekindle;
   the Church will fall. . . .

Let us not mock God with metaphor, analogy, sidestepping transcendence, making of the event a parable, a sign painted in the faded credulity of earlier ages:
let us walk through the door.[7]

Perhaps even preachers are reluctant to "walk through the door" if it means having to explain the resurrection or if it means getting caught up in doctrinal debate. Moreover, the resurrection is a scandal, a stumbling block, for all kinds of reasons. The resurrection involves mystery, and arguably the purpose of preaching, in claiming that the resurrection is central to the faith, is not to explain the mystery but to highlight it. Peter Short, the former moderator of my denomination, wisely said, "Don't look directly at the resurrection any more than you would look directly at the sun. You know what will happen. Besides, if you were capable of explaining it you would have so diminished the resurrection that it would no longer explain you."[8] Even Mark struggled with what to say, if indeed his original ending was 16:8: "They said nothing to anyone, for they were afraid." John M. Buchanan still finds persuasive the "old argument" for the resurrection: "Some transformation occurred in the lives of Jesus' followers such that those who were cowering in fear became fearless witnesses and martyrs. They became convinced that death did not defeat Jesus, that he was alive and present in the world, and that therefore there was nothing for them to fear, not even their own death."[9] Richard B. Hays notes, "The term *resurrection* in 1st cent. Judaism was understood to refer to the raising of a physical body, not merely a spiritual exaltation to heaven or a mystical visionary experience by Jesus' followers."[10]

One could maintain that if people trip in their faith journey, wisely it is not at the parting of the Red Sea, at the virgin birth, or at whether a woman can be healed of her bleeding by touching a garment. It should be in front of the empty tomb, asking, Is Jesus Christ alive or not? Other miracles comparatively fade in significance before this one, and no answer is more central to what we proclaim. Only this answer can bring certainty in other areas of the faith. If God can raise Jesus from the dead, why would we choose to deny the possibility of other biblical miracles? If God has raised Jesus, what miracles in our lives or in the very act of preaching are not possible? Might someone yet believe even now?

There may be other ways to understand the gospel, but they all seem to lead to the cross. As Paul said, "If Christ has not been raised, then our proclamation has been in vain and your faith has been in vain" (1 Corinthians 15:14). Many denominations today are in trouble with declining membership, increased overhead, spiraling litigations from immoral and other practices, and overburdened pastors. Preachers are pressured to try anything to make a difference, and some are tempted to abandon the sermon as we know it.

The purpose of this volume has been to suggest another approach, to invite preachers to consider preaching in a way that they may not have consciously employed and that involves joy and praise. Christ commissioned the church to preach the gospel, and for all of the changes in homiletics lately, the gospel arguably still has not become its conscious model. Preachers tend to teach the Bible, tradition, or topics relevant to today and may not also teach the connection of their biblical text or sermon to the gospel. The gospel gives people reason for faith and justice. Consequently the art of proclamation that has been so central to the church in the past remains mostly lost, and some churches long for the nourishment they might receive. Proclamation may offer potential to revitalize the church. These pages have been dedicated to the recovery and enhancement of proclamation.

Sermons that proclaim are as varied as individual snowflakes, yet they have in common one main feature: they transform by doing the gospel, and people experience that the good news is for them. If people know through our preaching that Christ dies on the cross for them and all of God's children, they no longer need to be in control. The assent of faith need be the only response, "I believe; help my unbelief!" (Mark 9:24.) As Luther said, "Glaubst du, so hast du" (believe it, and you have it). Having it, we may do it, and the world will conform more closely to God's loving will.

Notes

Opening Epigraph

1. Jean-Pierre Camus, "Third Panegyric Commemorating Saint Charles Borromeo," trans. James Waring de Bernieres McCrady, in *A History of Preaching*, by O. C. Edwards Jr., vol. 2 (Nashville: Abingdon Press, 2004), 280.

Chapter 1: A Challenge for Preaching

1. David Buttrick notably spoke of numerous matters that relate to subforms in his *Homiletic: Moves and Structures* (Philadelphia: Fortress, 1987). In my writing I have spoken about the Four Pages of a sermon (trouble in the Bible, trouble in our world, grace in the Bible, grace in our world) that are one way of addressing subform, though they are in the first instance a grammar of preaching. See *The Four Pages of the Sermon* (Nashville: Abingdon Press, 1999).

2. In the fall of 2006 the National Association of Evangelicals hosted a series of leadership conferences in forty-four cities warning pastors that teenagers in large numbers are abandoning the faith. They predicted that if current trends prevail, only 4 percent of current teenagers will become "Bible-believing Christians" as adults, down from 35 percent of the current baby boom generation. Laurie Goodstein, "Fearing the Loss of Teenagers, Evangelicals Turn Up the Fire," *New York Times*, October 6, 2006, national desk late edition—final, sec. A.

3. The Institute on Religion and Democracy, "Chart of Mainline Church Membership Decline: Church Membership 1960–2003," http://www.irdrenew.org/site/apps/nl/content2.asp?c=fvKVLfMVIsG&b=470745&ct=1571507 (accessed December 30, 2006). By contrast the same chart shows alone the Assemblies of God increasing by almost 75 percent to more than 2 million and the Southern Baptist Convention increasing by almost 50 percent to 16 million.

4. Nancy T. Ammerman, "Memory Verses: Teaching Children the Bible," *Christian Century* (April 3, 2007): 10.

5. Brian D. McLaren, review of *After the Baby Boomers: How Twenty- and Thirty-Somethings Are Shaping the Future of American Religion*, by Robert Wuthnow, *Christianity Today* (October 16, 2007): 51.

6. The United Church of Canada, the largest Protestant denomination in Canada, is the product of a union of the Methodists, Congregationalists, and two-thirds of the Presbyterians in 1925. The Evangelical United Brethren joined in 1968. At one time 25 percent of Canadians said they were affiliated with the United Church of Canada compared to 9 percent today.

7. Douglas John Hall, *The End of Christendom and the Future of Christianity* (Valley Forge, Pa.; Leominster, England: Gracewing, 1997).

8. CBC News, http://www.cbc.ca/stories/2004/01/11/elvis_church040111 (accessed November 6, 2005).

9. George Lindbeck, *The Nature of Doctrine: Religion and Theology in a Postliberal Age* (Louisville: Westminster, 1984).

10. Richard Lischer, *The End of Words: The Language of Reconciliation in a Culture of Violence* (Grand Rapids: Eerdmans, 2005), ix.

Chapter 2: Preaching as Good Teaching?

1. Alan of Lille, *The Art of Preaching*, Cistercian Fathers Series, no. 23, trans. Gillian R. Evans (Kalamazoo: Cistercian Publications, 1981), 16.

2. Ibid.

3. Richard L. Eslinger, *A New Hearing: Living Options in Homiletic Method* (Nashville: Abingdon Press, 1987), 14.

4. W. E. Sangster, *The Craft of the Sermon* (London: Epworth, 1964), 84–87; originally pub. 1951.

5. H. Grady Davis, *Design for Preaching* (Philadelphia: Fortress, 1958), esp. 15–16, 163–64.

6. David James Randolph, *The Renewal of Preaching* (Philadelphia: Fortress, 1969), 22–23.

7. Robert of Basevorn, *The Form of Preaching*, trans. Leopold Krul, O.S.B., in *Three Medieval Rhetorical Arts*, ed. James J. Murphy (Berkeley: University of California Press, 1971), 138.

8. Richard Baxter, "A Sermon of Repentance," in *Twenty Centuries of Great Preaching*, ed. Clyde Fant, vol. 2 (Waco: Word Books, 1971), 252–75.

9. Fred B. Craddock, *As One Without Authority*, rev. ed. (St. Louis: Chalice Press, 2001). First published 1979 by Abingdon Press.

10. Barbara Brown Taylor, "Hands and Feet," in *Home by Another Way* (Cambridge and Boston: Cowley, 1999), 121.

11. Ibid., 123.

12. Ronald J. Allen, *The Teaching Sermon* (Nashville: Abingdon Press, 1995).

13. Ibid., 19.

14. Ibid., 31–34.

15. Ibid., 35–37.

16. Ibid., 27.

17. Ibid., 29–30.

Chapter 3: Teaching Principles from the New Homiletic

1. Laurence Sterne, "The Prodigal Son," in *The English Sermon*, ed. Robert Nye, 3 vols., vol. 3, *1750–1850* (Cheadle Hulme, England: Carcanet, 1976), 81. Reprinted in *Tongues of Angels, Tongues of Men*, ed. John F. Thornton and Katharine Washburn (New York: Doubleday, 1998), 394.

2. James S. Stewart, "The Tenderness, Tenacity and Triumph of the Love of God," in his *Walking with God*, ed. Gordon Grant (Edinburgh: St. Andrew Press, 1996), 87–88.

3. St. John Fisher, "Dependence upon Divine Mercy," in *English Prose: Selections*, ed. Henry Craik, vol. 1, *Fourteenth to Sixteenth Century* (New York and London: Macmillan, 1916), 144. Reprinted in Thornton and Washburn, *Tongues of Angels, Tongues of Men*, 226–27.

4. In the early fourth century Rufinus used the same image in his *A Commentary on the Apostles' Creed*, section 16. See Philip Schaff, *Nicene and Post-Nicene Fathers*, second series, vol. 3, *Theodoret, Jerome, Gennadius, and Rufinus: Historical Writings* (Edinburgh: T. & T. Clark, 1889).

5. Even in this sermon this set piece stands alone and is not integrated to the material around it, not least because it is based on Job, not on the text of the sermon, which is John 20. Presumably this piece could easily fit in any sermon. St. Gregory the Great, "Homily 25," in *Forty Gospel Homilies*, trans. Dom David Hurst (Kalamazoo: Cistercian Publications, 1990), 196–97. Reprinted in Thornton and Washburn, *Tongues of Angels, Tongues of Men*, 132–33.

6. John M. McLaughlin, "Leviathan," in *Eerdmans Dictionary of the Bible*, ed. David Noel Freedman (Grand Rapids: Eerdmans, 2000).

7. C. H. Spurgeon, "God's First Words to the First Sinner," *The New Park Street and Metropolitan Tabernacle Pulpit Containing Sermons Preached and Revised by the Rev. C. H. Spurgeon During the Year 1861*, vol. 7 (Pasadena, Tex.: Pilgrim Publications, 1969, 1973), 514.

8. J. L. Austin, *How to Do Things with Words: The William James Lectures at Harvard University in 1955* (Cambridge, Mass.: Harvard University Press, 1962).

9. Horace Bushnell, *The Vicarious Sacrifice* (London: Richard D. Dickinson, 1880), 454.

10. George Campbell Morgan, "The Power of the Gospel," in *Great Sermons of the World*, ed. Clarence Edward Macartney (Peabody, Mass.: Hendrickson, 1997), 411–12; originally pub. 1926.

11. Another possibility is that the mission life of individual churches was discussed in worship services, but during announcements that went unrecorded. Henry Ward Beecher was the first pastor of Plymouth Church of the Pilgrims in Brooklyn in 1847, a station on the Underground Railroad. Not only did he invite antislavery giants like Sojourner Truth and Frederick Douglass to his pulpit, but during announcements, he often conducted a mock auction to raise money to buy slaves their freedom. See John Strausbaugh, "On the Trail of Brooklyn's Underground Railroad," *New York Times*, October 12, 2007, http://www.nytimes.com/2007/10/12/arts/12expl.html?_r=1&emc=eta1&oref=slogin (accessed October 12, 2007).

12. See Henry C. Potter, *Sermons in the City* (New York: E. P. Dutton, 1881).

13. Theodore Parker, "Poverty," in his *Sins and Safeguards of Society*, ed. Samuel B. Stewart, centenary ed. (Boston: American Unitarian Assoc., 1909), 185.

14. F. W. Robertson, "Selfishness in Balaam's Character," in his *Sermons on Bible Subjects* (London: J. M. Dent; New York: E. P. Dutton, 1906), 73.

15. Ernest Campbell, "Follow Me," in *A Chorus of Witnesses: Model Sermons for Today*, ed. Thomas G. Long and Cornelius Plantinga (Grand Rapids: Eerdmans, 1994), 170.

16. Thomas Guthrie, "Sins and Sorrows of the City," in Macartney, *Great Sermons of the World* (1997), 313–14.

17. Clarence Macartney, "Thomas Guthrie," in Macartney, *Great Sermons of the World* (1997), 305.

18. Charles Jefferson, "The Man at Bethesda," in *The New Crusade* (New York: Thomas Y. Crowell, 1907), 158.

19. Ibid., 160.

20. Ibid., 163.

Chapter 4: Teaching and Polar Language

1. See my "Biographia's Coherence: God, Self, and Coleridge's 'Seminal Principle,'" *Philological Quarterly* 72, no. 4 (Fall 1993): 451–69.

2. Stopford Augustus Brooke, ed., *Life, Letters, Lectures and Addresses of Fredk. W. Robertson, M.A., incumbent of Trinity Chapel, Brighton, 1847–1853* (New York: Harper, 1870), 315.

3. Joseph R. Jeter Jr., "Robertson, Frederick William," in *Concise Encyclopedia of Preaching*, ed. William Willimon and Richard Lischer (Louisville: Westminster, 1995), 420.

4. Horace Bushnell, "Our Gospel, a Gift to the Imagination," in *Horace Bushnell: Sermons*, ed. Conrad Cherry (New York: Paulist Press, 1985), 109.

5. Ibid., 99.

6. Augustine advocated that preachers follow the practices of a physician who "sometimes applies contraries, such as cold to hot, moist to dry, and so on. . . . Because man fell through pride, [God] applied humility as a cure. We were trapped by the wisdom of the serpent; we are freed by the foolishness of God. . . . We ill used our immortality, so that we deserved to die; Christ used His mortality well to restore us." Augustine, *On Christian Doctrine*, trans. D. W. Robertson Jr., Macmillan / Library of Liberal Arts (Upper Saddle River, N.J.: Prentice Hall, 1958), 15 (1.14.13).

7. John Chrysostom, "Excessive Grief," in *The World's Greatest Sermons*, comp. Grenville Kleiser, vol. 1 (New York: Funk & Wagnalls, 1909), 32–33.

8. Fulton J. Sheen, "The Beatitudes," in *The Electronic Christian: 105 Readings from Fulton J. Sheen* (New York: Macmillan, 1979), 33. Reprinted in Thornton and Washburn, *Tongues of Angels, Tongues of Men*, 679–80.

9. Brooke, *Life, Letters, Lectures and Addresses of Fredk. W. Robertson*, 315.

10. Horace Bushnell, "Preliminary Dissertation on the Nature of Language as Related to Thought and Spirit," in *God in Christ* (Hartford: Brown and Parsons, 1849), 55.

11. James Richmond, "Dialectical Theology," in *A New Dictionary of Christian Theology*, ed. Alan Richardson and John Bowden (London: SCM, 1983).

12. W. Foster-Harris, *The Basic Formulas of Fiction* (Norman: University of Oklahoma Press, 1963), 60; originally pub. 1944.

13. Anne Lamott, *Bird by Bird: Some Instructions on Writing and Life* (New York: Pantheon Books, 1984), xxi.

14. Ibid., 50.

15. Phillips Brooks, "Christian Charity," in his *The Candle of the Lord and Other Sermons* (New York: E. P. Dutton, 1899), 337.

16. John Henry Newman, "Sermon 2: Obedience Without Love, as Instanced in the Character of Balaam," in his *Parochial and Plain Sermons* (San Francisco: Ignatius Press, 1987), 744.

17. Dietrich Bonhoeffer, "The Judas Sermon," in *Dietrich Bonhoeffer: Selected Writings*, ed. Edwin Robertson (New York: HarperCollins, 1995), 79. Reprinted in Thornton and Washburn, *Tongues of Angels, Tongues of Men*, 597.

18. Samuel Taylor Coleridge, *Biographia Literaria*, Bollingen Series, ed. James Engell and W. Jackson Bate (Princeton: Princeton University Press, 1983), 314.

19. Ron Hansen, *A Stay against Confusion: Essays on Faith and Fiction* (New York: Perennial, 2001), 12.

20. Reinhold Niebuhr, "Sorrow and Joy according to the Christian Faith," in *Great Preaching Today: A Collection of 25 Sermons Delivered at the Chicago Sunday Evening Club*, ed. Alton M. Motter (New York: Harper and Brothers, 1955), 121–22.

21. Frederick Buechner, "The Magnificent Defeat," in his *The Magnificent Defeat* (New York: Seabury, 1966), 18.

22. Barbara Brown Taylor, "Beginning at the End: Matthew 20:1-16," in her *The Seeds of Heaven: Sermons on the Gospel of Matthew* (Louisville: Westminster John Knox, 2004), 106.

23. Bushnell, "Our Gospel, a Gift to the Imagination," 100.

24. Phillips Brooks, "The Fire and the Calf," in *The Protestant Pulpit: An Anthology of Master Sermons from the Reformation to Our Own Day* (New York and Nashville: Abingdon Press, 1947), 129–37. Reprinted in Thornton and Washburn, *Tongues of Angels, Tongues of Men*, 546.

25. C. L. Franklin, "Except I Shall See in His Hands the Print of the Nails and Thrust My Hand into His Side," in *Give Me This Mountain: Life Story and Selected Sermons*, ed. Jeff Todd Titon (Evanston: University of Illinois Press, 1989), 139–40. Reprinted in Thornton and Washburn,*Tongues of Angels, Tongues of Men*, 704.

Chapter 5: What Does the Bible Say about the Gospel?

1. Gerald Kennedy, "God's Good News," in Motter, *Great Preaching Today*, 82–92.

2. R. G. Lee, "A Plain Speech," in *Billy Sunday Speaks*, ed. Karen Gillen (New York: Chelsea House, 1970), 13.

3. Luke typically uses the infinitive *euangelizesthai* (to proclaim), sometimes with a specific christological-soteriological meaning "to proclaim the good news" (e.g., Luke 9:6; Acts 14:7). See G. Strecker, *"euangelizo,"* in *Exegetical Dictionary of the New Testament*, ed. Horst Balz and Gerhard Schneider, vol. 2 (Grand Rapids: Eerdmans, 1991), 69–70; originally pub. 1981.

4. On the pre-Pauline compositions, see G. Strecker, *"euangelion,"* in *Exegetical Dictionary of the New Testament*, 2:70–74, esp. 71.

5. A. B. Luter Jr., "Gospel," in *Dictionary of Paul and His Letters: A Compendium of Contemporary Biblical Scholarship*, ed. Gerald F. Hawthorne, Ralph. P. Martin, and Daniel G. Reid (Downers Grove, Ill.,: InterVarsity Press, 1993), 370.

6. See Christopher R. Seitz, "'We Are Not Prophets or Apostles': The Biblical Theology of B. S. Childs," in *Word Without End: The Old Testament as Abiding Theological Witness* (Grand Rapids: Eerdmans, 1998), 102–9, esp. 107–8.

7. Kevin J. Vanhoozer, *The Drama of Doctrine: A Canonical Linguistic Approach to Christian Theology* (Louisville: Westminster John Knox, 2005), 388.

8. Ellen F. Davis, *Wondrous Depth: Preaching the Old Testament* (Louisville: Westminster John Knox, 2005), 68.

9. Richard B. Hays, "Resurrection," in *The New Interpreter's Handbook of Preaching*, ed. Paul Scott Wilson et al. (Nashville: Abingdon Press, 2008).

10. Ibid.

11. G. D. Yarold, *Risen Indeed: Studies in the Lord's Resurrection* (London: Oxford University Press, 1959), 103.

12. Thomas F. Torrance, *Preaching Christ Today: The Gospel and Scientific Thinking* (Grand Rapids: Eerdmans, 1994), 34.

13. Ibid., 32.

14. Martin Luther, "Sermon VIII," in *The Sermons of Martin Luther*, ed. and trans. John Nicholas Lenker, vol. 8, *Sermons on Epistle Texts from Trinity Sunday to Advent* (Grand Rapids: Baker), 224.

15. Ibid., 230.

16. Ibid., 233–34.

17. Ibid., 236.

18. Ibid.

19. Martin Luther, *Luther's Works*, vol. 52, *Sermons II*, ed. Hans J. Hillerbrand (Philadelphia: Fortress, 1974), 132.

20. William H. Willimon, *The Intrusive Word: Preaching to the Unbaptized* (Grand Rapids: Eerdmans, 1994). See also his *Peculiar Speech: Preaching to the Baptized* (Grand Rapids: Eerdmans, 1992).

21. L. Susan Bond reviews many of the key issues in her *Trouble with Jesus: Women, Christology, and Preaching* (St. Louis: Chalice Press, 1999).

22. See Deanna A. Thompson, *Crossing the Divide: Luther, Feminism, and the Cross* (Minneapolis: Fortress, 2004).

23. See Sally Brown, "Soteriology," in Wilson et al., *The New Interpreter's Handbook of Preaching*.

24. Willimon, *Intrusive Word*, 42.

25. Carol M. Norén, *In Times of Crisis and Sorrow* (San Francisco: Jossey-Bass, 2001), 11. She is citing a brochure by Christopher Seitz for a 2001 conference on scholarly engagement with Anglican doctrine, "Nicene Christianity: The Future for a New Ecumenism," Charleston, S.C., 2001.

26. Harold Wells, *The Christic Center: Life-Giving and Liberating* (Maryknoll, N.Y.: Orbis, 2004), 1.

27. Douglas John Hall, *The Cross in Our Context: Jesus and the Suffering World* (Minneapolis: Fortress, 2003) 113, italics in original.

28. Ibid., 112.

Chapter 6: Practical Helps in Teaching the Gospel

1. Phillips Brooks, *Lectures on Preaching* (Manchester: James Robinson, 1899), 262.

2. See Lucy Lind Hogan, *Graceful Speech: An Invitation to Preaching* (Louisville: Westminster John Knox, 2006), 191–95; at least three homileticians address gospel in varying ways in *What's the Matter with Preaching Today?*, ed. Mike Graves (Louisville: Westminster John Knox , 2006).

3. O. Wesley Allen, *Preaching Resurrection* (St. Louis: Chalice Press, 2000), 2.

4. David L. Bartlett, *What's Good about This News? Preaching from the Gospels and Galatians* (Louisville: Westminster John Knox, 2003), 2.

5. See, in particular, Edward Farley, "Preaching the Bible and Gospel," *Theology Today* 51, no. 1 (April 1994): 90–104; and Edward Farley, "Toward a New Paradigm for Preaching," in *Preaching as a Theological Task: World, Gospel, Scripture*, ed. Thomas G. Long and Edward Farley (Louisville: Westminster John Knox, 1996), 165–75.

6. Charles. L. Campbell, *Preaching Jesus: New Directions for Homiletics in Hans Frei's Postliberal Theology* (Grand Rapids: Eerdmans, 1997), 192.

7. André Resner, *Preacher and Cross: Person and Message in Theology and Rhetoric* (Grand Rapids: Eerdmans, 1999).

8. André Resner, e-mail message to author, March 13, 2006.

9. Richard Lischer, *A Theology of Preaching: The Dynamics of the Gospel*, rev. ed. (Eugene, Ore.: Wipf and Stock, 2001), 26.

10. David Buttrick, *A Captive Voice: The Liberation of Preaching* (Louisville: Westminster John Knox, 1998), 51; see 38–53.

11. David Buttrick, *Preaching the New and the Now* (Louisville: Westminster John Knox, 1998), 57; see 105–12.

12. James F. Kay, "The Word of the Cross at the Turn of the Ages," *Interpretation* 53, no. 1 (January 1999): 50; see 44–56.

13. Stephen H. Webb, "A Hyperbolic Imagination: Theology and the Rhetoric of Excess," *Theology Today* 50 (1993): 56–67.

14. Farley, "Preaching the Bible and Gospel," 90–104; and "Toward a New Paradigm for Preaching,"165–75.

15. Farley, "Preaching the Bible and Gospel," 101.

16. Buttrick, *A Captive Voice*. His first two chapters ("Preaching and Bible" and "Preaching and Church") are among the best theological treatments of preaching in recent memory. He says, "We are hearing more and more apologetic sermons trying to justify unlikely passages as being, nevertheless, Word of God" (11).

17. Michael Rogness and David Lose, "Seven Marks of a Good Sermon," http://www.luthersem.edu/story/story_article.asp?article_id=39&issue_id=8&m=1782 (accessed June 8, 2006).

18. David J. Lose, *Confessing Jesus Christ: Preaching in a Postmodern World* (Grand Rapids: Eerdmans, 2003), 222.

19. Ibid.

20. Gordon W. Lathrop, *The Pastor: A Spirituality* (Minneapolis: Fortress, 2006), 50–51.

21. John Calvin, *Institutes*, ed. John T. McNeil, trans. Ford Lewis Battles, vol. 22, *The Library of Christian Classics* (Philadelphia: Westminster, 1960), 1.3.580–81.

22. Karl Barth, *Church Dogmatics*, trans. G. T. Thompson (Edinburgh: T. & T. Clark, 1936), 1.1.98–140.

23. Daniel L. Migliore, *Faith Seeking Understanding: An Introduction to Christian Theology* (Grand Rapids: Eerdmans, 1991), 46.

24. Brevard S. Childs, *Biblical Theology of the Old and New Testaments: Theological Reflection on the Christian Bible* (Minneapolis: Fortress, 1992), 67.

25. Preachers arguably are not prophets; the preached word does not come directly to them, and prophecy is not a function of ecclesial office. See Seitz, "We Are Not Prophets or Apostles."

26. See my *The Four Pages of the Sermon*, 155–74; *The Practice of Preaching*, rev. ed. (Nashville: Abingdon Press, 2007), 39–55.

27. See my *God Sense: Reading the Bible for Preaching* (Nashville: Abingdon Press, 2002).

28. I have spoken of these matters in some detail in my discussion of a gospel hermeneutic in *The Practice of Preaching*, rev. ed., chap. 13.

29. Gardner Taylor, "Shaping Sermons by the Shape of Text and Preacher," in *Preaching Biblically: Creating Sermons in the Shape of the Text*, ed. Don Wardlaw (Philadelphia: Westminster, 1983), 140.

30. Ellen F. Davis, *Wondrous Depth: Preaching the Old Testament* (Louisville: Westminster John Knox, 2005), 70.

31. See my *Practice of Preaching*, rev. ed., 251–56.

32. C. H. Dodd, *The Apostolic Preaching and Its Developments* (London: Hodder and Stoughton, 1936), 17. He seemed to add at least two other points: that Jesus "taught and worked miracles" (27–31) and that he issued "an appeal for repentance, the offer of forgiveness and of the Holy Spirit, and the promise of 'salvation'" (23).

33. Ibid., 74.

34. Ibid., 55.

35. David Buttrick, "Proclamation," in Willimon and Lischer, *Concise Encyclopedia of Preaching*, 385.

36. Lucy Atkinson Rose, *Sharing the Word: Preaching in the Roundtable Church* (Louisville: Westminster John Knox, 1997), 55; see also 40–41, 43–44.

Section 3: Becoming Better Proclaimers

1. I have argued this more fully in *The Practice of Preaching*, rev. ed., 39–55, 260–62.

Chapter 7: What Is Proclamation?

1. Gerhard Ebeling, *Luther: An Introduction to His Thought* (Philadelphia: Fortress, 1970), 257.

2. Karl Barth, *Homiletics*, trans. Geoffrey W. Bromiley and Donald E. Daniels (Louisville: Westminster John Knox, 1991), 51.

3. Ibid., 50.

4. Ibid., 51.

5. Dodd, *The Apostolic Preaching and Its Developments*, 47; see 17.

6. James S. Stewart, *A Faith to Proclaim* (London: Hodder and Stoughton, 1953), 36.

7. Rudolf Bultmann and five critics, *Kerygma and Myth*, "The Mythological Element in the Message of the New Testament and the Problem of its Re-interpretation," Part II: Demythologizing in Outline, 2. The Event of Jesus Christ, (c) The Resurrection, http://www.religiononline.org/showchapter.asp?title=431&C=293 (accessed June 22, 2006).

8. Barth, *Church Dogmatics*, 1.1.55.

9. Emil Brunner, *Truth as Encounter* (Philadelphia: Westminster, 1963), 180–81.

10. Emil Brunner, *The Divine Human Encounter* (Philadelphia: Westminster, 1943); original German *Warheit als Begegnung* (Zurich: Zwingli-Verlag, 1938). I cite a new enlarged edition, *Truth as Encounter*.

11. Emil Brunner, "Intellectual Autobiography," in *The Theology of Emil Brunner*, ed. Charles W. Kegley, The Library of Living Thought, vol. 3 (New York: Macmillan, 1962), 12.

12. Brunner, *Truth as Encounter*, 179.

13. Ibid., 178.

14. Ibid.

15. Ibid., 180.

16. Ibid., 179.

17. Ibid., 121.

18. Gerhard Ebeling, *Theologie und Verkündigung* (Tübingen: J. C. B. Mohr [Paul Siebeck], 1962); English ed., *Theology and Proclamation: A Discussion with Rudolph Bultmann*, trans. John Riches (London: Collins, 1966). Citations are from this latter edition.

19. Ebeling, *Theology and Proclamation*, 13–14.

20. Ibid., 15.

21. Ibid., 19–20.

22. Ibid., 21.

23. Ibid., 20.

24. Ibid., 24.

25. Ibid., 31.

26. Ibid., 79.

27. Ibid., 32.

28. Ibid., 79.

29. Ibid., 53.

30. Ibid.

31. Ibid., 80.

32. Gerhard O. Forde, *Theology Is for Proclamation* (Minneapolis: Fortress, 1990), 2.

33. Ibid.

34. Ibid.

35. Ibid., 3.

36. Ibid.

37. Ibid., 147.

38. Ibid., 148.

39. Ibid., 155.

40. Ibid., 156–57.

41. Ibid., 5.

42. Ibid., 164.

43. See my discussion of these terms in *The Four Pages of the Sermon*.

44. Karl Barth, "Saved by Grace," in his *Deliverance to the Captives* (London: SCM, 1961), 36–37.

45. Frederica Mathewes-Green, *At the Corner of East and Now: A Modern Life in Ancient Christian Orthodoxy* (New York: Jeremy P. Tarcher/Putnam, 1999), 146–47. Cited in Mike Graves, "God of Grace and Glory," in *What's the Matter with Preaching Today?*, ed. Mike Graves (Louisville: Westminster John Knox, 2004), 112.

46. William H. Willimon, *Proclamation and Theology* (Nashville: Abingdon Press, 2005), see for instance 5, 7–8.

47. Davis, *Design for Preaching*, 110–11, my enumeration.

48. Richard A. Jensen, *Thinking in Story: Preaching in a Post-literate Age* (Lima, Ohio: C.S.S. Publishing, 1993), 73. See also his *Telling the Story: Variety and Imagination in Preaching* (Minneapolis: Augsburg, 1980), esp. chap. 3, "Proclamatory Preaching," 53–93.

49. Jensen, *Thinking in Story*, 74. Jensen is reviewing what he said in his *Telling the Story*.

50. Jensen, *Thinking in Story*, 75.

51. David J. Lose, "Preaching as Proclamation," in Wilson et al., *The New Interpreter's Handbook of Preaching*.

52. See, in particular, Farley, "Preaching the Bible and Gospel," 90–104; and "Toward a New Paradigm for Preaching," in Long and Farley, *Preaching as a Theological Task*, 165–75.

53. Campbell, *Preaching Jesus*, 192.

54. Rose, *Sharing the Word*, 83.

55. Eugene L. Lowry, *The Sermon: Dancing the Edge of Mystery* (Nashville: Abingdon Press, 1997), 37.

56. Ibid., 39.

57. See Lose, *Confessing Jesus Christ*, 62–63.

58. Joni Sancken, a doctoral student in homiletics at Emmanuel College in the University of Toronto, made this comment in a personal conversation, November 15, 2000.

59. Todd Townshend, "The Sacramentality of Preaching: Homiletical Uses of Louis-Marie Chauvet's Theology of Sacramentality" (Th.D. diss., University of Toronto, 2007), 7 n. 5.

Chapter 8: Proclamation and Sermon Subforms

1. Brooks, *Lectures on Preaching*, 1.

2. Henry Ward Beecher, *Lectures on Preaching* (London: T. Nelson and Sons, 1872), 16.

3. Brooks, *Lectures on Preaching*, 5.

4. Ibid., 128.

5. Ibid., 130.

6. Ibid., 114.

7. Ibid., 115.

8. Ibid., 160.

9. Ibid.

10. Ibid., 161–62.

11. Ibid., 115.

12. Ibid.

13. Ibid., 131.

14. Ibid., 147.

15. Ibid., 129–30.

16. Ibid., 132.

17. Ibid., 132–33.

18. See my *Preaching and Homiletical Theory* (St. Louis: Chalice Press, 2004), 69–70.

19. In fact, contemporary genre theory in literary criticism embraces many of the notions that Brooks articulates. See chap. 8 of this book.

20. One exception to this is celebration in African American traditions. Homiletics may also speak of illustrations and stories, biblical text and our world, of sermon "moves" and "pages," and similar kinds of ideas that have formal implications without each of these functioning necessarily as forms or genres.

21. Richard Bartlett, "Texts Shaping Sermons," in *Listening to the Word*, ed. Gail R. O'Day and Thomas G. Long (Nashville: Abingdon Press, 1993), 153. Cited in Graves, *What's the Matter with Preaching Today?*, 27.

22. Allen, "Shaping Sermons by the Language of the Text" in Wardlaw, *Preaching Biblically*, 37.

23. Don M. Wardlaw, "Shaping Sermons by the Context of the Text," in Wardlaw, *Preaching Biblically*, 63–71, esp. 69. Just as Christ undergoes sacrifice and limitation and is exalted, the Philippian Christians are encouraged to follow the same example.

24. Taylor, "Shaping Sermons by the Shape of Text and Preacher"in Wardlaw, *Preaching Biblically*, 141. Taylor cites *revelant* as Kyle Haselden's term.

25. Tom Long, *Preaching and the Literary Forms of the Bible* (Philadelphia: Fortress, 1989), 24. See also how he responds to these questions in each of his chapters dealing with the following literary forms: psalms, proverbs, narratives, parables of Jesus, and epistles.

26. Ibid., 95–101.

27. Ibid., 121.

28. Graves, *What's the Matter with Preaching Today?*, 7. Graves refers to Donald L. Hamilton, *Homiletical Handbook* (Nashville: Broadman, 1992), 178.

29. Graves, *What's the Matter with Preaching Today?*, 24. Note too his book's title.

30. Richard F. Ward, *Speaking from the Heart* (Nashville: Abingdon Press, 1992), 76–77. Cited by Graves, *What's the Matter with Preaching Today?*, 11.

31. Graves, *What's the Matter with Preaching Today?*, 31. See also his discussion of "form-sensitive," 8–12.

32. Ibid., 72.

33. Charles Rice, "Shaping Sermons by the Interplay of Text and Metaphor," in Wardlaw, *Preaching Biblically*, 101.

34. William Carl III, "Shaping Sermons by the Structure of the Text," *Preaching Biblically*, 101.

35. Graves, *What's the Matter with Preaching Today?*, xvii.

36. Fred Craddock, "When the Roll Is Called Down Here," in *Creative Styles of Preaching*, ed. Mark Barger Elliott (Louisville: Westminster John Knox, 2000), 14–18.

37. Augustine is quoting Cicero's *Orator* 21:29. Saint Augustine, *On Christian Doctrine*, trans. D. W. Robertson Jr., Macmillan / Library of Liberal Arts (Upper Saddle River, N.J.: Prentice Hall, 1958), 136 (4.12.27). George Campbell in his *Philosophy of Rhetoric* (1776) adapted Augustine's aims of speaking: "to enlighten the understanding, to please the imagination, to move the passions, or to influence the will." See Craig Loscalzo, "Rhetoric," in Willimon and Lischer, *Concise Encyclopedia of Preaching*, 411.

38. Augustine, *On Christian Doctrine*, 136 (4.12.27), 137 (4.12.28).

39. Ibid., 136 (4.12.27).

40. Ibid., 133 (4.9.23).

41. Ibid., 143 (4.17.34). Robertson translates Augustine's Latin original *submissus* as "subdued."

42. Ibid., 143 (4.17.34), 145 (4.19.38)

43. Ibid., 143 (4.17.34).

44. Ibid., 137 (4.12.28).

45. Ibid., 143 (4.28.35), see also 146 (4.20.39).

46. Ibid., 146–47 (4.20.39), 152–55 (4.21.45–46). He says that all of Galatians is in the simple style except for the beginning and the end (moderate) and 4:10-20, which is in the grand.

47. John Wesley, "Preface to Sermons on Several Occasions" in *The Works of John Wesley*, vol. 5 (Grand Rapids: Zondervan, n.d.), 1–6. Reprinted in Edwards, *A History of Preaching*, 2:363.

48. Augustine, *On Christian Doctrine*, 163 (4.26.57). Fred B. Craddock may have been offering a simplified version of Augustine when he implied that language has two types, one communicates information and the other communicates feelings. Craddock, *Preaching* (Nashville: Abingdon Press, 1988), 186.

49. Augustine, *On Christian Doctrine*, 162 (4.26.56).

50. Ibid., 163 (4.26.57), see also 145 (4.18.38).

51. Augustine's examples of the moderate style may be found in Augustine, *On Christian Doctrine*, 148–50 (4.20.40–41), 155–56 (4.21.47–48).

52. "Her sincere disposition was not stained by any traces of deceit. She was humble in heart, grave in discourse, prudent in mind, sparing in speech, studious in learning. She placed her hope, not in the uncertainty of wealth, but in the prayer of the poor man. . . . She customarily sought not man but God as the guide to her mind. She injured no one, but had good will toward all; she assented to her elders, and did not envy her equals; she fled boasting, followed reason, loved virtue. When did this one injure her parents, even with a glance? When did she quarrel with her relatives? When did she disdain the humble? When did she deride the weak? When did she avoid the needy?" Ibid., 155–56 (4.21.47).

53. Ibid., 156.

54. Ibid., 145 (4.18.38). His examples of the grand style may be found at 150–52 (4.20.42–44), 156–58 (4.21.49–50).

55. Ibid., 150 (4.20.42).

56. Ibid., 162 (4.25.55).

57. As he says, "*caesa* and *membra* and *circuitus.*" See Ibid., 152 (4.20.44), 130–32 (4.7.18–20).

58. Ibid., 162 (4.25.55).

59. Ibid., 158–59 (4.22.51).

60. For purposes of simplicity I have omitted from this chart his three kinds of speech (judicial, demonstrative, and deliberative) and the issues at stake with each (justice, honor, and expediency). Aristotle associated these three styles with past, present, and future in *Rhetoric* 1.3.1–4; 1358b.

61. Robert Stephen Reid says, "The interesting question is whether the grand or majestic style is really in play [today]—for this is the sermon style of the preacher who is centered on the vision for who we are called to be and will not surrender that vision, but pursues it using all the possibilities of language to call people to live into that vision—calling them to act on what they say they believe." E-mail message to author, January 17, 2007. In his *The Four Voices of Preaching: Connecting Purpose and Identity behind the Pulpit* (Grand Rapids: Brazos Press, 2006), Reid places aspects of African American preaching in all four "voices."

62. Lucy Lind Hogan, "Rethinking Persuasion: Developing an Incarnational Theology of Preaching," *Homiletic* 24, no. 2 (Winter 1999):. 1–12; and Richard Lischer, "Why I Am Not Persuasive," *Homiletic* 24, no. 2 (Winter 1999): 13–16.

63. Lose, *Confessing Jesus Christ*, 200–207.

64. Ibid., 206.

65. Ibid., 202.

66. Mary E. Lyons, "Style," in Willimon and Lischer, *Concise Encyclopedia of Preaching*, 460.

67. Ibid., 460.

Section 4: Trouble Genres of Proclamation

1. The six categories belong to John Frow, *Genre: The New Critical Idiom* (London: Routledge, 2005), 9–10. They have been applied to sermons here.

Chapter 9: Condemnation

1. St. John Fisher, "Dependence upon Divine Mercy," in Craik, *English Prose*, 1:144, see also 1:143.

2. Jonathan Edwards, "Sinners in the Hands of an Angry God," in *Jonathan Edwards: Basic Writings*, ed. Ola Elizabeth Winslow (New York: New American Library [Meridian Books], 1966), 65–66.

3. C. H. Spurgeon, "On Conversion as Our Aim," Lecture 23 (Lecture 10, second series), in *Lectures to My Students*, Ministry Resources Library (Grand Rapids: Zondervan, 1954), 342.

4. Anonymous, "Homily 2: The End of the World," in *The Vercelli Book Homilies: Translations from the Anglo-Saxon*, trans. James Schonewise (Lanham, Md.: University Press of America, 1991), 28–29.

5. Christmas Evans, "The Triumph of Calvary," in Macartney, *Great Sermons of the World* (1997), 268–69.

6. T. DeWitt Talmage, "The Broken Pitchers," in his *500 Sermons*, 20 vols. (New York: Christian Herald, 1900), 12:328–29.

7. Ralph Waldo Emerson, "Sermon XIII," in *The Complete Sermons of Ralph Waldo Emerson*, vol. 1, ed. Albert J. von Frank, intro. David M. Robinson (Columbia: University of Missouri Press, 1989), 148, my italics.

8. Charles G. Adams, "Faith Critiques Faith," in *Power in the Pulpit: How America's Most Effective Black Preachers Prepare Their Sermons*, ed. Cleophus J. LaRue (Louisville: Westminster John Knox, 2002), 24.

Chapter 10: Lament

1. William Sloane Coffin Jr., "Alex's Death," in *Sermons from Riverside* (January 23, 1983). Reprinted in Thornton and Washburn, *Tongues of Angels, Tongues of Men*, 746.

2. Kathleen S. Smith, *Stilling the Storm: Worship and Congregational Leadership in Difficult Times* (Herndon, Va.: Alban Institute, 2006), 57.

3. Ibid.

4. F. W. Dobbs-Allsopp, "Lament," in Freedman, *Eerdmans Dictionary of the Bible*, 784–85.

5. Sally A. Brown and Patrick D. Miller, eds., *Lament: Reclaiming Practices in the Pulpit, Pew, and Public Square* (Louisville: Westminster John Knox, 2005).

6. See C. Clifton Black, "The Persistence of the Wounds," and Robert C. Dykstra, "Rending the Curtain: Lament as an Act of Vulnerable Aggression," in Brown and Miller, *Lament*, 47–58, 59–69.

7. Joachim Begrich, "Das priesterliche Heilsorakel," 1934, cited by Clinton McCann Jr. and James C. Howell, *Preaching the Psalms* (Nashville: Abingdon Press, 2001), 73.

8. McCann and Howell, *Preaching the Psalms*, 75.

9. Luke Powery, *The Holy Spirit and African American Preaching* (Th.D. thesis, University of Toronto, 2007), 198.

10. James L. Mays, *Psalms*. Interpretation: A Bible Commentary for Teaching and Preaching (Louisville: John Knox, 1994), 21.

11. Sally A. Brown, "When Lament Shapes the Sermon," in Brown and Miller, *Lament*, 28. She draws on Walter Brueggemann and notes that there are laments like Psalm 88 that express no hope. She suggests four different types of sermons based on biblical laments: (1) an exploration of the effect of suffering on "our relationships, including our relationship with God," (2) a pastoral lament that stresses "the cry for anguish and plea for help," (3) the critical-prophetic lament that will accent "protest, imprecation, and self-examination," and (4) the theological-interrogatory lament that will focus on "the interrogation of the divine nature and purpose" (29).

12. On possible links between David's life and the psalms, see Patrick D. Miller, *Interpreting the Psalms* (Philadelphia: Fortress, 1986), 53–57.

13. Mays, *Psalms*, 22.

14. Miller, *Interpreting the Psalms*, 57–62.

15. Norén, *In Times of Crisis and Sorrow*, 11.

16. Nancy J. Duff, "Rediscovering Lamentation as a Practice in the Church," in Brown and Miller, *Lament*, 4.

17. Nicholas Wolterstorff, *Lament for a Son* (Grand Rapids: Eerdmans, 1987), 5–6.

18. Niebuhr, "Sorrow and Joy," in Motter, *Great Preaching Today*, 129.

19. John Chrysostom, "Homily II," in *The Homilies of St. John Chrysostom on the Statues*, trans. Members of the English Church, Library of Fathers, vol. 9 (Oxford: John Henry Parker, 1842), 31–32.

20. John Wesley, "Sermon on the Mount, I," *The Works of John Wesley*, vol. 1, ed. Albert Outler (Nashville: Abingdon Press, 1984), 486.

21. Ibid., 487.

22. Hugh Martin, "The Hidden Life," in *Modern Scottish Pulpit: Sermons by Ministers of Various Denominations*, vol. 2 (Edinburgh: James Gemmell, 1880), 101.

23. Charles Booth, "When Good People Do Bad Things," in *Outstanding Black Sermons*, vol. 4, ed. Walter S. Thomas (Valley Forge: Judson, 2001), 20.

24. John Watson [Ian Maclaren], "The Glory of the City," in *The Inspiration of Our Faith* (New York: A. C. Armstrong & Son, 1905), 262–65.

25. Morton, *Modern Scottish Pulpit*, 66.

26. Ibid.

27. Leonard Lovett, "How Far Is the Promised Land?" in *Outstanding Black Sermons*, vol. 3, ed. Milton E. Owens Jr. (Valley Forge:: Judson, 1982), 44-45.

Chapter 11: Stern Exhortation

1. M. B. Thompson, "Teaching/Paraenesis," in Hawthorne, Martin, and Reid, *Dictionary of Paul and His Letters*, 922. He identifies agreement of J. I. H. McDonald and D. E. Aune.

2. See ibid.

3. See Herman G. Stuempfle, *Preaching Law and Gospel* (Philadelphia: Fortress, 1978), 20–33.

4. John Calvin, *Calvin: Institutes of the Christian Religion*, ed. John T. McNeil, trans. Ford Lewis Battles, 2 vols. (Philadelphia: Westminster, 1960), 1:354, see also 1:355.

5. Ibid., 1:356.

6. Ibid., 1:357.

7. Brooks, *Lectures on Preaching*, 129, 132.

8. Augustine, "Sermon 5: Christmas," *St. Augustine: Sermons for Christmas and Epiphany*, trans. Thomas Comerford Lawler, Ancient Christian Writers, no. 15 (Westminster, Md.: Newman Press, 1952), 87.

9. Augustine, "Sermon 17: New Year's Day," in Lawler, *St. Augustine*, 149.

10. Augustine, "Sermon 14: Christmas," in Lawler, *St. Augustine*, 133–34. Apparently it was the custom in Hippo to exchange presents at the new year, and Augustine also discourages this, encouraging Christians to give to the poor, people who will not be able to give something in return (152).

11. John Chrysostom, "The Sixth Instruction," in *St. John Chrysostom: Baptismal Instruction*, trans. Paul W. Harkins, Ancient Christian Writers, no. 31 (London and Westminster, Md.: Paulist Newman Press, 1963), 97–98.

12. Quoted and translated by Sabina Flanagan, *Hildegard of Bingen, 1098–1179: A Visionary Life* (New York: Routledge, 1990), 174–75. From J.-P. Migne, "S. Hildegardis," in *Patrologiae Cursus Completus*, vol. 197 (Paris: Garnier, 1882), 243–44.

13. John Howe, "The Redeemer's Tears," in Macartney, *Great Sermons of the World* (1997), 109.

14. George Whitefield, "Sermon 17: Jacob's Ladder," in *Eighteen Sermons Preached by the Late Rev. George Whitefield, A.M.* Taken in verbatim short-hand and faithfully transcribed by Joseph Gurney, rev. A. Gifford (Lexington, Ky.: Thomas T. Skillman, 1825), 281–301. Reprinted in Edwards, *A History of Preaching*, 2:359.

15. Margaret Guenther, *Holy Listening: The Art of Spiritual Direction* (Cambridge, Mass.: Cowley, 1992).

16. Eugene Peterson, *Working the Angles: The Shape of Pastoral Integrity* (Grand Rapids: Eerdmans, 1993). See the section on spiritual direction, 149–202.

17. J. J. G. Kippen, "Confession of Sins: The Sure Condition of Forgiveness and Cleansing," in *Modern Scottish Pulpit*, 275.

Chapter 12: Testimony

1. Thomas Hoyt Jr., "Testimony," in *Practicing Our Faith: A Way of Life for a Searching People*, ed. Dorothy C. Bass (San Francisco: Jossey-Bass, 1997), 92.

2. Ibid.

3. "Testimony," in *The Eerdmans Bible Dictionary*, ed. Allen C. Myers (Grand Rapids: Eerdmans, 1987).

4. Martin C. Albl, "Testimony," in Freedman, *The Eerdmans Dictionary of the Bible*.

5. John M. Buchanan, "The 'I' in Sermons," *Christian Century*, March 6, 2007, 3.

6. James Fodor, *Christian Hermeneutics: Paul Ricoeur and the Refiguring of Theology* (Oxford: Caledon Press, 1995), 1.

7. Thomas G. Long, *Testimony: Talking Ourselves into Being Christian* (San Francisco: Jossey-Bass, 2004), 6.

8. Hoyt, "Testimony," in Bass, *Practicing Our Faith*, 94.

9. Ibid., 101. In his chapter, Hoyt explores testimony in each of these expressions.

10. The best study of this is André Resner Jr., *Preacher and Cross: Person and Message in Theology and Rhetoric* (Grand Rapids: Eerdmans, 1999).

11. Anna Carter Florence, *Preaching as Testimony* (Louisville: Westminster John Knox, 2007), xiii.

12. Lose, *Confessing Jesus Christ*, 62.

13. Ibid., 189.

14. Ibid., 197–99.

15. Ibid., 200–204, esp. 204.

16. Ibid., 207.

17. Ibid., 205.

18. Ibid., 195, see also 221.

19. Ibid., 218.

20. John Knox, "The First Temptation of Christ," *The World's Great Sermons*, comp. Grenville Kleiser, vol. 1 (New York: Funk and Wagnalls Co., 1909), 196–97.

21. John Calvin, "Sermon 9 on Job 19:26-29," in *Sermons from Job by John Calvin*, sel. and trans. Leroy Nixon (Grand Rapids: Eerdmans, 1952), 123–24. Reprinted in Edwards, *A History of Preaching*, 2:266–67.

22. Henry Ward Beecher, "Spared!" in Clarence Edward Macartney, ed., *Great Sermons of the World* (Boston: Stratford Company, 1926), 497–510. Reprinted in Thornton and Washburn, *Tongues of Angels, Tongues of Men*, 507.

23. Charles Finney, "God's Love for a Sinning World," in *Sermons on Gospel Themes* (Oberlin, Ohio: E. J. Goodrich, n.d.), 12–13.

24. Dwight Lyman Moody, "Come," in *The Best of D. L. Moody* (Chicago: Moody Press, 1971), 168–69. Reprinted in Thornton and Washburn, *Tongues of Angels, Tongues of Men*, 562–63.

25. Fleming Rutledge, "The Master and the Best Man," in her *The Bible and The New York Times* (Grand Rapids: Eerdmans, 1998), 42.

26. Hugh Reed, "Ways and Means," a sermon preached on Sunday, July 4, 2004, in *Festival of the Word! Messages of Inspiration and Wisdom from the Summer Sermon Series at Timothy Eaton Memorial Church, Toronto, Canada* (Toronto: Timothy Eaton Memorial Church, 2004), 7.

27. Joseph Sittler, "The View from Mount Nebo," in *The Care of the Earth, and Other University Sermons* (Minneapolis: Augsburg, 1964), 80–81. Cited in Hoyt, "Testimony," in Bass, *Practicing Our Faith*, 99.

28. H. Beecher Hicks Jr., "The Preacher's Predicament," in Thomas, *Outstanding Black Sermons*, 4:42.

29. James A. Forbes Jr., "The Battle of Bethlehem," in Owens, *Outstanding Black Sermons*, 3:35.

Chapter 13: Prayer

1. Augustine, "Sermon 14: Christmas," in Lawler, *St. Augustine*, 132.

2. Jean-Pierre Camus, "Third Panegyric Commemorating Saint Charles Borromeo," in Edwards, *A History of Preaching*, 2:280–81.

3. John-Baptist Massillon, "On the Small Number of the Saved," in *Sermons*, last London ed. (Boston: Waite, Peirce & Co., 1845), probably 46, 48.

4. Ibid., 52–53.

5. Beecher, "Spared!" in Macartney, *Great Sermons of the World* (1926), 497–510. Reprinted in Thornton and Washburn, *Tongues of Angels, Tongues of Men*, 511.

6. Washington Gladden, "The Eternal Kingdom," in his *The Lord's Prayer: Seven Homilies* (Boston: Houghton, Mifflin, 1881), 59–81. Reprinted with standardized spelling in Edwards, *A History of Preaching*, 2:523–24.

7. Walter J. Burghardt, S.J., "Do We Deserve Peace?" in his *Tell the Next Generation* (New York: Paulist Press, 1980), 20.

8. Ibid., 25.

9. C. L. Franklin, "Except I Shall See in His Hands," in Titon, *Give Me This Mountain*, 138–44. Reprinted in Thornton and Washburn, *Tongues of Angels, Tongues of Men*, 706.

10. Trinette V. McCray, "Walking in Ordered Steps," in Thomas, *Outstanding Black Sermons*, 4:61–62.

11. Warren H. Stewart Sr., *Interpreting God's Word in Black Preaching* (Valley Forge: Judson, 1984), 43.

Chapter 14: Nurturing Exhortation

1. Spurgeon, "On Conversion as Our Aim," 341.

2. Johannes Thomas, "*Parakaleō/paraklēsis*," in *Exegetical Dictionary of the New Testament*, vol. 3, ed. Horst Balz and Gerhard Schneider (Grand Rapids: Eerdmans, 1993 [German, 1982–83]), 24. He quotes O. Schmitz and G. Stählin, Theological Dictionary of the New Testament, 5:791.

3. Johannes Thomas says that *paraklēsis* in the verb form in the active voice in the New Testament takes various subjects: Messiah, God, the spirit of God, the Scriptures, the missionary call to salvation, the charismatic, and the church. Thomas, 24. As examples of each type of active voice, he cites Luke 2:25; Rom. 15:5; 2 Cor. 1:3; Acts 9:31; Rom. 15:4; Heb. 6:18; 12:5; 1 Thess. 2:3; Rom. 12:8; 1 Cor. 14:3; 1 Tim. 4:13; Acts 4:36; Phil. 2:1; Acts 13:15. I am also grateful to Professor Terry Donaldson of Wycliffe College, University of Toronto, for his guidance with these two terms.

4. Ibid., 25.

5. Ibid.

6. Calvin, in McNeil and Battles, *Calvin: Institutes of the Christian Religion*, 1:360–61 (section 2: 7.12).

7. Ibid., 1:361, my italics. This passage is a reflection on "your word is a lamp to my feet / and a light to my path" (Psalm 119:105).

8. As Calvin says, "Believers in whose hearts the Spirit of God already lives and reigns." Ibid., 1:360.

9. Ibid., 1:361.

10. Merwyn S. Johnson, "Calvin's Handling of the Third Use of the Law and Its Problems," in *Calviniana: Ideas and Influence of Jean Calvin*, ed. Robert V. Schnucker (Kirksville, Mo.: Sixteenth Century Journal Publishers, 1988), 46.

11. Luther, *Works*, ed. Jaroslav Pelikan and Helmut T. Lehmann (St. Louis: Concordia Press; Philadelphia: Fortress, 1955), 26:329. Cited in Stuempfle, *Preaching Law and Gospel*, 33.

12. Thomas, 26.

13. Ibid., 27.

14. Augustine, "Sermon 350: On Charity," in *The Works of Saint Augustine: Sermons*, trans. and notes by Edmund Hill, vol. 10 (Brooklyn: New City Press, 1995), 108–9.

15. St. Gregory the Great, "Homily 25," in Hurst, *Forty Gospel Homilies*, 198–99.

16. John Winthrop, "A Model of Christian Charity," in *Winthrop Papers*, vol. 2, 1623–1630 (Boston: Massachusetts Historical Society, 1931), 294–95.

17. Fant, *Twenty Centuries of Great Preaching*, 2:420–21.

18. Bushnell, *Horace Bushnell: Sermons*, ed. Cherry, 57. The squared brackets in the text indicate a change of the 1903 edition.

19. Bushnell, *The Vicarious Sacrifice*, 451–76.

20. Morgan, "The Power of the Gospel," in Macartney, *Great Sermons of the World* (1997), 416.

21. Valerie Brown-Troutt, "She Had Neither Father nor Mother," in Elliott, *Creative Styles of Preaching*, 28.

22. Adams, "Faith Critiques Faith" in LaRue, *Power in the Pulpit*, 26–27.

23. Clarence James, "You Don't Miss Your Water Until Your Well Runs Dry," *African American Pulpit* 3, no. 2 (Spring 2000): 160–61. I am grateful to Basil E. Coward for bringing this quotation to my attention and its similarity to Adams: Basil E. Coward, "Unique Characteristics of Black Preaching" (Th.M. Extended Essay, Toronto School of Theology, April 12, 2007), 28.

24. Teresa L. Fry Brown, "Just Preach," *African American Pulpit* 3, no. 2 (Spring 2000): 64. Cited by Coward, "Unique Characteristics of Black Preaching," 30–31.

25. Vashti M. McKenzie, "Wanted: Palm-Tree Preachers for the New Millennium," *African American Pulpit* 3, no. 2 (Spring 2000): 98. I am grateful to Coward, "Unique Characteristics of Black Preaching," 31, for bringing this quotation to my attention and its similarity to Brown.

26. Fleming Rutledge, "Help My Unbelief," in her *Help My Unbelief* (Grand Rapids: Eerdmans, 2000), 9.

27. Ibid., 4. She is citing her class notes from Union Theological Seminary in 1974.

Chapter 15: *Proclamatory Statements*

1. Lose, *Confessing Jesus Christ*, 222.

2. Ibid., 223.

3. *Fasciculus Morum: A Fourteenth-Century Preacher's Handbook*, ed. and trans. Siegfried Wenzel (University Park: Pennsylvania State University Press, 1989), part 3:10, 201–13. Reprinted in Edwards, *A History of Preaching*, 2:197.

4. Ibid., 201.

5. Virgil, *Eclogues*, trans. Barbara Hughes Fowler (Chapel Hill and London: The University of North Carolina Press, 1997), 11. The great humanist Erasmus continued to encourage preachers to read the "profane authors" for their eloquence and demonstration of rhetorical excellence; he listed Demosthenes, Cicero, Aristotle, Plato, Virgil, and the tragedians, Tacitus, Seneca, and Plutarch. "Erasmus: A Résumé of Ecclesiastes," in Manfred Hoffman, *Rhetoric and Theology: The Hermeneutic of Erasmus* (Toronto: University of Toronto Press, 1994), book 2 (1:4), 78–81.

6. John Wesley, "Reproving Our Neighbour," in his *Sermons on Several Occasions*, vol. 2 (London: Fisher, Son, & Co., n.d.), 108–9.

7. John Dobie, "Christ's Message of Mercy to the Men of Jerusalem," in *Modern Scottish Pulpit*, 2:142.

8. John Jasper, "The Stone Cut Out of the Mountain," in *John Jasper: The Unmatched Negro Philosopher and Preacher*, by William E. Hatcher (New York: Revell, 1908; reprint, New York: Negro Universities Press, 1969), 108–20. Reprinted with standardized spelling in Edwards, *A History of Preaching*, 2:434.

9. Karl Barth, *Deliverance to the Captives* (New York: Harper and Bros., 1961), 65–66. Cited by Lose, *Confessing Jesus Christ*, 223.

10. John Knox, "The Source and Bounds of Kingly Power," in *Masterpieces of Pulpit Eloquence*, comp. Henry C. Fish, Pulpit Eloquence Library, vol. 1, pt. 2 (Cleveland: F. M. Barton, 1907), 145.

11. John Watson [Ian Maclaren], "The Continuity of Life," in *The Mind of the Master* (New York: Dodd, Mead and Company, 1896), 313.

12. McCray, "Walking in Ordered Steps," 4:68.

13. Desmond Tutu, "Sermon by Archbishop Desmond Tutu at Southwark Cathedral," Anglican Communion News Service, http://www.anglican communion.org/acns/news.cfm/2004/2/6/ACNS3772 (accessed November 16, 2007).

Chapter 16: Doxology

1. The Westminster Catechism (Shorter Catechism), in *The Constitution of the Presbyterian Church (U.S.A.), Part I, Book of Confessions* (Louisville: The Office of the General Assembly, 1996), 181 (7.001). This claim is made on the basis of 1 Corinthians 10:31 ("So, whether you eat or drink, or whatever you do, do everything for the glory of God") and Romans 11:36 ("For from him and through him and to him are all things. To him be the glory forever").

2. Augustine, "Sermon 5," in Lawler, *St. Augustine*, 85–86. A similar passage is in "Sermon 10," 113.

3. Thomas à Kempis, "Taking Up the Cross," in Macartney, *Great Sermons of the World* (1926), 64–65. Reprinted in Thornton and Washburn, *Tongues of Angels, Tongues of Men*, 199–200.

4. Melito of Sardis, "Homily on the Passover," in *The Christological Controversy*, ed. and trans. Richard A. Norris, Sources of Early Christian Thought (Philadelphia: Fortress, 1980), 41–42. Reprinted in Edwards, *A History of Preaching*, 2:13–14. The translation uses the word in at every place I have inserted the words *as was*; even given early church trust in typology and in the Old Testament as prophetic of Christ, this substitution is easier for us to understand.

5. Isaac Barrow, "Of Submission to the Divine Will," in *Selected English Sermons: Sixteenth to Nineteenth Centuries*, ed. Hensley Henson (London: Oxford University Press, 1939), 167–84. Reprinted in Thornton and Washburn, *Tongues of Angels, Tongues of Men*, 327–29.

6. Robert H. Muir, "The Secret of Faith's Victory Only to Be Found in the Object of Faith," in *Modern Scottish Pulpit*, 2:11.

7. Fleming Rutledge, "The Faces of Love," in her *Help My Unbelief*, 92.

8. William A. Johnson, "Faith Makes the Difference," in *Outstanding Black Sermons*, vol. 2, ed. Walter B. Hoard (Valley Forge: Judson, 1979), 55–56.

9. Barbara C. Harris. *Parting Words: A Farewell Discourse* ([city?], Mass., Cowley, 2003), 64–65. I am indebted to Basil E. Coward for bringing this to my attention.

10. Caesar A. W. Clark, "The God of Amen," *The African American Pulpit* 3, no. 3 (Summer 2000): 11. Cited by Coward, "Unique Characteristics of Black Preaching," 19.

11. Coward, "Unique Characteristics of Black Preaching," 21.

12. Dan Corner, "100 Biblical Names and Titles of Christ," http://www.evangelicaloutreach.org/jesustitles.htm (accessed June 6, 2007).

13. Dr. S. M. Lockridge, *That's My King!*, a DVD by Igniter Media Group; see Worship House Media, http://www.worshiphousemedia.com/index.cfm?hndl=details&tab=MM&id=2862.

Chapter 17: Celebration

1. Henry H. Mitchell, *Celebration and Experience in Preaching* (Nashville: Abingdon Press, 1990), 62. See also Frank A. Thomas, *They Like to Never Quit Praisin' God: The Role of Celebration in Preaching* (Cleveland: United Church Press, 1997).

2. See "Rejoice," in *Vine's Complete Expository Dictionary*, by W. E. Vine, Merrill F. Unger, and William White (Nashville: Thomas Nelson, 1996).

3. R. P. Martin, "Hymns, Hymn Fragments, Songs, Spiritual Songs," in Hawthorne, Martin, and Reid, *Dictionary of Paul and His Letters*, 420–21. Martin notes that the line between hymn and poem is a fine one and sets out some criteria to distinguish them.

4. John Wesley, *The Works of John Wesley*, editor in chief Frank Baker (Oxford: Clarendon Press, 1975–). See the following sermons: in vol. 1: Sermon 8 (p. 245); 12 (312); 28 (630); in vol. 2: 43 (169); 53 (346); 54 (372); 57 (412); 67 (548); in vol. 3: 82 (167); 99 (413); and in vol. 4: 124 (119); 129 (167); 132 (200).

5. John Wesley, "Human Life a Dream," in his *Sermons on Several Occasions*, vol. 2 (London: Fisher, Son, & Co., n.d.), 552.

6. Ibid. The editor of vol. 2, Albert Outler, made this remark concerning the end of Sermon 53 (2:346).

7. See Mitchell, *Celebration and Experience in Preaching*.

8. The forthcoming book by Luke Powery is an adaptation of *The Holy Spirit and African American Preaching* (Th.D. thesis, University of Toronto, 2007).

9. Melito of Sardis, "Homily on the Passover," in Norris, *The Christological Controversy*, 33–47. Reprinted in Edwards, *A History of Preaching*, 2:17–18

10. Augustine, "Sermon 2," Lawler, *St. Augustine*, 73–74. A similar passage is in "Sermon 10," 113–14. See also "Sermon 12," 121.

11. John Chrysostom, "Paschal Sermon," http://www.monachos.net/library/John_Chrysostom,_Paschal_Homily, (accessed September 20, 2007); rendered in stanza format by M. C. Steenberg.

12. Martin Luther, "Sermon on the Raising of Lazarus, John 11:1-45," in *Luther's Works*, vol. 51, *Sermons I*, ed. and trans. John Doberstein (Philadelphia: Fortress,

1959), 46–47; reprinted in Thornton and Washburn, *Tongues of Angels, Tongues of Men*, 231.

13. John Calvin, "On the Final Advent of Our Lord Jesus Christ and other Sermons," in his *The Deity of Christ*, trans. Leroy Nixon (Grand Rapids: Eerdmans, 1950), 298–99.

14. James Kerr, "The Broadchurchism of the Gospel," in *Modern Scottish Pulpit*, 2:45.

15. Gerard Manley Hopkins, "And Joseph and His Mother Marveled," in his *The Sermons and Devotional Writings of Gerard Manley Hopkins*, ed. Christopher Devlin, S.J. (London: Oxford University Press, 1959), 34–38.

16. William Holmes Borders Sr., "Handicapped Lives," in *Best Black Sermons*, ed. William M. Philpot (Valley Forge: Judson, 1972), 23–24.

17. Vashti Murphy McKenzie, "Same No More," in Thomas, *Outstanding Black Sermons*, 4:78–79.

18. Richard Lischer, *The Preacher King: Martin Luther King, Jr., and the Word That Moved America* (New York: Oxford University Press, 1995).

Chapter 18: The Effects of Genres of Proclamation

1. Spurgeon, *Lectures to My Students*, 105.

2. David Duff, ed., *Modern Genre Theory* (London and New York: Longman, Pearson Education, 2000), xiii.

3. Goethe used this classification, although only recently did Gerard Genette establish that in neither Plato nor Aristotle was lyric actually a genre. See Gerard Genette, "The Architext," in Duff, *Modern Genre Theory*, 210–16. See also Duff, "Introduction," 3.

4. Friedrich Schlegel, *Literary Notebooks 1797–1801*. Cited by Peter Szondi, "Friedrich Schlegel's Theory of Poetic Genres: A Reconstruction from the Posthumous Fragments," in Szondi's *On Textual Understanding and Other Essays*, trans. Harvey Mendelsohn (Manchester: Manchester University Press, 1986), 93.

5. Tzvetan Todorov, "The Origin of Genres," in Duff, *Modern Genre Theory*, 197.

6. Roman Jakobson, "The Dominant," in *Language in Literature* (Cambridge, Mass.: Belknap Press, 1987), 41.

7. Todorov, "The Origin of Genres," 201.

8. Frow, *Genre*, 2.

9. Ibid., 3.

10. Ibid., 18–19. "It is central to human meaning-making. . . . No speaking or writing or any other symbolically organized action takes place other than through the shapings of generic codes, where 'shaping' means both 'shaping by' and 'shaping of': acts and structures work upon and modify each other." Frow, *Genre*, 10.

11. Søren Kierkegaard, *Purity of Heart is to Will One Thing*, trans. Douglas V. Steere (New York: Harper and Row, 1956), 181.

12. See also Frederick Buechner, *Telling the Truth: The Gospel as Tragedy, Comedy, and Fairy Tale*; C. S. Lewis, *God in the Dock*.

13. See, for instance, Kevin J. Vanhoozer, *The Drama of Doctrine: A Canononical-Linguistic Approach to Christian Theology* (Louisville: Westminster John Knox, 2005).

14. Various people have spoken of the theological movement of sermons, including Milton Crum, Eugene Lowry, Richard Lischer, Bryan Chappel, myself, and others. See Wilson, *Preaching and Homiletical Theory*, esp. 87–103.

15. Wilson, *The Four Pages of the Sermon*. I have spoken recently and in detail about the implications of gospel as a genre in *The Practice of Preaching*, rev. ed. (Abingdon Press, 2007) 162–83, and will not duplicate it here.

16. Lose, *Confessing Jesus Christ*, 74. He uses the term *confession of faith* in ways similar to what we mean by *proclamation*, and he conceives of the sermon in four stages: "The first deals with *approaching* the text on behalf of the congregation. The second describes our *listening* for the text's distinct confession of faith. The third concerns *discerning* what that confession may mean in light of the rest of the canon, the community's context, and one's hermeneutical experience and expectations. The fourth involves *articulating* that new confession for the community so as to actualize the text and offer it to the community to be appropriated through the power of the Holy Spirit" (189).

17. Ibid., 206–7.

18. Ibid., 222.

Chapter 19: Proclamation

1. Michael Pasquarello III, *Christian Preaching: A Trinitarian Theology of Proclamation* (Grand Rapids: Baker Academic, 2006), 138. He says that "the story becomes gospel today—good news—when it is remembered and reactualized in the church's proclamation, liturgical celebration, and common life" (139). He does not necessarily use the term *proclamation* as we do here.

2. Kenneth Cmiel, *Democratic Eloquence: The Fight over Popular Speech in Nineteenth-Century America* (Berkeley, Los Angeles, and Oxford: University of California Press, 1990).

3. Edwin Griffin Parker, *The Golden Age of American Oratory* (Boston: Whittemore, Niles, Hall, 1857).

4. Timothy Steele, *Missing Measures: Modern Poetry and the Revolt against Meter* (Fayetteville: University of Arkansas Press, 1990), 7.

5. I am grateful in these paragraphs to an e-mail conversation with Professor Robert Stephen Reid, January 23, 2007.

6. Ibid.

7. Jackson W. Carroll, *As One with Authority: Reflective Leadership in Ministry* (Louisville: Westminster John Knox, 1991), 14.

8. Alice P. Matthews, *Preaching That Speaks to Women* (Grand Rapids: Baker Academic, 2003), 40. Matthews bases her comments on Carol Gilligan, especially *In a Different Voice* (Cambridge: Harvard University Press, 1982).

9. Matthews, *Preaching That Speaks to Women*, 30.

10. Ralph Waldo Emerson, "Quotation and Originality," in *Letters and Social Aims* (Boston: James R. Osgood and Company, 1874), 159–60.

11. See Michael Kelly, ed., "Mimesis," in *The Encyclopedia of Aesthetics*, vol. 3 (Oxford: Oxford University Press, 1998), 233. The focus here is on Derrida's notion of difference or mimesis.

12. Raymond Bailey, "Plagiarism," in Willimon and Lischer, *Concise Encyclopedia of Preaching*, 374. In the Middle Ages, when many clergy lacked adequate education, preaching the sermons of the church fathers was often viewed favorably. By the 1500s the practice of preaching the sermons written by others became so widespread that King James published an edict commanding that preachers preach an original sermon once a month. Paulina Kewes in her *Plagiarism in Early Modern England* (Houndmills, Basingstoke, Hampshire; and New York: Palgrave Macmillan, 2003) traces the history of contemporary understandings of plagiarism from Elizabethan times. She discusses plagiarism in relation to translations of the Bible, historiography, drama, poetry, and sermons.

13. Walter Ong, *Orality and Literacy*.

14. Cleo LaRue, personal conversation, May 15, 2002.

15. Michael Taussig, *Mimesis and Alterity* (New York: Routledge, 1993), xiii.

Chapter 20: Fulfilled in Your Hearing

1. James S. Stewart, *A Faith to Proclaim* (London: Hodder and Stoughton, 1953), 36.

2. David J. Lose, "Preaching as Proclamation," in Wilson et al., *The New Interpreter's Handbook of Preaching*.

3. See most recently, Joseph M. Webb, *Preaching Without Notes* (Nashville: Abingdon Press, 2001).

4. I have attempted to do exactly this in *The Practice of Preaching*, rev. ed., 247–62.

5. Spurgeon, "On Conversion as Our Aim," 341.

6. Ibid., 341.

7. John Updike, *Telephone Poles and Other Poems* (New York: Alfred A. Knopf, 1969), 72.

8. Peter Short, "Life Stirred Up Out of the Dust," *United Church Observer* (April 2004): 19.

9. John M. Buchanan, "Sound of Easter," *Christian Century* (April 3, 2007): 3.

10. Richard B. Hays, "Resurrection," in Wilson et al., *The New Interpreter's Handbook of Preaching*. He agrees with N. T. Wright, *The Resurrection of the Son of God* (Minneapolis: Fortress, 2003), whom he cites.

Proclamation CD Contents

Readers on the CD: The Reverend Scott Hoezee, Director, Center for Excellence in Preaching, Calvin Theological Seminary, Grand Rapids, Michigan; The Reverend Margaret Jenista, Associate Pastor, Third Christian Reformed Church, Kalamazoo, Michigan; Professor Luke Powery, Princeton Theological Seminary; and Professor John Rottman, Calvin Theological Seminary

Contents

Track 1: Introduction by Paul Scott Wilson.

Track 2: Scott Hoezee reading an example of Condemnation from T. DeWitt Talmage, "The Broken Pitchers,"[1] and Lament from John Watson [Ian Maclaren], "The Glory of the City."[2]

Track 3: John Rottman reading an example of Testimony from Hugh Reed, "Ways and Means,"[3] and Prayer from Trinette V. McCray, "Walking in Ordered Steps."[4]

Track 4: Margaret Jenista reading an example of Nurturing Exhortation from Fleming Rutledge, "Help My Unbelief,"[5] and Proclamatory Statements from John Dobie, "Christ's Message of Mercy to the Men of Jerusalem."[6]

Track 5: Luke Powery reading an example of Doxology from Melito of Sardis, "Homily on the Passover,"[7] and Celebration from John Chrysostom, "Paschal Sermon"[8] and Valentino Lassiter, *Martin Luther King in the African American Preaching Tradition.*[9]

Track 6: Scott Hoezee with an example of Proclamatory Statement from his sermon from John 21, "Always," and an example of Celebration from his sermon from Matthew 28, "Soar We Now."

Track 7: John Rottman with two examples of Testimony from his sermon from Luke 10 on "The Good Rottman."

Track 8: Margaret Jenista with an example of Nurturing Exhortation from her sermon, "Cheering for the Underdog," based on Revelation 5, and an example of Celebration from her sermon, "Bring It On," based on John 13.

Track 9: Luke Powery with an example of Lament from his sermon from Isaiah 5, "Unmet Expecations," and an example of celebration from his sermon on Psalm 20, "Victory Shout."

---

1. T. DeWitt Talmage, "The Broken Pitchers," in his *500 Sermons*, 20 vols. (New York: Christian Herald, 1900), 12:328–29.

2. John Watson [Ian Maclaren], "The Glory of the City," in *The Inspiration of Our Faith* (New York: A. C. Armstrong & Son, 1905), 262–65.

3. Hugh Reed, "Ways and Means," a sermon preached on Sunday July 4, 2004, in *Festival of the Word! Messages of Inspiration and Wisdom from the Summer Sermon Series at Timothy Eaton Memorial Church, Toronto, Canada* (Toronto: Timothy Eaton Memorial Church, 2004), 7.

4. Trinette V. McCray, "Walking in Ordered Steps," in Walter S. Thomas, ed., *Outstanding Black Sermons*, vol. 4 (Valley Forge: Judson Press, 2001), 61–62.

5. Fleming Rutledge, "Help My Unbelief," in her *Help My Unbelief* (Grand Rapids, Michigan, and Cambridge, U.K.: William B. Eerdmans Publishing Company, 2000), 4.

6. John Dobie, "Christ's Message of Mercy to the Men of Jerusalem," in *The Modern Scottish Pulpit*, 142.

7. Melito of Sardis, "Homily on the Passover," in Richard A. Norris, Jr., ed. & trans., *The Christological Controversy, Sources of Early Christian Thought* (Philadelphia: Fortress, 1980), 33–47. Reprinted in O. C. Edwards Jr., *A History of Preaching*, vol. 2 (Nashville: Abingdon Press, 2004), 13–14. The translation uses the word "in" at every place I have inserted the words "as was."

8. John Chrysostom, "Paschal Sermon" viewed on the worldwide web at http://www.monachos.net/library/John_Chrysostom,_Paschal_Homily, September 20, 2007. In the public domain; rendered in stanza format by M. C. Steenberg.

9. Valentino Lassiter, *Martin Luther King in the African American Preaching Tradition* (Cleveland: The Pilgrim Press, 2001), 38.

Index of Key Biblical Texts

Subject Index

Edwards, Jonathan, 29, 116
Elijah, 221
Embodiment, 4, 211, 223, 252
Emerson, Ralph Waldo, 122–23, 244
Emotion. see Passion
Epistles, 55–57
Eschatology, 67–68, 83, 120, 219
Eslinger, Richard L., 18
Esther (Hadassah), 182–83
Evangelism, 10, 38, 61
Evans, Christmas, 119
Evil, 12
Exegesis, 18, 71
Exhortation. See Nurturing exhortation; Stern exhortation
Expository. See Sermon, expository

Faith
    acts 1 and 2 levels of, 233, 250
    barriers to speaking the, 9–13
    characterization and, 5
    difference made by, 207
    -wooing address, 85
Farley, Edward, 68
Fasciculus Morum, 192
Finney, Charles, 156
First-to-second person address, 90, 188, 191
Fisher, St. John, 29, 116
Florence, Anna Carter, 151
Fodor, James, 150
Forbes, James A., 162
Forde, Gerhard O., 86–87, 188, 249
Form
    content and function of, 97–100
    criticism of, 227
    hybrid, 210, 214–217
    organic, 97–98
    See also Sermon, form
Form sensitive, 102
Foster-Harris, W., 44
Four pages of a sermon, 177, 234
Franklyn, C.L., 51, 172

Genette, Gerard, 276n3
Genres
    of the Bible, 100–3, 112

creativity and, 228–30
frames as, 230–31
gospel as, 234
history of, 228–29
major/minor, 229–30
movement as, 232–34
naming guidelines for, 112
of prayer, 165
proclamation, 113, 227–35
purity of, 229
of sermons, 6–7, 96–100
in sermons. See Sermon, subforms
world projection and, 230–32
Gloria Patri, 200
God
    as adversary, 48, 49, 94
    anger of, 29, 115, 116–25
    attributes of, 204, 208–9
    as center of the sermon, 78
    conversation with, 162
    law and, 85
    meeting, 186, 188
    names of, 204
    power of, 181, 182
    sovereignty of, 117, 199, 231
    as speaker, 114, 188, 191–92, 195, 228
    teaching about, 17
    See also Holy Spirit; Jesus Christ; Trinity
Gomer, 28
Gospel, 53–76
    actualized, 83, 196, 234, 237
    Bible texts as, 68, 71–73, 251
    definition of, 53, 66–67, 88
    doing the, 81, 87, 94, 115, 135, 190, 211, 228, 231–32, 234–35, 247, 255
    epistles and the, 55–57
    foolishness of the, 12
    as genre, 234
    Gospels and the, 58
    grace and, 71, 228
    heart of the, 82–83
    hermeneutic, 263n28
    humiliated, 248
    identity of Jesus and the, 192
    intertextuality and the, 252
    joy and the, 198, 205, 210, 211, 214

Mitchell, Henry, 210
Moody, Dwight Lyman, 157
Moral issues, 142. See also Social justice
Morgan, George Campbell, 34, 182
Morton, Andrew, 134
Moses, 50, 136, 178, 203, 211, 221, 242
Movie-making, 27
Muir, Robert H., 205.
Musicality. See Rhythm
Mystery, 46–47, 92

Narrative, 18, 21–22, 36, 38, 122, 221
  point form and, 32
New Hermeneutic, 18
New Homiletic, 3, 5, 21, 24, 36, 52, 65,
  72, 78, 90, 241, 242
  Bible genres and, 100–3
  concrete language and, 37
  gospel and the, 78, 241, 251
  purpose of preaching, 241, 251
  Romantics and the, 18, 29
  styles and the, 107–9, 238
  teaching principles in the, 26–39
Newman, John Henry, 45
Newton, John, 158
Nicene Creed, 223
Niebuhr, Reinhold, 47, 129
Noah, 178, 207, 221
Norén, Carol, 63, 128
Novel, the, 36, 38, 121
Nurturing exhortation, 174–87, 215, 220

"Old" Homiletic, 18, 241
Old Testament, 57–58
Orality, xv–xvi, 4–6, 19, 238, 245

Paradox, 43–46
Parainesis, 138, 175
Paraklesis, 175, 176
Paralytic, Healing of, 87
Parker, Theodore, 35
Pasquarello, Michael, III, 236
Passion, xv–xvi, 4, 183, 202, 204, 211,
  212, 237, 252
Pastoral ministry, 144
Pentecost, 137

Performative language, 34, 188, 230,
  231, 247, 249. See also Embodi-
  ment; Gospel, doing the
Persuasion, 103, 105–7, 108, 109, 238
Peter, 222
Peterson, Eugene, 144
Picture-painting, 27, 38
Plagiarism, 244, 278n12
Plot, 18, 23, 221
Point Form, 19
  narrative and, 32
Potter, Henry C., 35
PowerPoint, 20
Powery, Luke, 127, 214
Prayer, 165–73, 202
  celebration as, 210–11
  creeds as, 170
  hymns as, 170
  of illumination, 165, 166–67
  of invocation, 165
  Lord's, 170
Preach, 184–85
Preacher
  anger of, 117, 118, 131
  authority of, 240–43
  character of, 151, 162
  ethos of, 151
  as prophet, 263n25
  role of, 7, 9, 22, 242
  self-disclosure of, 161–62
  as servant, 242
Preaching
  African American, 6
  orality and, xv–xvi
  passion and, xv–xvi, 4, 183, 202, 204,
  211, 212, 237, 252
  propositional, 18, 21, 22, 32–33, 40
  Puritan, 19–20
  purposes of, 11, 28, 103–9, 241, 251
  roundtable, 240
  text, 73
  transformational, 91, 247
Proclamation,
  authority issues of, 240–43
  barriers to, 9–13
  confessional, 92, 277n16
  congregation and, 10

Proclamation (*continued*)
content of, 96
creativity and, 246
definition of, xi, xiii,1–2, 76, 81, 84, 85, 112
delivery of, 250
doing the gospel to, 81, 87, 94, 190, 211, 228, 231–32, 234–35, 247, 255
doing the text to, 86
features of, 91
first-to-second person address in, 90, 188, 191
form in, 96
genres of. See Sermon, sub-genres of the gospel, 90, 94–95, 188
as highest goal of preaching, 78
individualistic, 253
language of, 90
listener emphases for, 90
loss of, 237–38
Lutheran, 85–88, 90–91, 188
movement to, 234
New Homiletic and, 90
opposition to, 90–91
prerequisite of, 36
questions concerning, 250–53
recovery of, 113–15, 236–46
as sacrament, xi, 86–87, 91
Spirit and, 93–94, 247–48
style of, 96
teaching and, 83, 89–90, 92–94, 248–49
trouble of, 94–95, 112–45
two kinds of, 87–88
worlds projected by, 41, 231–32
Proclamatory statements, 188–98, 215
Prodigal son, 27
Propositional preaching. See Preaching
Puritan/s, 180–81

Randolph, David, 18
Rauschenbush, Walter, 35
Redemptive suffering, 129
Reed, Hugh, 159
Reid, Robert Stephen, 108, 238, 267n47
Religion,
good / bad, 184
traditional, 9

Repetition of others, 246
Resner, André, 66
Resurrection. See Jesus Christ
Revelation, xii
Reversal, 125
Rhetoric, Ciceronian, 237–38, 266n23
Rhetorical devices, 106, 112
accumulation, 118
comparison and contrast, 40–43, 259n6
contradiction, 46–48
identification, 45
inversion, 123
paradox, 43–46
parallelism, 5, 105, 118–19, 125, 155, 179, 200
repetition, 183, 204
reversal, 125
rhyme, 214
rhythm, 120, 202, 211, 219, 221
short phrases, 179, 183, 201, 212
Rhyme, 214
Rhythm, 120, 202, 211, 219, 221, 237
Rice, Charles, 102
Richards, I. A., 18
Robert of Basevorn, 19
Robertson, F. W., 36, 43
Rogness, Michale, 68
Romantics
English, 18, 29, 40, 43–44, 97, 229
German, 229
Rose, Lucy, 75, 91
Rufinus, 258n4
Rutledge, Fleming, 158, 186, 206

Sacrament, xi, 86–87
Saint Francis of Assisi, 10
Salvation, 34–35
Sangster, W.E., 18
Sanken, Joni, 92
Sarai, 133
Schlegel, Friedrich, 229
Schleiermacher, Friedrich, 35
Scripture
fulfilled, 93, 176, 188, 247–255
theological reading of, 71–72